THOMAS BECKET

S. THOMAS OF CANTERBURY

THOMAS BECKET

ARCHBISHOP
OF
CANTERBURY

By
WILLIAM HOLDEN HUTTON, D.D.

*Dean of Winchester ; Honorary Fellow of S. John's
College, Oxford ; A Chaplain of the Order
of S. John of Jerusalem ; Honorary
D.C.L. Durham*

✠

CAMBRIDGE
AT THE UNIVERSITY PRESS
MCMXXVI

CAMBRIDGE
UNIVERSITY PRESS

University Printing House, Cambridge CB2 8BS, United Kingdom

Published in the United States of America by Cambridge University Press, New York

Cambridge University Press is part of the University of Cambridge.

It furthers the University's mission by disseminating knowledge in the pursuit of
education, learning and research at the highest international levels of excellence.

www.cambridge.org
Information on this title: www.cambridge.org/9781107661714

© Cambridge University Press 1926

First published by Sir Isaac Pitman and Sons, Ltd. 1910
New Edition, revised and enlarged, published by the Cambridge University Press 1926
First published 1926
First paperback edition 2014

A catalogue record for this publication is available from the British Library

ISBN 978-1-107-66171-4 Paperback

PREFACE

THIS biography is the result of an endeavour to sift and restate what has long been known about the great Englishman whose life has been written, perhaps, more frequently than that of any other hero of the Middle Age. It was originally published in a series I was then editing, called *Makers of National History*, the object of which was to illustrate the importance of individual contributions to national development, in action and in thought. It was published by Sir Isaac Pitman and Sons, Ltd., in 1910, and has long been out of print. With their cordial consent I have revised it for the present edition, taking note of much that has been published since then. Many kind friends have written to me during the last fifteen years about my book, and here I venture especially to thank that most learned and generous helper of others, Dr Reginald Lane Poole.

Thirty-seven years ago I published on the same subject a volume (*S. Thomas of Canterbury*, D. Nutt, second edition, 1899) of translated extracts from the contemporary biographers and other choniclers. I have not now used the translations I then made, but have either translated the Latin anew or used, with revision, the translations made more than eighty years ago by Mr R. H. Froude and Dr J. A. Giles, to whom (the latter in spite of some unforgotten blunders) in the nineteenth century we owe the revival of interest in the great chancellor and archbishop. Perhaps the Early Victorian style of some of these versions may even be preferred to the Wardour Street English of a modern translator. The importance of the original biographies themselves is so great, second indeed only to that of their subject, that I have given to them a separate treatment at the end of this book.

I have added foot-notes of detailed reference only to letters quoted or when there was some special reason for observing the particular authority who was responsible for the original statement. To have mentioned each biographer who stated each fact would have been of interest only to special students, who would already know without being told. But the analysis and criticism of the Becket literature is a fascinating subject in itself.

I desire particularly to render the homage of affection and respect to Dr A. J. Mason, whose kindness to me extends over many years, and to assure him that while I venture, rather diffidently, to differ from his conclusions as to the Bones of Becket, I feel deeply indebted to him, as all scholars do, for his work in this and many other fields which his learning has adorned.

A few pages in this book have been already printed in past years in the *Times Literary Supplement*, the *Guardian* and the *Church Quarterly Review*: I thank the Editors for sanctioning the reprinting here.

Becket is worthy of a biography in several volumes. This book claims only to have been written from the original literary sources and after visits to the chief scenes of its hero's life, and to tell briefly the tale of a full and passionate life.

I should like to add one plea—that all who read this book would set themselves to stamp out the use, for the family name of the archbishop, of the barbarism "À Becket": the "A" has no contemporary, or early, authority whatever, and is as ugly as it is useless.

W. H. HUTTON

THE DEANERY, WINCHESTER.
S. John Baptist's Day, 1926

CONTENTS

PLATES

CORRIGENDUM

P. 57, l. 8. *For* Godfrey *read* Geoffrey.

THOMAS BECKET

CHAPTER I

YOUTH AND TRAINING

AMONG MAKERS of National History may certainly be ranked the saints of the Christian Church. Mohammedanism and Hinduism, and other religions, too, have had their great typical figures who have deeply influenced the ideals, and to some extent the history, of the peoples of the East. But wherever Christianity has gone the influence of its heroes has been even more profound. They have exemplified national characteristics while they have elevated the nations and inspired them with a higher impulse of consecration or sacrifice. All over Europe history has been made or modified by men and women whose life was moulded by the doctrine of Christ; and beyond the bounds of our continent the progress of the world has been as strongly affected by missions as it has by crusades, by a Francisco Xavier and a Livingstone, as by a Warren Hastings or a Captain Cook. Most of all, perhaps, was this true in the Middle Ages, when a society scarcely emerged from barbarism rallied to the voice of "picturesque and emancipated individuals." They championed romantic causes: they indicated principles that had been passed by in neglect.

The history of the Middle Age is full of such lives. The history that was then written is, indeed, largely biography; and the most tame and jejune of monastic chroniclers will show a spark of fire when he names the heroes he has known. In England the names of

Cuthbert and Oswald and Dunstan, as of Henry II and Simon de Montfort and Edward I, have been kept alive by this personal touch of enthusiasm in those who wrote of them; and everywhere about the country local legend has preserved and embellished the memory not only of its heroes but of its saints. Chiefest among all these, there can be no doubt at all, stands Thomas of Canterbury, incomparably the most popular English hero of the Middle Age; and he was a hero because he was regarded as a saint.

Of few characters in all history is the life-story better known. At least ten contemporary biographies are extant, and it would be easy to increase that number if we counted the fragments of original information in other writings of the age. Besides this, we have an almost unique collection of letters relating to Becket, written by himself, his friends and his enemies. Of no other personage in the Middle Ages would it be so easy to compile the "Life and Letters." The fact that the material is so large and that it has been familiar for so long does not render the task of the modern biographer altogether an easy one. He must disclaim any idea of throwing a new light on a career that has long been so well known. But the interest of the life is still so fresh and vigorous, it is so typical an example of medieval interest and passion, and it is even to-day so little removed from a concern with problems that have not ceased to be of importance in national life, that it may well be told again, and that, if it may be, without political or ecclesiastical prejudice, and with the sole aim of setting forth the truth.

Thomas of London, for so he called himself all his

life, even after he was archbishop of Canterbury, was born on December 21st, S. Thomas's Day, most probably in 1118, and was baptised after vespers that evening. His father was Gilbert Becket, a Norman descended from a family of gentle blood, settled at Thierceville, who had come from Rouen, where he had traded, to settle in London as a citizen and merchant. His mother was a native of Caen, of burgher birth, and named Mahatz (or Matilda) or, according to one writer, Roesia. The house in which he was born was in Cheapside[1]; and all through his life he was proud of being a Londoner. Though some called him Becket, the surname of his father,[2] he always styled himself "of London," whether he was chaplain to the archbishop, chancellor of the realm, or primate of all England.[3] Thus, though of Norman birth, he ranked as an Englishman. His contemporaries were proud of him as the first man born on English soil who, after the Norman Conquest, became archbishop of Canterbury.[4]

His father and mother, it seems, were notable people: the mother beautiful, discreet, a good and pious ruler of the house, who taught her child from earliest years to fear the Lord and to invoke the Blessed Virgin as his patroness, and put his trust, after Christ, in her. His father was successful in business, and was also a port-

[1] It was on the site of what is now the Mercers' Hall.

[2] The name occurs three or four times, applied to himself, in the biographies—once in Grim's account of his last moments.

[3] Mr Walter Rye made an attempt in 1923 (*Times Lit. Supp.* April, 1923) to claim for the archbishop a "Norfolk parentage." This was conclusively disproved by Mr J. H. Round.

[4] The curious may have observed, in 1926, that of the last eight archbishops of Canterbury and York only two were born on English soil of English parents.

reeve of the city. He was, as says Guernes of Pont Ste Maxence, among "les barons de la cit,"[1] possessing, that is, the freedom of the city. Yet he lived simply, and his famous son spoke in later years of the home and family as humble. Later centuries, seeking to cradle their hero in wonders, told that Becket was a knight who had been on Crusade and his wife a Saracen princess, who had followed him alone to England, knowing only the words Gilbert and London: but the story belongs to three centuries after his birth. More credible are the stories of his mother's dreams that he would be great and a saint: perhaps they helped to bring about their own fulfilment.

At ten years old he was sent to school at the house of canons, at Merton in Surrey, whose prior, Robert, his teacher, became his friend for life and lived to see him die.

A story of his childhood at Merton is told by William Fitz-Stephen, who was with him, it would seem, for many years, and must have heard many things from his own lips. No doubt as years went on—for very likely Fitz-Stephen did not write till nearly twenty years after his master's death—the tale was coloured by the knowledge of what the boy became. One day, it runs, the father came to see his son, and to the prior's indignation, kneeled before him. "Dost thou fall at thy son's feet, O mad old man?" said Robert.[2]

---

[1] Cf. Fitz-Stephen: "habitatores aliarum urbium cives, hujus barones dicuntur."

[2] The learned Bishop G. F. Browne in letters to me in 1915 raised doubts as to the identity of the Robert so often referred to. It is possible no doubt that there were two, but I am not convinced that the archbishop's teacher, confessor, and friend to the last were different persons.

"He should do thee the worship that thou dost to him." But the father held his peace, and afterwards in private said, "I know what I do; for in the Lord's sight the boy will be great." Thomas's schooldays were certainly happy, for in later years he induced the king to erect and endow the priory, and he kept his old teacher Robert constantly about him to the end of his life.

But he was not at school only in the country. He became a scholar of one of the three famous London schools of which Fitz-Stephen speaks, where the standard of education was high and it was a privilege to be admitted. What the boys learnt one does not discover in detail, but of their games Fitz-Stephen, himself a Londoner, has left a lucid account. Not only did they play football on half holidays, and that so furiously that the citizens, even the haughty officials, crowded to watch and wished themselves boys again, but they indulged, with the masters' assistance, in cock-fighting—and that, it seems, within the school itself: it was for many centuries the appropriate amusement of Shrove Tuesday.[1] "We have all been boys," says Fitz-Stephen, and he doubtless includes his hero Thomas among those who enjoyed the boys' amusements.

London, indeed, was full of amusement. Besides cock-fighting and football, there were theatrical spectacles in which were shown the doings of holy con-

[1] So much so that when Mrs Holmes, wife of the President of S. John's College, Oxford, left money in the eighteenth century to provide chickens on Shrove Tuesday for the Fellows' table, some have asserted that they were really intended to be fought, not eaten.

fessors and martyrs; on Sundays in Lent there was tilting, in which not only schoolboys but courtiers mingled, and at Easter time were sports on the Thames, when boatloads of lads tried to strike a shield fixed on a post in midstream. On summer days they ran and jumped and shot arrows, and even threw stones; and at night they danced with girls till moonrise. In winter they had sports on the ice, and sometimes broke an arm or a head. In all these pleasures, we are to take it, young Thomas played his part; and he watched the horsefair at Smithfield, and the frequent fires among the wooden houses. He took a meal now and then at the great restaurant by the river bank, the first of so long and famous a line; he joined in the verse-contests of the schools, where Fescennine licence was mixed with Socratic salt; and, like Fitz-Stephen, who tells us of all these things with abundance of quotations from Vergil and Horace, Ovid and Persius, and the modern Geoffrey of Monmouth (no doubt all known to him also), he was doubtless shocked at the immoderate potations of fools.

Such was the London in which Gilbert Becket's boy grew up. He could compare it with Paris, for there, too, he went, it seems, to school. He learnt, we know, how to ride and tilt, and we are sure that his mind dwelt on the memories of martyrs and confessors. But chiefly was the city the great mart of commerce for all nations, and in this, too, Thomas was to bear part. His father was a gentleman, yet, some say (though Fitz-Stephen denies it), made his living as a merchant; and his kinsman Osbert, with the cognomen "Eightpence" (Huit-deniers, Octodenarii), a rich man in trade, honoured among courtiers—though Christian usurers were supposed not to exist, one is almost tempted to think he may have been a money-lender on the sly—as well as citizens, and holding a knight's fee in Kent, now took him to serve for three years among his clerks. The years were probably 1139 to 1142. He obtained experience also of the sheriff's business; Osbert, it may be, was sheriff.[1] He served as secretary or "notary" also to Richer of Laigle, a knight who was a friend of his parents, and with whom he had often been out hunting as a boy, once indeed narrowly escaping with his life through his horse falling into a millstream.[2]

So life passed till he was about twenty-three. He was quick to acquire, ready to remember, and well learned in the "seven liberal arts." While he was at work among the lawyers he had amassed a good knowledge of law and yet had kept up the knowledge that came from his old school books. He was already one whom men noticed and for whom a bright future was predicted.

To look upon he was—so says the Icelandic Saga, which probably embodies the work of Robert of Cricklade, a scholar who may have known him well— "slim of growth and pale of hue, dark of hair, with

[1] "Practically at the head of the government of London," said Mr Round in the *Athenaeum* in a note on Mr Radford's *Thomas of London*.

[2] Guernes de Ste Maxence, 216–19, records this, and so does Roger of Pontigny (*Materials*, iv, 8) with, it seems, a little gloss. See Walberg, *Guernes de Ste Maxence*, pp. xxix–xxxi. Richer, it is interesting to note, was one of the benefactors of the great church of S. Stephen, Caen, the foundation of William the Conqueror.

a long nose and straightly featured face; blithe of countenance was he, winning and loveable in all conversation, frank of speech in his discourse, but slightly stuttering in his talk, so keen of discernment and understanding that he could always make difficult questions plain after a wise manner. Of such wondrously strong memory was he that whatsoever he had heard of sentences and law-awards he could cite it at any time he chose to give it forth. By reason of these great gifts of God which we have told of even now it was easily understood by wise men that he was predestined to a high station in the church of God."

Theobald, archbishop of Canterbury, came from the same district, perhaps the same village, in Normandy, as Gilbert Becket. It was natural that he should know and be reminded of the clever young man. Of how he came to call him into his household there are different accounts: it was the request of the father himself, or of two of his friends, archdeacon Baldwin and master Eustace, from Boulogne. He came with one of the primate's servants or officials to Harrow, one of the manors of the see of Canterbury, and there was admitted into the family of the archbishop. So he put aside his sports and set himself to learn from wise men in the life of religion.

It was a household of learned men, some of whom were to be the teachers, some the friends, some the rivals, of Thomas Becket. Chief among them was Roger of Pont l'Evêque, a good scholar but an ambitious and jealous man, who would often "break out into contumely" against him, and nicknamed him, after the knight with whom first he came to the house, "clerk Baillehache," as a token of contempt. The joke has lost its savour by now, for we know nothing of the knight after whom it seemed comic to name this young clerk; but to Edward Grim, when he wrote the biography of Becket, the humour seemed of bitter omen. "In good truth," he says, "Thomas did, at a later time and a fitting opportunity, take the axe in hand, yet rather the sword of S. Peter himself, wherewith he hewed away Roger and his associates from the communion of the faithful, so that, as they also made plaint to the king, he left them not so much as the power to make the sign of the cross to bless their food."

Archbishop Theobald had, like not a few of his great predecessors in the chair of S. Augustine, and especially the famous Theodore of Tarsus, made of his house a school of literary and ecclesiastical learning. Thomas of London found it a congenial home. His mother, who had such high ambition for him to serve God, was dead. He had seen something of the world, and thought, no doubt, as young men will, that he had seen all that was worth seeing. Now, as the Icelandic Saga says in its quaint fashion of speech, "he waxeth weary with such way of living, in that he perceiveth how, in many things, the deeds of worldly lords turn straight against the right and the honour of learned folk." At Canterbury, or in one of the archbishop's manors, in the circle of learned clerks, he would find peace. Yet he did not live apart from common secular affairs. We hear of him at Colchester some time between 1141 and 1148,[1] and witnessing a confirmation of the church

[1] Dr J. H. Round in *Trans. of Essex Archaeol. Soc.* xv, pt. 2.

of Glinde to the monks of Bec between 1143 and the latter year.[1] Theobald had had his share of political troubles, and he had seen his power practically superseded by Henry of Winchester, king Stephen's brother, and papal legate. In 1143 he resumed his authority, for the new Pope, Celestine II, gave him the legation which the bishop of Winchester had held under his predecessor; in 1144, under Lucius II, it lapsed again. In 1148 he did an act of bold defiance to king Stephen, for in spite of the refusal of permission to leave England, he crossed the Channel secretly, and attended on the Pope's summons at Rheims for a Council in mid-Lent. Roger of Pont l'Evêque and Thomas of London were his companions. In later years Becket quoted this boldness as an example of how kings might be defied.[2] Eugenius III, indeed, had no fear of the king of England. He had already deposed an archbishop of York and consecrated another in his stead—no matter that the deposed archbishop was afterwards famous among saints as S. William of York; he now suspended Henry of Winchester and threatened to excommunicate Stephen. Theobald was the sufferer: he was banished, and the event of a prelate and a king at deadly feud, not for the first time nor by many a time the last, was another object lesson to the young clerk. The party of Theobald was strengthened by the adherence of the Cluniac Gilbert Foliot, abbat of

[1] Dr R. L. Poole in *Hist. MSS. Comm. Various Collections*, vii, 31.
[2] In a letter to Cardinal Boso, 1166, *Materials for the History of Archbishop Becket*, vi, 57-9.

Gloucester, who now by papal authority was appointed, and then consecrated by the primate, bishop of Hereford. He did homage not to Stephen, king of the English, but to Henry, duke of the Normans, the son of Matilda, daughter of king Henry I, widow of Henry V the Emperor, and wife of Geoffrey of Anjou, who had so long fought for the English throne.

This first coming of Henry of Anjou into near connection with the life of Thomas was ominous of future history. It was in a matter of Church authority that they were first brought near, and through Gilbert Foliot, who was to be a chief supporter of the one against the other. The event, it seems, brought Stephen to submission. Theobald came back to England and there was peace.

Thomas had been to Rome with Theobald in 1143, yet it was some time before he won the archbishop's complete confidence. Twice, it seems, the jealous Roger caused him to be dismissed, but Walter, archdeacon of Canterbury, the archbishop's brother, sheltered him, and he was soon restored to favour. The School of Canterbury was not only a school of literature, where learned clerks gathered to study and teach, bringing their learning from foreign Universities or going to Paris or Bologna to perfect themselves: it was also a school of politics, where the interests of Henry of Anjou were always kept in mind and where— by Thomas himself, it is said—the plan of Stephen to crown Eustace, his son, in 1152, was foiled by the refusal of Theobald. The School of Canterbury was pledged to the succession of the Angevin heir, now the claimant of rights that had been his mother's, for his father died in 1151. It was the training ground of politicians as well as of priests. Peter of Blois, though he knew it was the house of God and the gate of heaven, where was all righteousness, prudence, and learning, described how "all the knotty questions of the kingdom were referred to us, and when they are discussed in the hearing of all, each of us without strife or wrangling sharpens his wits to speak on them well."

Living and studying in this circle of wits, Thomas of London, while still only in minor orders, received the church of S. Mary-le-Strand, by the gift of John of Pageham, bishop of Worcester, and by that of the archbishop himself the church of Otford, in Kent. He was also a prebendary of S. Paul's, and in 1154 also of Lincoln, when he was ordained deacon and succeeded Roger of Pont l'Evêque[1] as archdeacon of Canterbury.

For the office of archdeacon, "oculus episcopi," it was necessary, or at least customary, to receive a training in Church law, and Theobald, "the real founder of the medieval canon law jurisprudence" in England, had already sent Thomas to study at Bologna and Auxerre.

The age was marked by a great revival in the study of law, the Roman law never forgotten and the canon law at this time codified. In Italy[2] lay teachers had never died out, and the revival found them at work and increased their numbers. In France, where the ecclesiastical schools and the monasteries directed

---

[1] Who succeeded Walter when he was made bishop of Rochester in 1148 (Gervase Cant. i, 133).

[2] See Rashdall, *Universities of Europe*, ii, 329, whom I am here largely following.

education, it was different. There Becket had already been a student, and was to be again. In Northern Italy there was a continuous municipal life, with all the traditions of freedom which that implied. Roman law, too, had lasted on, and was taught in the schools. Becket, who had already studied it at Canterbury, now came to the Italian schools, where the tradition had never died.

Bologna was a school of general arts, and it had a law school as well, to which came students already grounded in general learning in other lands. Between the general education and the technical stood the art of composition, *Dictamen*, which men studied all over Europe. But law made the great fame of Bologna in the twelfth century; and traditionally Irnerius was the founder of its greatness, living himself probably till 1130, the contemporary of Gratian, the great canonist. A chronicler of the day[1] says that at the request of the great countess Matilda of Tuscany, whose memory was fragrant for centuries, he "renewed the books of the laws, which had long been neglected, and, in accordance with the manner in which they had been compiled by the Emperor Justinian of divine memory, arranged them in divisions, adding perchance between the lines a few words here and there." This means probably that Matilda fostered a law school at Bologna to support papal claims as a contrast to imperial Ravenna. Thus, in spite of Bologna's ancient seal— "Petrus ubique pater legumque Bononia mater"—the early Bolognese doctors were Imperialists.

The reference to the hero of the lawyers, Justinian,

[1] Richard of Ursperg, Pertz, *Scrip*. xxiii, 342, cited by Rashdall.

is to be interpreted as involving the study of the Digest; and the work of Irnerius and his scholars was directed to a study, both critical and professional, of Roman law, to the organisation of a law school, and to its separation from other studies. Side by side with the study of Roman law, the law of the Empire, there grew the systematisation of canon law, the law of the Church. Ivo of Chartres, and others, had already produced summaries of this. Now, about 1142, Gratian produced his *Decretum*, a text-book of Church law, to balance the text-books of Roman law, and to support the papalist position in the war of investitures. Having the civil law among its sources, the Church law both imitated it and reacted from it; and now it was made into a system, apart from it, and apart also from theology. When Becket in later years turned back to the study of canon law which he now began, his friends saw in it something of a defection from the true studies of a primate or, perhaps, a priest.

But for an archdeacon it was meet to study both. "Bologna owed its fame as much to the canon law as to the civil law; and that school of canon law originated, as we have seen, in the triumph of all that is represented by the name of Hildebrand. Even in the Imperialist Civilian of Bologna there was hardly anything in common with the modern anti-clerical."

As yet there was no University in the modern sense, but the lectures of Irnerius were its beginning: men, already scholars who had studied elsewhere, were pupils again here, and "a stream of young archdeacons, at the age at which in England a boy is articled to an attorney," were among his hearers. Delightfully said a great historian—"Many and varied were their experiences; but invariably they get into debt and write home for money; some of them fall in love and become the quasi-husbands of Italian ladies; some get a bad character for learning the Italian art of poisoning; some are killed in frays with the natives; some remain abroad and become professors; all more or less illustrate the scholastic question which John of Salisbury propounds, 'Is it possible for an archdeacon to be saved?'"[1] He generously adds: "There are some few exceptions." Thomas of London was certainly one of them.

It is not difficult to-day to reconstruct something of his life at Bologna. If he did not hear lectures from that brick pulpit on the wall of San Stefano, from which it is traditionally reported that Irnerius gave his discourses, he would certainly attend the law teachers at the monastery within. He must have worshipped in the ancient church beside it, The Holy Sepulchre, and in the crypt with its ancient columns and the ancient basilica, and in the church of the Holy Trinity read the inscription on the font in the *atrio di Pilato*, which names the Lombard Luitprand, and walked in the beautiful cloisters, all belonging to that great sevenfold building which is the glory of the city to-day. He must have gazed upon the wonderful twin towers, Asinelli and Carisenda—

"Qual pare a riguardar la Carisenda
    Sotto il chinato, quando un nuvol vada
    Sopr' essa sì, che ella incontro penda."

[1] Stubbs, Lectures in *Medieval and Modern History*, p. 303.

He would have stood in the square where now rises the huge mass of San Petronio; and one may well imagine him turning away, with that acute sensitiveness of smell to which his biographers testify, from the odours of the "street of ancient fish" hard by.

From Bologna, so it seems from William Fitz-Stephen—but the chronology is hazy—he went to Auxerre, still studying the canon law,—the beautiful Auxerre which we know, with its three churches of the Middle Ages—S. Etienne, S. Germain, S. Eusèbe —that rise high above the houses which cluster up the hill from the river, stripped now of many treasures, but keeping a brave front in the fight for religion in the rich and peaceful country of the vine. It may well be that Becket worshipped in the churches and walked with the bishop in that splendid arched terrace of his, which looks upon the garden and across the broad river.

Then he was called back to England, and the active life began again. At Canterbury now he found a new scholar, John of Salisbury, philosopher, theologian, and wit, who was to be for all the rest of his life his adviser, sometimes his critic, always his candid friend. John of Salisbury, who was probably a little younger than Thomas of London, had studied at Paris under Abailard and many masters, among them Robert of Melun, and another, Adam of Petitpont, who was also to receive a bishopric from Henry II—S. Asaph, as Robert had Hereford, avoiding it, however, "for fear of the Welsh," and preferring the security of Abingdon. Twelve years John spent in study, then he taught, and acted as secretary to Peter, abbat of Montier-la-Celle, outside Troyes. In 1154 he returned to England, commended by S. Bernard to archbishop Theobald, and then "for thirty years he continued to live the central figure of English learning." Of him we hear much more when he was with his friend Becket in exile. Beside John of Salisbury was John the Kentishman, who became in 1162 bishop of Poitiers, and in 1181 archbishop of Lyons, but remained till his death rector of Eynesford, in Kent, Ralph of Sarr, and some of those who were afterwards to win fame as biographers of their distinguished companions. Theobald himself had the traditions of Bec, where he had been first monk, than abbat, and he was the link between the memories of Lanfranc and Anselm and the claims of his own successor. In 1149 he brought, probably from Bologna, Vacarius, of whom Becket may well have told him, to lecture on Justinian, and to make textbooks from the Code and the Digest. The court of the archbishop was indeed a school of Church law, armed at all points, with an eye to the civil law itself, against the supremacy of the lay power.

In 1152 the School won its first triumph. Stephen demanded that his son Eustace should be crowned, while he himself was still alive, to secure the succession. Theobald was supported by Eugenius III in his refusal, and he had the lore of his clerks at his back. Stephen put him in prison; he escaped over sea and took with him the chiefest of his advisers, Thomas the archdeacon; and he used the familiar weapon, a threat of interdict, to procure his return.

Thomas, one may be sure, was at his side throughout. All was done, says Gervase of Canterbury, by the subtle providing and insight of Thomas the clerk. It was not long before he should have his reward.

Events moved rapidly. Henry of Anjou married Eleanor of Aquitaine, the divorced wife of Louis VII, king of the Franks. The Pope stood out against the succession of Eustace. Henry came over to England to press his claims in person and met king Stephen at Wallingford, and spoke with him face to face, across the Thames or some side channel, where the stream was narrow. Already duke of the Normans, count of Anjou, and lord through his wife of the rich lands of Southern Gaul, he was now recognised as heir to the English kingdom. Within a few weeks Eustace died, and the treaty was confirmed: Henry was to rank as Stephen's son, his justiciar, and his undoubted successor. Again a few months, and Stephen was dead, and Henry II was crowned at Westminster on Sunday, December 19th, 1154.

One of the last of those who chronicled the stark deeds of the Norman kings,[1] and who had set down the horrors of the strife of the nineteen winters of king Stephen, ended his book, ready to give a new one to the new king. All England was of his mind. A new age was felt to begin with the gallant young warrior who had won the heritage of Norman and Angevin, of Languedoc and England.

With the new era in the State went changes in the Church. Roger of Pont l'Evêque, who had gone to Rome on Stephen's behalf in 1152, and had tried to stir up strife between king and archbishop, was an un-

[1] *Henry of Huntingdon*, pp. 291–2.

congenial companion to Theobald as well as Thomas, and, after the way of good men, the archbishop made his dislike show itself only in further favour. Aided by Robert the dean and Osbert the archdeacon, he procured Roger's election to the archbishopric of York on the death of Henry Murdac, and he consecrated him in Westminster Abbey on October 10th, 1154, within a few days of Stephen's death. Roger was home again from Rome with his pall in time to see Henry of Anjou crowned in the same place. He was succeeded as archdeacon of Canterbury by Thomas Becket.

The archdeaconry of Canterbury was, as it is, the highest rank in the English Church after the bishops and abbats (or deans). It was worth an hundred pounds a year, a great sum, and its new possessor became in theory what he had no doubt long been in fact, the "eye of the archbishop." To give Becket weight in the northern province also he was given the provostship of Beverley, succeeding in this as in the archdeaconry his old rival, Roger, now of York.

Thomas Becket was now a rich and prosperous clerk. Some say that Theobald was training him to be his own successor. At least he was rewarding him very fully for the work he had done and giving him opportunity to do more. Years later, when Gilbert Foliot taunted him with owing his rise solely to the king's favour, he answered that he had already the archdeaconry, the provostship, "churches in plenty, prebends more than one, and other benefices not a few," and was not poorly furnished with this world's goods. Men thought this no reflection on a minister of Christ.

Feudalism had touched the Church, and benefices, ecclesiastical as well as lay, were regarded much as fiefs of which men could discharge the duties, if need be, by deputy. "The average conscience of the time was fully satisfied if the holder of several benefices provided a competent person to do the duties of each. If Thomas did this at Beverley and Otford, and where-ever else he held preferment, he would not reach the standard either of primitive or of modern morality; but he would fully satisfy the morality of his own age." So Mr Freeman,[1] whose name those who were his scholars and friends can never mention without affection and honour, well expressed the defence that fifty years ago was called for by an attack on the "accumulation of preferments." One may be sure that the arch-bishop who gave the preferments thought it was in no way wrong that Thomas should hold them.

But Theobald saw in him the power of much greater usefulness if he should serve the State. The new king was young. Those round him were thought to be hostile to the Church, which had been the real ruler of England, so far as England was ruled at all, during the later years of Stephen. Theobald asked the advice of those who best knew the king, the two Norman bishops, Peter of Bayeux and Arnulf of Lisieux, and set before them the virtues of his archdeacon, the son of his old fellow-countryman. Wise and bold and faithful was Thomas of London, and sweet were his manners; and then, the archbishop dreaded that Henry would treat England as a conquered land, and knew that Thomas was staunch for the freedom of the

Church. Already Henry knew something of him; it seems possible that the archdeacon had already acted as his chamberlain. Thomas, to hold his new offices, had needed at last to proceed above minor orders and had been ordained deacon. He was, under inviolable vows, the Church's man. He now became the king's man, too, for Henry II made him chancellor of England.

CHAPTER II

THOMAS THE CHANCELLOR

IT was probably at the beginning of 1155 that Thomas of London became chancellor, and certainly it was within a year of his having received the archdeaconry of Canterbury. He was from the first a partner with the king in the restoration of law to the land.

Years later his enemy Gilbert Foliot charged him with having bought the office as a stepping-stone to the primacy of all England. The charge cannot be proved or disproved to-day. That he paid a large sum on his appointment is most probable: it was one of the ways by which medieval kings tried to secure the fidelity of their servants. Yet Fitz-Stephen says expressly that the chancellorship could not be bought. That Thomas saw in the post an avenue to the archbishopric very likely means no more than that he knew Theobald would be glad to think of him as his successor. It could hardly have been foreseen how warm a friendship with his new master would make the appointment probable.

From the first Henry took most kindly to the clever scholar whom the archbishop had sent to be at the head of his secretaries. Often he would come to his house, when the day's work or hunting was over, riding into his hall, drinking a health and away again, or jumping over the table to take a seat by his chancellor's side. Henry was only twenty-one, still an impulsive boy: Thomas, every record shows, had a boy's heart. When they rode out together they played together, scrambling in the streets while courtiers and people wondered. Fitz-Stephen tells how once Henry dragged off his chancellor's cape to give to a poor man, and they fell to fighting over it: Thomas would not give up the new scarlet and grey hood without a struggle. It was the boyish friendship which made the hard work of the official, and the jealousies which beset him, endurable. And even then we soon hear that he wished to give up his honours and return to the archbishop. "Clear-sighted as the blessed Thomas was in all his wisdom, he saw all along how the great folk of England bore him foul thought, a fair mien notwithstanding. Hence it is written that he prayed archbishop Theobald, often times with tears, that he might be taken back into his service, so as to withdraw his neck from under the yoke of the thraldom of standing between the Church and the king's men. This, however, the archbishop could not grant him, saying that, by the spiritual reward which awaited him, he was the more needed for the Church the heavier the trials were that he must needs endure."[1]

The office of chancellor ranked next to the justiciar. "Who knows not," wrote his old master, Peter of Celle, "that you are second from the king in four realms?" In the first place, he was chief of the royal chaplains, yet his duties, it seems, went no further than the charge of the chapel, for Thomas remained a deacon. The Church, however, was especially in his charge. Revenues of vacant bishoprics and abbeys were in his hands, to account for to the treasury. Thomas,

[1] *Thomas Saga*, i, 58.

says Fitz-Stephen, caused the king to delay appointments as little as possible. Petitions to the king for the most part passed through his hands also. He kept the king's seal, but in the treasury, whence it could not go forth but by the justiciar's order. When he sealed, he sealed publicly, in the eyes of all, alike in the Curia and in the Exchequer. At the Exchequer nothing great could be done without his consent and advice. His clerk kept the roll of the chancery, and he was responsible, with the treasurer, for the accounts. All councils he attended or could attend: even when not summoned he might enter. No official had so wide a responsibility, for where the justiciar, or the treasurer, had no concern he was employed. So intimate was his association with the king and with all the king's business that, says Fitz-Stephen slyly, "If by the grace of God his well-spent life should win its mercies he need not die, if he liked, without being bishop or primate."

Thomas as chancellor was certainly always in the public eye: he was known as the king's chief adviser, and men fawned upon him for his favour. Arnulf of Lisieux writes a letter—the first in the long Becket correspondence—

"I have received your highness's epistle, every word of which seemed to me to drop honey, and to be redolent with the sweetness of affection. I was delighted to find that I had not lost the privilege of our early intimacy, either by the wide distance which separates us, or by the multitude of affairs in which you are involved. I was delighted, I say, because the matter is put beyond all doubt, because of your letter, which it would be unworthy of me to suspect either of flattery or of falsehood. The same interest in you exists also in my bosom, which though it has seldom an opportunity of exemplifying itself by deed, yet still lives in the devoted yearnings of the will. For in friendship, it is the will alone which is concerned, and there is no room for questions of bartering, lest our affection be thought to be prostituted or mercenary. Friendship is complete in the purity of its own existence, and gains but slight addition[1] from being demonstrated in deed; it is but little exposed to the caprices of fortune and derives its own dignity from itself. So true is this, that it is seldom found among the rich, for it hates riches and seems to attach itself to the single-minded and to the poor. It is, indeed, a rare virtue, and therefore the more precious; but nowhere is it more rarely found than between those who are invited to administer counsel to kings, and to transact the business of kingdoms. For, to say nothing of other points, ambition sits with anxious weight upon their minds, and whilst each fears to be outstripped by the vigilance of the other, envy springs up between them, which, ere long, fails not to become open hatred. For it is an old feature in the character of the envious, that they look upon others' success as their own ruin, and whatever others gain they think has been subtracted from themselves. Envy ever suffers torment, and dissembles its hidden pains under a smiling look, and thus a deceitful exterior cloaks secret treachery. Moreover, if the favour of the prince is changed, and he begins to look on a man with a clouded brow, all the support of his companions fails him, the applause and

[1] Reading "crementi."

obsequiousness with which they crowded round him die away; those from whom he expected consolation, insult him; and when occasion offers, remind him of the wrongs he had once done them: nay, his very benefits are designated as acts of injury. Such is the sea on which you are sailing; such the turmoil amid which your life is cast, wherein you will have to guard against the siren smiles of those who applaud you, and the venomed strains of flatterers. From all these you have but one way to escape—sincere faith accompanied with uprightness in well-doing; seek rather, with the Apostle, to obtain glory to yourself from the testimony of a good conscience, than the uncertain honours of public report, and of slippery and popular applause. Popularity departs from a man more rapidly than it came; whereas those other virtues, though they may be unpalatable in acquiring, yet lead to a happy sequel. I write to you thus plainly, not because I would, according to the proverb, teach Minerva letters: but in speaking to a friend, I could not restrain the current of my thoughts, particularly when urged by the impulse of my mind to offer you my congratulations."[1]

The work which Thomas of London was first called on to share with his master and friend was a work of reconstruction. The young king appealed to the memory of his grandfather's rule. Already he had in his mind the "avitae consuetudines" which became famous in the Constitutions of Clarendon. England was to be brought back to the good days of Henry I.

---

[1] I have used the rather cumbrous translation of Dr Giles, for it well conveys the artificial air of the original.

Those who had seized Crown lands and royal rights or secured control of royal towns were dispossessed. William of Newburgh, fairest of all the chroniclers, and very well informed, says that the grants they showed from Stephen were disallowed, as those of an usurper. The first of the Angevins, like the first of the Normans, disavowed his predecessor on the throne, and looked beyond him for his "antecessor." The foreign mercenaries were driven forth from the land. Again the justices started on their errand, the eyre, as under Henry I, and now rather to judge than to exact money: the young king himself, some say, supervising them. Henry was interested in the legal development of his day; he attended the greater trials in his own court, and learned by practical experience something of the needs for legal reform which he would soon endeavour to supply. He was not a little of a financier, too: the new financial expedients of his reign may well have owed something to his initiation. One of his early acts was to restore the weight of the coinage. In both law and finance Becket's experience would be of value. In all the work of government no man would be brought more closely into association with the king than the chancellor. The chief of the secretaries, if he were also a personal friend, would be the chief man in the realm. Theobald's aim was fulfilled. At the young king's side there stood a man of steadfast soul, determined, active, and with religion ever at the heart of his life.

Thomas of London, as the chroniclers describe him, was, at the age of thirty-seven, a handsome and impressive personage. He was tall, with a long thin face and a high forehead, lighted by bright piercing eyes, with the white hands, and with the grace of movement, the dignity of manner, which marked the noble. His courtesy was perfect, not that of outer show which cares not for friends or guests save as pawns in a game of ambition, but the courtesy of the heart, kindly, considerate, searching out ways to benefit as well as to please those with whom he had to do. The chroniclers speak enthusiastically of the affection he won. William Fitz-Stephen, in a long eulogy, says—[1]

"High was the favour of the chancellor, whether among the clergy, knights, or people. He might have had all the parochial churches that were vacant, both in the towns and castles, for no one would deny him, if he would only ask: but he showed such greatness of mind in repressing all views of interest, that he disdained to forestall the poor priests or clerks, or take from them the opportunity of gaining those churches for themselves. His great mind rather aimed at great objects, such as the priorship of Beverley, and the presentation to the prebends of Hastings, which he got from the Count of Eu, the Tower of London, with the service of the knights belonging to it, the castellanship of Eye, with its service of two hundred and forty knights, and the castle of Berkhamsted." The Pipe Rolls of the fifth, sixth and seventh years of Henry II show him also as holding this, and in the later year the abbey of Ramsey.

To continue Fitz-Stephen—
"He generally amused himself, not as if it were a business but carelessly, and as it might happen with

---

[1] *Materials*, iii, 20 *sqq.*

hawks and falcons, or dogs of the chase, and in the
game of chess,

'Insidiosorum ludebat bella latronum.'

Martial, xiv, 20.

"The house and table of the chancellor were common
to all of every rank who came to the king's court, and
needed hospitality: whether they were honourable
men in reality, or at least appeared to be such. Hardly
any day did he dine without the company of earls and
barons, whom he had invited. He ordered his hall to
be strewed every day with fresh straw or hay in winter,
and with green branches in summer, that the numerous
knights, for whom the benches were insufficient,
might find the floor clean and neat for their reception,
and that their rich garments and beautiful linen might
not take harm from its being dirty. His board shone
with vessels of gold and silver, and abounded with rich
dishes and precious wines, so that whatever there
might be either for eating or drinking was recommended by its rarity; no price was great enough to deter
his agents from purchasing them. But amid all these
he was himself singularly frugal, so that his rich table
provided rich alms for those who partook thereof:
and I have heard from his confessor, Robert, the
venerable canon of Merton, that from the time of his
becoming chancellor, no excess ever stained his life.
This, too, was a subject on which the king was continually tempting him night and day; but as a man of
prudence, and ordained of God, he was ever sober in
the flesh, and had his loins girt. As a wise man, he
was bent on administering the government of the king-

dom, and whilst busied in so many matters, both public and private, he might rarely yield to such seduction. For says the poet—

'Otia si tollas, periere Cupidinis arcus.'

Ovid, *Rem. Amor.* 139.

A modest man, indeed, was the chancellor—a foe to depravity and uncleanness; and when a clerk of his, of high birth, Richard of Ambly, had carried off the wife of a friend, who had been long absent beyond the sea, and persuaded her that her husband was dead, he removed him from his house and his friendship, and caused him to be kept prisoner in the Tower of London, where he was detained for some time loaded with irons."

To the medieval monk it perhaps seemed strange that any man out of the cloister should live a pure life. Thus, the Saga,[1] derived no doubt from the Cricklade prior, speaks with an air of more surprise than does Fitz-Stephen—

"The holy fathers have made plain that a chaste monk is like unto a knight who keepeth his wealth and life in a close stronghold. But he who liveth chastely in the world signifieth a knight who fighteth with sword and shield in open field and receiveth a greater reward the more glorious victory he gaineth; for that indeed is a more wondrous art to stand on the embers being unburnt than to shun the fire and be unscathed. Both these signs point to that laudable man the blessed Thomas. He was placed by the lord king in the way of such a good hap and fulness of this

---

[1] *Thomas Saga Erkibyskups*, ed. Magnusson, i, 50 *sqq.*

world's bliss as hath been before told, and yet he wore over his breast nevertheless such a trusty hauberk of virtue through God's abiding with him that he never departed from a life of purity and holy endeavour; for if in the daytime the fulfilment of many duties hindered he would get up anight-tide to worship his Creator. And how he was wont to bring his God the sacrifice of praise and of a pure life appeareth from two tales which now follow concerning this matter.

"So Robert writes, that there was a certain person, a nigh kinsman of his, who sought the king's court about the time in which the story goeth. He had on hand certain affairs on the happy issue of which he deemed that much might lie. He setteth his mind, as many a man in England now listed, on first seeing the chancellor Thomas, to expound to him the nature of his affairs, and to pray him for some furtherance thereof. Now by reason of his reaching the town not till the day is far spent, a laudable custom forbiddeth to go before such a mighty man at late eventide, wherefore he betaketh him to his chamber. But in early morn, already when day was abreaking, he bestirreth himself for the carrying out of his errands. Now the way taketh such turn that he must needs go by a certain church, and he seeth lying before the door a man prostrate in prayer even unto earth. And when as he stands bethinking him of this sight there comes upon him, as ofttimes may happen, some sneeze or a kind of coughing. And forthwith starts he who lay kneeling on the ground and rises straightway up, then lifteth his hand up to God and thus ends his prayer, and thereupon walks away thence to his own chamber.

The new-comer was right eager to know who of the townspeople might follow such worthy ways, and therefore he taketh an eye-mark against the dawn both of his growth and the manner of attire he wore, that he might the rather know him if he should happen to see him afterwards. Nor did that matter long await true proof, for no sooner hath he leave to see chancellor Thomas than he well perceiveth that the very growth and raiment which he had noted before belongeth to no man but to him alone; for even now Thomas putteth off his over-garment as though he had just entered the room. This person testified to his kinsman Robert when he came home what virtue and godly fear he had found in the blessed Thomas, straight against the thinking of most people; and hence it came to pass that the prior put this deed into his writings."

He then tells a story which originally appears in Guernes of Pont Ste Maxence, and which is given also by William of Canterbury. It was evidently a tale that was well known: Avice, the king's mistress, would be observed by many eyes—

"In a certain thorpe named Stafford[1] there was a certain lady, goodly and of great wealth. It was talked of among the household folk of king Henry that on this lady he had set a fond eye aforetime. But now that love is somewhat waning and waxing colder the king cometh the seldomer, and, he having turned away, it so happeneth oftentimes that chancellor Thomas

---

[1] About 1180 there was founded near Stafford a priory of S. Thomas the Martyr, by a certain Gerard of Stafford "pro salute animae meae et uxoris meae et parentum nostrorum." M. Walberg in his edition of Guernes, p. 222, suggests that there may here be some connection with this Avice, of whom nothing is known.

taketh harbour in this same township. And when he happens to be staying there this lady sendeth him many seemly gifts for his table. From this the host, with whom the chancellor was wont to be harboured, thinketh that she is minded by this kindness to win for her a new lover. And such great heed giveth he to this thought that once upon a time, when the chancellor hath taken up his dwelling in his house, he getteth up amidnight, taketh a lantern, and goeth to the chamber which the chancellor had, entereth it, listeneth about, and hearing nought thinketh now that surely the chancellor must have gone away. But the very time he turneth up the light of his lantern and beginneth to spy about it is proven that such is the case not altogether since before the very bed he seeth a bare-footed man, prostrate on the floor, on whom after kneeling and praying sleep had fallen. And soon he perceiveth that here lieth Thomas the chancellor, and it was proven here, in truth, that he was a man of pure life and good manners, whom a misdoubting man thought to be like even unto himself. Blessed is the soul that deceiveth the world yet serveth its Maker...."

Such tales proved that if Thomas had "put off the deacon" he still lived the life of a servant of God. And prior Robert of Cricklade, from whose record these stories reached Iceland, added the more general praise—

"...Unto this the lord Thomas added such bounty to needy folk and foreigners that he yielded them in their hardships unstinted comfort in gifts of money, although it were hidden from the knowledge of the multitude. But to lords and great men he chose to give his gifts openly. For these things, as might be looked for, the poor loved him even as a father, but lords held him in honour as their equal, and revered him as their superior. At this time those only deemed themselves well bestead in England who were partakers of his kindness. For this reason he had the power much to give and many to comfort, that the king made him, for his own living and profit, a grant of a fee, which men nowadays call barony, and is as large a fief as that which belongeth to him who is called a baron of the king's realm. But it is worthy of mention, that for all this kingly favour, and the manifold grants which have been told now awhile, many lords in England bore Thomas a sullen mind, although openly they showed themselves blithe enough; for two things preyed inwardly upon them, firstly, the king's favour towards the chancellor, and secondly, this, that they might not as at this time wreak as much evil against the Church as they had a mind to; and who these folk were became manifest enough when the crash befell whereby the king's friendship brake."

And a few words of the faithful Edwin Grim, a man not vocal, as Carlyle might have said, but writing with a certain stiffness of pen that is a testimony to truth, may be added to complete the picture.[1]

"The poor and the oppressed found ready access to him: the cause of the widow did not come before him in vain: he gave justice and protection to the weak and needy. He had so large a following of chosen knights and dependents of all sorts, that the royal palace seemed empty in comparison; the king himself

[1] *Materials*, iii, 363–4.

was left almost alone, and sometimes complained to the chancellor that his court was drained."

Such was Thomas as contemporaries saw him in the days of his power. His fame was resplendent among the Londoners. It was he who restored the Tower, now in his custody, as it had so long been in that of the Mandevilles.

Fitz-Stephen, who told of how the foundations of the great fortress were cemented by blood, says—

"Thomas the chancellor caused the Tower of London, which is the seat of the Monarchy, and was become almost a ruin, to be put into repair; and proceeded with such marvellous rapidity that this great work was completed between Easter and Whitsuntide; so many carpenters and other workmen were labouring together, and made such a din in their haste to finish their labours, that even those who were standing close together could hardly hear one another speak."

The eye-witness, one sees, was a London citizen.

The greatness of the things he planned, the vigour with which he carried out what he had designed, no less than the courage with which he fought "the beasts of the Court," made the simple monks who knew him, like William of Canterbury, in later years, think that there was no wonder men considered him half a sorcerer. Yet those who knew him saw that he had "the breastplate of righteousness." Thus, John of Salisbury might dedicate both the "Statesman's Book," and the defence of logic, to the man who, after four years as chancellor, was seen to be a light of the clerical order, as scholar and as judge, at the king's right hand, and who quashed unjust laws and set always the public good before private gain.[1]

We are not without examples of the part played by Thomas of London in judicial business. In 1156 he was itinerant justice in three shires. The Pipe Roll accounts for the profits of the pleas heard in Lincolnshire by him with Robert Beaumont, earl of Leicester, one of the young king's chief advisers; for those in Essex, where he sat with Henry, earl of Essex, the constable; and in Kent where he judged with Essex and also apparently alone. It seems probable that he held pleas again in later years, up to 1158.

In the Chancery we know practically nothing of what he did, beyond the vague phrase of John of Salisbury, which can only be regarded as a punning anticipation of the later equitable jurisdiction of the chancellor. The utmost that can be said is that Becket's personal eminence added very greatly to the

---

[1] The *Policraticus* was completed before September, 1159; the *Metalogicus* a little later. Both were dedicated to the chancellor. [See Mr C. C. Webb's splendid edition, 1909.] In his Introduction John of Salisbury thus eulogises Becket, sending his book to him as Ovid his to Augustus—

> Ergo quaeratur lux cleri, gloria gentis
> Anglorum, regis dextera, forma boni.
> Quaesitus regni tibi cancellarius Angli,
> Primus sollicita mente petendus erit
> Hic est qui regni leges cancellat iniquas,
> Et mandata pii principis aequa facit.
> Si quid obest populo uel moribus est inimicum,
> Quicquid id est, per eum desinit esse nocens.
> Publica priuatis qui praefert commoda semper,
> Quodque dat in plures, ducit in aere suo.
> Quod dat habet, quod habet, dignis donat: uice uersa
> Spargit, sed sparsae multiplicantur opes.
> Utque uirum uirtus animi, sic gratia formae
> Undique mirandum gentibus esse facit.

importance of the office of chancellor, and thus did something to add to its judicial work, of which in his day very little is known.

But of the work as a whole it has been said with scarce a trace of exaggeration that it was primarily administrative, and that during the years when Becket held the office "the Angevin chancery became the most perfect piece of administrative machinery that Europe had known."[1]

But in the ordinary judicial work of the Curia Regis he played a more prominent part. The case of Battle Abbey looks big in some of the modern biographies, because it may be used to support a theory of the chancellor's indifference to the interests of the Church. In May, 1157, Henry II heard at Colchester the suit between the bishop of Chichester and the abbat of Battle, as to whether the special privileges conferred by William the Conqueror involved exemption from episcopal control. Richard de Lucy, the justiciar, argued the case of his brother the abbat against Hilary, bishop of Chichester, who spoke very volubly for himself. The chancellor acted as clerk of the court, read documents, asserted the abbat's rights—which were really those of the Crown—and also took his place among the judges of the Curia, who advised the king as to the ultimate decision. The judgment was not formally given: the bishop was induced to withdraw his claim to jurisdiction and to state that this was done voluntarily. Becket, writing years later to the Pope, says he was compelled to receive back to communion

[1] By Dr T. F. Tout in his brief and brilliant lecture on *The Place of St Thomas of Canterbury in History* (Manchester, 1921).

without absolution the abbat, whom he had excommunicated, and to give him the kiss of peace. In the account which the *Chronicle of Battle* gives to the trial, it would seem as if the chancellor was in favour of the abbat. There has been a good deal of unnecessary dispute about the explanation. It is clear enough that while Becket was generally in favour of episcopal authority over monasteries and so far in sympathy with the bishop, he knew that in the case before the court a special exemption had been granted, which, whether it was given wisely or not, was valid. His view was that of archbishop Theobald and was sanctioned by subsequent popes.[1] And at the utmost his responsibility was that of one among several judges. The chancellor was not yet, as chancellor, a judge himself.

Nor was he a financial officer apart from others. A chancellor of the exchequer was still to come: Becket was the chancellor in the exchequer as elsewhere, having there his roll and the king's seal. His clerk played an important part. He himself was the channel through which writs for the king's remission of debts to the Crown were issued, and disbursements on account of the king were often made through him. He acted in fact as a trusted secretary in this as in other matters. The special financial importance of his work is not great. Not till he became archbishop did he issue writs of remission ("perdona") in his own name.

But he was already found useful, for his tact and

---

[1] The authority is the *Chronicle of Battle*, of which the parts bearing on the question are reprinted in *Materials*, iv, 244 *sqq*. Dr Radford in *Thomas of London before his Consecration*, discusses the facts and criticises Fr. John Morris, *S. Thomas of Canterbury*, ii, note D.

graciousness, his insight and determination, in diplomatic business. He is first found as sending his deputy to welcome the Norwegian ambassadors who came in the second year of the king's reign, and to pay for their entertainment: one of those rare instances of relation with Scandinavia since the time of Swegen and Cnut which the chroniclers cherish, giving quaint details of the wild doings of the northern kings and rebels. Herbert of Bosham, who knew him from this time, bore a letter to the Roman Emperor in Germany, Frederic I, to which he was witness.[1]

In 1156 Thomas accompanied the king when he reduced his younger brother Geoffrey to submission, taking from him Mirabeau and Chinon, where (says Benedict of Peterborough) he destroyed the castles— a destruction which did not prevent their soon being built up again. Great aid gave Thomas the chancellor, says Gervase of Canterbury. In the first Welsh war of the reign, July to September, 1157, when Henry led his troops in person, Thomas was with him. The first disaster, in which Henry of Essex, the constable, threw down the royal standard and fled, was redressed by a march along the coast, which prevented the Welsh, who were chiefly dependent on England for corn, getting supplies, and reduced them to submission, Owain Gwynnedd doing homage for North Wales. Henry returned by Chester, Thomas still with him, bearing the repute of an inspired sagacity.[2]

[1] See *Materials*, v, addenda, p. xxvi *a*.
[2] Cf. John of Salisbury, *Policraticus*, ii, 144: "Cum adversus Vivicollinos Britones regia esset expeditio producenda, in quo te consultus aruspex praemonuit, etc."; and see *It. Camb.* ii, 7, 21 f. R.S., *An. Camb.* 20, R.S.

The chancellor was next sent on embassy to Louis VII, king of the Franks, to negotiate the marriage between the English king's eldest surviving boy, Henry, and Margaret, the French king's little daughter, the debatable land of the Vexin to be her dowry, one of the few negotiations for child-marriage in that age which was brought to completion. It was an occasion for ostentation, of which Thomas, who certainly loved splendour, was not slow to avail himself. He would impress the Frankish king, "that the person of him who sent might be honoured in him who was sent and that of the envoy in himself." There were two hundred knights, clerks, butlers, servants, sons of English nobles, as pages and squires, and the whole train bore the appearance of an armed force, dressed in new clothes and bright armour. Thomas himself had twenty-four suits of raiment, which he wore, it would seem, but once, and then lavishly gave away. He took his own chapel furniture, the sacred vessels, the altar ornaments and books; the carpets and hangings for his own chamber, the gold and silver plate, from cups and plates to salt-cellars; bags and boxes full of money, and barrels of beer, a liquid clear and of a better colour and taste than wine, thinks Fitz-Stephen, and much admired by the French.

"Each waggon had a dog chained to it, great, strong and terrible, which seemed fit to subdue a bear or a lion." The English mastiff was, in sooth, a famous beast. Each sumpter horse had a monkey on it ("humani simulator simius oris," as Claudian says), and footboys ("fruges consumere nati") led the way into every village singing their own English ballads after the same fashion that they used at home. After them came hounds in couples and greyhounds at leash, so that the French might see the English manner of *la chasse*. The waggons full of stores rattled over the stones, and then the grooms riding the sumpter animals, and sticking their knees in, as still the English way is. When all this noise had stirred the phlegmatic French, they would rush from their houses and ask what it meant. The English chancellor, going on embassy to the king of France,[1] was the answer. Wonderful, indeed, must the English king be who has so grand a chancellor! And so they stood at their doors while the squires came by with their knights' shields and war-horses, and other squires with the hawks on their wrists: then the servants, then the knights and clerks, a-horseback, two and two: then, last of all, the chancellor with his household friends about him.

The way to Paris was a sort of triumph, and, when Thomas was arrived there and lodged in the Temple he must outdo the French in munificence, supplying his own food by trick, when the king ordered that no one should take payment from the English envoys, and feasting in an incredible excess of luxury, worthy of the riches of Solomon. A hundred pounds was given for a single dish of eels, says Fitz-Stephen, and expects his readers to believe and tremble; from the which, you may gather, he adds, that the table of the chancellor was both sumptuous and sufficient.

Becket remembered the scholars and their masters,

---

[1] Fitz-Stephen says "regem Franciae": it would be an unusual phrase among the Franks at that time, and no English king yet called himself "rex Angliae."

for he once had studied at Paris; and he remembered too that English scholars are usually in debt, for he paid their creditors. He gave "tips" in fact right royally: as one reads of Hannibal after the slaying of Hasdrubal, when he sent envoys to Rome (says Fitz-Stephen, a little mixed), saying to them "Ite, et omnem mortalem explete pecunia."

And so the embassy was successful. What Thomas asked, that was granted. The dower was agreed on, the Vexin with several castles, including the famed Gisors, to be held by the Templars till the marriage should take place. This seemed to be a settlement of the bitter question about frontiers; in such a form at least it came into the Saga of Iceland, for—"by his wisdom and law-pleading, Thomas wrought a settlement as to the landmark laid down of old between France and Normandy."[1]

In all this there may well be exaggerations. Henry II certainly took part in the negotiations himself. But there is no reason why Becket should not have been, as Fitz-Stephen makes out, a special envoy, and have brought back, as Robert of Torigny says, the little maid who was to marry king Henry's son. There was certainly a diplomatic victory.

In the other foreign questions of the year Thomas may have had no concern. He was probably at work in England. But the next year, 1159, included one

---

[1] Some have thought that there were other matters in debate with Louis at this or other times during the first year of Henry II, among them the seneschalship of France. Cf. Davis, *England under the Norman and Angevin Kings*, pp. 202–3. But M. Luchaire (*Institutions monarchiques*, i, 176) shows that the counts of Anjou never claimed this office.

of the great events of his life, the campaign in Southern Gaul. Already he had shown himself eager for the defence of the king's island realm: he had himself given to Henry three fine ships, fully fitted. He was as eager for the strength of the military force. In the short war with Geoffrey he had shown this. Now he was to bring his financial skill to bear.

The claim of Henry to the county of Toulouse was characteristically complicated and weak. It seems that William VIII, duke of Aquitaine, had mortgaged the country of Toulouse to his wife's uncle, Raymond of S. Giles. Whether or not the money had been repaid, Eleanor, Henry's wife, duchess of Aquitaine, had claimed the return of the land, and Raymond, the grandson of the mortgagee, had held to the possession. Henry of Anjou was ready to establish his power over all Southern Gaul, by alliance or by conquest. He treated with Raymond, count of Barcelona, husband of Petronilla, queen of Aragon, for the marriage of his boy Richard (born at Oxford hardly a year before) with their baby girl; he secured the support of the count of Blois, and of Montpellier and Nîmes, and he gathered a mighty force together. The gathering was largely Becket's work.

Under Henry I, compensation in lieu of military service had occasionally been taken from those whose duty it was to provide knights for the king's wars, and it had become a custom to allow the ecclesiastical tenants (and sometimes those who held by subinfeudation) to compound in money for the knight service This was the scutage. Already it had been used by Henry II in 1156, when a levy was made from ecclesiastics holding by knight-service. Now it was again imposed, on mesne tenants and on the churches, two marks being charged on the knight's fee in lieu of service. In this there was nothing new. But what was new, and what needs apology all through Thomas's later life, when his friends were pleading his unbroken attachment to the Church, was the *donum* now demanded, an arbitrary tax, under colour (in true medieval fashion) of a gift, demanded from the Church. There were no less than eight measures for exacting money employed in 1159, of which six were arbitrary[1]; and the *donum* from the Church tenants in chief, irrespective of their fees, and from some of the religious houses who held in frank-almoign, not by military tenure, was the most arbitrary of all. A large sum was thus drawn from the Church, and for this action men said that the great churchman who was chancellor was responsible.[2] Foliot, bishop of London, in the vehemence of his remonstrance with Becket, his archbishop,

[1] See Round, *English Historical Review*, vi, 633–6, and *Feudal England*, pp. 262 *sqq.*

[2] John of Salisbury in the *Policraticus* (ed. Webb, ii, 424), thus speaks of the Toulouse expedition: "Maior enim es quam ut debeas aut possis (licet iam sic ceperit multos) capi tendiculis eius. Rex illustris Anglorum Henricus secundus, maximus regum Britanniae, si initiis gestorum fuerit exitus concolor, circa Garonnam et (ut dicitur) te auctore te duce fulminat, et Tolosam felici cingens obsidione non modo Prouinciales usque ad Rodanum et Alpes territat, sed, munitionibus dirutis populisque subactis, quasi uniuersis praesens immineat, timore principes Hispanos concussit et Gallos. In tantis rerum tumultibus quaeso custodi innocentiam et uide et dicta et praedica aequitatem; nec amore nec odio, timore uel spe declines a uia recta." But John takes a rather different view of the matter when he explains, and apologises for, his hero's action, in a letter to Bartholomew, bishop of Exeter, written in 1166. (*Materials*, v, 376 *sqq.*).

in 1166, spoke of Becket as chancellor holding the
sword of State and plunging it into the bosom of Holy
Mother Church when he stripped her of so much money
to pay for the expedition against Toulouse. It was a
charge to which no satisfactory reply could be given.
The demand was an arbitrary one, and Becket was at
least partly responsible for it. He was serving the
king, and he thought only of serving him to the best
of his power. John of Salisbury's defence that he
yielded to the king's will under compulsion and was
only the minister, not the contriver, of iniquity, will
not bear consideration.

The chancellor certainly threw himself into the war
with a most unclerical enthusiasm. Now indeed did
he—as Herbert of Bosham[1] says of him during his
chancellorship—"put off the deacon," and that most
conspicuously. He had been with the king in January
at Argentan, and in June was with him at Saintes.
Early in July he was at Agen, where he alone attested
a grant to the bishop of Rochester. He led seven
hundred knights of his own, and fought with the best
of them. He pressed on to Toulouse with the utmost
vigour, and when there urged the king to attack and
capture the city, for Louis, his suzerain, was within
the walls. Henry had scruples. Becket had none; nor
indeed was there any occasion for them, for if war once
involved the suzerain it was absurd to pretend that his
rights, or his dignity, were respected. When Henry
broke up the siege, the chancellor followed him to
Cahors, and received the charge of the captured city;
and when Henry withdrew from the campaign Thomas

[1] *Materials*, iv, 173.

continued it, stormed castles, crossed the Garonne, and subjugated districts to the Angevin lord.

The war ended by a truce, and king and chancellor turned their attention to the Norman frontier, where Becket, with his knights, twelve hundred mercenaries, and four thousand followers ("servientes") was foremost in the attack. Guernes of Pont Ste Maxence, who lived to write the glory of Thomas's life as a martyr, saw him unhorse many French knights, and he overthrew and despoiled a gallant warrior, Engelram of Trie. He led his men, and they were always the most daring and the most victorious in the army. "Who can tell how he inflicted death and confiscation of goods? Supported by a strong band of knights, he attacked cities, destroyed towns, gave vills and farms to the devouring flames, and showed himself merciless to the foes of his master, wheresoever they arose": so wrote Edward Grim, when he had seen the fierce warrior become a saint and die a martyr's death.

He would prosecute the war to the end, and the only hope of peace, wrote John of Salisbury, depended on his judgment. Well might Theobald be offended by the long absence from the archdeaconry which was spent in such a way.[1] But peace was made within a few months: perhaps Thomas hurried it on because of the significant advice that he should return before the archbishop died.

But, high though he seemed in favour, he was not always able to remain in perfect accord with the king.

---

[1] *Materials*, v, 13. On the letters of John of Salisbury at this time see the valuable paper by Dr R. L. Poole in *Proceedings of the British Academy*, xi.

He had not so entirely "put off the deacon" that he could set aside Church law when it seemed to speak clearly. In his own case, he could disobey canons and appear on a battlefield; but when what seemed immutable Christian laws were in danger, he could stand firm. Henry wished to marry Mary, daughter of the count of Blois, though she was abbess of Romsey, to Matthew of Boulogne, brother of the count of Flanders. Becket forbade the sacrilege and contested it to the utmost of his power, but in vain.[1] He was, it seems, stricter than the Pope, for a dispensation was given. It may have been at the same time that Thomas also interfered in regard to the marriage of William, Henry II's brother, to the countess of Warenne, widow of king Stephen's son, and prevented it, on the ground of consanguinity, which act was remembered by one of his murderers, Le Breton, who cried as he struck him, "Take that, for the Lord William's sake, the king's brother."[2] But the date of the affair is uncertain, and its significance, as given in the *Draco Normannicus* of Stephen of Rouen, who attributes to it a great part of Henry's anger against Becket, is greatly exaggerated.

[1] The story is in Robert of Torigny, and in Herbert of Bosham, Robert speaking of Matthew as winning Boulogne by this marriage.

[2] A late reference to this is interesting. In the *English Historical Review*, viii, 85, Dr Macray gave an account of one of the Hereford MSS. of the fourteenth century: a sermon of archbishop Stratford, preached to monks at Canterbury in 1341. This makes Le Breton give as reason for murdering Becket that he had prevented William, Henry's brother, marrying countess Warenne, because her late husband was son of king Stephen, and Stephen and Matilda were cousins. This came from "libro quodam conscripto de vita sua apud Osneyam." Stratford says that if this is true it ought to be noted ("valde notandum").

Thomas held his archdeaconry and his chancellor-ship till the death of the archbishop. In the former office he cannot have been very active; nor, perhaps, was there even then an excessive laboriousness demanded from the archdeacon of Canterbury. But Theobald was not inclined to bear his absence patiently. There are letters of his in 1160 and in 1161 demanding his return. The primate of all England laments, as his days close in, the evil customs of monetary exaction which hang round the archbishopric—especially an exaction called "second aids": will the archdeacon forgo his share of these, that the archbishop's soul may have peace? And again, when will he return to his duties? He is altogether inexcusable and nigh unto cursing, unless his absence be excused by the king himself on the ground of necessity and public usefulness. And again John of Salisbury writes of the archbishop's anger at the prolonged absence; and yet with a sort of trembling respect, for if all that is said by those who return from the court be true, the king and the whole court depend entirely on his counsel, and it is said that he is given the revenues of three vacant sees. Still, the friend adds the personal advice to return. We do not know if it was obeyed.

As to the chancellorship, again details are lacking. The legal reforms which make the reign of Henry II second in importance only to that of Edward I in our medieval history belong to the time when Becket's secular service was over. Dr Stubbs used to attribute the Grand Assize, by which the use of a jury to determine the right to land in dispute was instituted (and of which the date is not certainly known, and the

account appears only in Glanville, *de Legibus Angliae*),
to the period of Thomas's political employment; and
it was argued that this act must have been prior to the
Constitutions of Clarendon, which show, in the Assize
Utrum, the custom of a jury in civil suits. But it has
been shown more probably that that Assize was issued
in the Great Council at Windsor in April, 1179.[1] It is
indeed, improbable that if Thomas were the author of
so important a measure there would be no record
among his biographers that the *regale beneficium* was
his work.

The main interests of these years lay among foreign
affairs. The third marriage of Louis VII, with Alice
of Champagne, arrayed more enemies against Henry,
for it linked the house of the Frankish king to the
enemies of Anjou in central France. The retort was
the enforced marriage of Margaret and Henry, the
children of the rival kings, and Henry's seizure of the
frontier castles, followed by a short war and the seizure
of castles, after the English king's constant policy.
Then matters were patched up as usual. It was
neither party's interest as yet to have a war to the
knife.

Before this came an event almost equally familiar,
a Schism in the Papacy. Adrian IV, the English Pope,
died. Frederick the emperor had Victor IV chosen by
his party: "divinum non verita judicium," says William
of Newburgh. Alexander III was the Pope of the
Hildebrandine party: the English and French kings
accepted him: he fled from Italy and took refuge in

---

[1] See Round, *Athenaeum*, Jan. 28th, 1899, accepted by Davis,
England under the Norman and Angevin Kings, pp. 280-1.

France. Complications arising on all sides kept Henry busy abroad from August, 1158, and probably his chancellor was often at his side. During the king's "absence from England, which lasted till January, 1163, the country was administered by the justices, the queen or the young Henry occasionally presiding at the Court or Councils. The country was quiet, and the business of justice and taxation went on without difficulty."[1] This was soon to be changed.

Theobald, archbishop of Canterbury, had long been sick. Again and again in the last months of his life had John of Salisbury written in his name to beg the king to spare the chancellor that he might visit him before he died and that the Lord's anointed himself would come to his servant's bedside. But neither Henry nor Thomas came, and Theobald died without seeing him whom his soul desired, yet not without still thinking of him as his successor. On April 18th, 1161, he passed away. He was buried in his own cathedral church. In 1174 his body was translated to the nave. In 1787, according to the custom at Canterbury[2] of opening the graves of archbishops, his bones were again seen and identified. Long before that the dust of his successor had been scattered to the winds.

---

[1] Stubbs, *Constitutional History*, i, 458.
[2] Cf. Archbishop Herring and S. Anselm, *Hist. MSS. Com. Report on Various MSS.* i, 226–31, and *Life of Archbishop Benson*, ii, 301–2.

CHAPTER III

THE ARCHBISHOPRIC

THEOBALD had prayed Henry to give him a worthy successor. For some time the king seems to have hesitated. Several months passed during which we have no knowledge of what was in his mind. Men had long suspected the chancellor of desiring the primacy. He had known himself, as had others, that the dead archbishop had looked for him to succeed. But now the king and he went about their ordinary business, and if they ever spoke of the matter we know nothing of what they said. We do not know if they were much together during these months; but early in April, 1162, the signature of the chancellor shows that he was with the king at Rouen, and there the prior of Leicester told him of the rumour at Court that he should be archbishop. A month later Henry was at Falaise, and designing to secure the succession of his young son, who had long been in the chancellor's charge among many young sons of nobles whom, after the custom of the great medieval prelates, he brought up in his household, teaching them religion, and gentle manners and warlike exercises. The king sent for the chancellor, who, as was customary, had charge of the vacant see. He was to be sent to England, to deal with the Welsh, and to see that prelates and nobles did homage to the king's son.

Henry gave the commission, and then when Thomas came to take leave, had received his orders and turned to depart, at last he spoke. Herbert of Bosham tells the story, no doubt from Thomas's own lips, but with his own prolixity. The Saga's picturesque words are to the same effect. The king called him back "and they talk thus privily: 'Thou knowest not yet fully all things concerning thy journey. My will is fully settled that thou be Canterbury's archbishop.' At this the blessed Thomas smileth somewhat,[1] pointing to the armhole of the kirtle he wore, saying deftly: 'Behold, my lord, what a religious and holy person you are minded to install in that exalted seat, and over the many monks and holy persons who worship God there. But in sooth it were better that you should not set your mind so hard on this change in me, for if this ever should come to pass by the long-suffering of God, surely your favour would depart from me speedily. And withal you have in your realm such laudable persons as that my fleshly feebleness fareth low before their feet. It might come to pass, too, my lord, should my affairs take this shift, that I might turn out right unlike, and of a different mind, to him who now standeth here before you; yea, and many would they be who would give themselves to carrying slander between us. I therefore pray, in all humbleness, that you go somewhere else.' Having thus spoke, he boweth to the king and walketh out of the chamber."

The protest and warning were in vain. Bonitho[2] tells a similar tale of Hildebrand. Henry would listen

---

[1] Robertson (*Becket*, p. 38) noted this, but Dr Radford (*Thomas of London*, p. 198, note) criticised him, not observing this authority, which goes beyond Herbert here in detail.

[2] *Monumenta Gregoriana* (Jaffé), p. 657.

to no objection when his mind was made up, now or ever. Several advisers, including his mother, had already warned him against the choice, but in vain. He repeated his decision in public, and to Richard de Lucy, his faithful justiciar, he commended the chancellor as he would commend his own son. With him into England he sent the bishops Walter of Rochester, Hilary of Chichester, Bartholomew of Exeter (all names often repeated in the letters of the later years), and the abbat of Battle, whose rights king and chancellor had secured. Richard de Lucy lived to be excommunicated by the man whose interest he was now pledged to serve.

Whether or no he had looked forward to the primacy Thomas was now reluctant to receive it. He had come to know the king so thoroughly, he had come perhaps to know the manner in which he designed to deal with the Church, that he would fain have drawn back when the moment came. He was warm-hearted, impulsive, affectionate; his letters in later years must be hypocritical indeed if they do not prove a real love for his friend and master: he would dread the breach of friendship, and, if there were anything in his life to show a trace of personal timidity we might think that he would dread the issue of a conflict with such a king. But he dreaded, one may be sure, the conflict itself, not its issues. Yet there is nothing to show that he foresaw in any detail the nature of the conflict. Some of his biographers think, too, that the flesh was weak: he shrank from the hard life that lay before a true shepherd of the flock. He had put off the deacon: he feared to put on the priest—still more, the primate.

But he gave way. The Cistercian Henry of Pisa, cardinal and papal legate, pressed on him to yield. He must not give up the opportunity of doing such great service to the Church. Guernes says that Becket's resistance was overcome by Henry of Winchester, the king's aged kinsman and wise counsellor. He yielded, and having once accepted the charge he was not the man to withdraw an inch from its demands. He went to England prepared for all that lay before him.

But first he did his last act of faithfulness in a lay charge. He induced the bishops and abbats to swear fealty to the young Henry, and himself "did homage to him first of them all, saving only his allegiance to the king, so long as he should live and wish to stay at the head of the realm."

Meanwhile the king's will was being carried out. The justiciar and the bishops went to Canterbury[1] and there Richard de Lucy addressed the monks of Christ Church. They knew the king to be most observant of the things of God, he said, and to regard the Church of Canterbury with filial love, humbly and faithfully. He gave them his leave to choose a new archbishop, and prayed that they should make a wise choice, for otherwise grave dangers would befall the whole Church. Then the prior and the older and wiser monks withdrew to consider, and very soon saw that they must do nothing without the counsel of the bishops and the justiciar. They returned to ask advice,

---

[1] This account comes from Anonymus I (*Materials*, iv), whom Mr Freeman (*Contemp. Rev.* 1878) and Fr. John Morris (*Life*, 1885 ed.) identify with Roger, a monk of Pontigny, who is said by Thomas of Froidmont to have written a life of Becket. The identification is accepted by M. Walberg in his edition of Guernes.

and, the advice given, all with one voice, bishops and monks, chose Thomas the chancellor. But when the whole chapter considered the matter, many, says Herbert of Bosham, were against such a choice: the chancellor, they said, was better fitted to wield a sword than to rule a great Church; and, besides, Canterbury had always been designed—by S. Augustine himself—to be a monastic church, and should not be ruled by a secular. But the opposition did not prevail, and the election was unanimous.

Then the choice was submitted to the bishops at Westminster, May 23rd, 1162. All the bishops, abbats and priors of the province were summoned, and with them, in the refectory of the abbey, sat young Henry, the king's son. One only protested against the choice, and that was Gilbert Foliot, bishop of Hereford, a stern and learned monk, once of Cluny, strict and bitter, and an ascetic who never took wine or meat. He declared that Thomas who had been a persecutor of the Church, must not be chosen: he had destroyed the Church, held her in despite, and scattered her goods: the monks had done wrong in choosing him. Foliot had already refused to administer the diocese of London when the bishop, Richard de Belmeis, was paralysed; it was, as it seemed, only with reluctance, a little later, that he accepted the see when it became vacant. Some had named him as the fit successor of Theobald. His opposition to the choice of Thomas, recalled again with bitterness four years later, was overcome.

Henry, bishop of Winchester, a Cistercian, once legate, and a statesman among the most prominent in the days of Stephen, announced the bishops' assent to the election, and adjured Thomas to serve the Heavenly King better and with stronger will than he had served the earthly. "So Saul the persecutor became Paul."

The formal assent of the king was given by the child Henry. Full release from all secular obligations was prayed and granted.[1] Thomas accepted the charge; some say that he then declared that he would defend the liberties of the Church against the king.

It was the Wednesday after Whit Sunday. He prepared at once to go to Canterbury. As he rode thither, with attendants clerk and lay, he spoke to Herbert of Bosham, as perhaps to others, bidding him to show him always how others judged him and to tell him always when he acted wrongly: "four eyes," he said, "are better than two." He told, too, a dream he had had the night before of a venerable man who intrusted to him ten talents. His mind was dwelling on what faithfulness should mean in his new charge, and how he should attain to it. When the journey ended he was received at Canterbury "as the custom is, with hymns and spiritual songs."

The Ember fasts of Wednesday and Friday prepared for the ordination as priest on Saturday. In the cathedral church, Walter, bishop of Rochester, and the vicar of the Church of Canterbury for episcopal acts during the vacancy of the see, ordained him to the priesthood.

Next day he was consecrated by Henry, bishop of

---

[1] It seems impossible, in face of an accumulation of testimony, to doubt this, though the place and date may be doubtful. Cf. Radford, *op. cit.* p. 220, note 1.

Winchester, assisted by Nigel of Ely, the famous statesman of the ministerial house founded by Roger of Salisbury, the servant of Henry I, Robert of Bath, Jocelin of Salisbury, William of Norwich, Hilary of Chichester, Richard of Lichfield, Bartholomew of Exeter, Robert of Lincoln, Walter of Rochester, Nicholas of Llandaff, David of S. David's, Gilbert of Hereford, and Godfrey of S. Asaph. Roger of Pont l'Evêque, archbishop of York, his old rival, had claimed the right of consecration as inherent in his see; but the claim was rejected because Roger had made no profession of obedience to Canterbury. A claim is said to have been made by a Welsh bishop, as senior by consecration of all the bishops, but the dates confute the story. On Sunday, June 3rd, 1162, the octave of Pentecost, Thomas of London was consecrated and enthroned as archbishop of Canterbury.

Immediately afterwards, contrary to what would in later years have been considered orthodox custom but in accord with the usage of the day, he said "his first mass" in the chapel of the Blessed Trinity at the east end of the cathedral church.

"This chapel," says Fr. Morris,[1] who made a loving study of Canterbury as it was in Becket's day, "was his favourite resort when he was in Canterbury. Here he said mass both before his exile and after his return. Here he would come to assist privately at the office of the monks in choir, and he would frequently retire to the same chapel for prayer. On a screen on the right of the high altar, between it and the chapel of the blessed Trinity, lay S. Odo; on the left, S. Wilfrid; by

[1] *Life of S. Thomas of Canterbury*, i, 69.

the south wall of the chapel was the resting-place of Lanfranc, and by the north wall that of Theobald. Beneath was the crypt, containing on the south side an altar dedicated to S. Augustine, the Apostle of England, and on the north side the altar of S. John the Baptist. Between these two altars in the crypt S. Thomas was buried the day after his martyrdom, and there his body lay until the site of the chapel he had loved best in life was prepared to receive his shrine. The altar-stone was prized on which the Saint had said his first mass, and of it an altar was made that was dedicated to S. John the Evangelist."

The mass in that chapel was remembered in the consecration of that special day. Gervase of Canterbury tells that the new archbishop instituted the festival of the Holy Trinity to be for ever observed on the octave of Pentecost. Hitherto where such a special festival had been observed the dates had been different in different places, and the Roman Church (which still numbers the Sundays after Pentecost) had not observed it. The usage begun by Becket spread over the whole Church; and John XXII accepted it for all the churches under his supremacy in the fourteenth century. After the consecration of the new choir at Canterbury in 1220 the whole of the cathedral church, which had before from time to time been so called, bore permanently the dedication to the Holy Trinity.[1]

So Thomas entered upon his great charge. And he entered on it in the spirit of renunciation. If he was

---

[1] Cf. Dr R. L. Poole in *English Historical Review*, xv, 86, but see *Materials*, vi, 418, where a letter of Alexander III is addressed to the Convent of the Holy Trinity.

not yet a monk he was soon to become a regular. The monks of Christ Church, ever eager to find fault, murmured that he still wore the secular habit; one of his household told him a dream which ordered him to change his garb: it is not likely that he needed such a warning. Within a few days of his consecration, it seems probable—for he was certainly a secular priest when he was consecrated—he went to the abbey of Merton, laid down "his costly weeds" and took "the black cappa and white surplice with the ordination of a canon regular." This was the habit of the Augustinian canons: a monk, strictly speaking, Becket never became, though he wore the Cistercian cowl, four years later, at Pontigny. We have no reason to suppose that he ever took monastic vows; if he had done so his biographer would be sure to have told it. His garb, as Guernes says, was partly regular, partly secular. But a life of rule he certainly adopted.

Consecrated on June 3rd, 1162, he received the pallium from Alexander III, in exile at Montpellier, on August 10th. Thus the English State and Church and the Roman pontiff had combined to confer, or recognise his powers. He entered upon his work with a determination to cast off all that had been purely secular in his life. His biographers without exception see that there was a real change, a real renunciation. "Sinner that I am," says Herbert of Bosham, "for having attempted to describe him, who have not myself been with Moses to the top or Joshua to the foot of the mount." What this involved William Fitz-Stephen thus tells—[1]

[1] *Materials*, iii, 37 *sqq.*

"The archbishop, in his consecration, was anointed with the visible unction of God's mercy, and putting off the secular man, was clothed in Jesus Christ; he cast aside the temporal duties of the chancellor; and how to discharge the functions of a good archbishop alone occupied his thoughts.

"To this end he kept watch over his mind with all diligence: his words were serious for edification of the hearers; his works were those of mercy and piety; his thoughts, those of righteousness and equity. Clad in sackcloth of the coarsest kind, reaching to his thighs and covered with vermin, he mortified his flesh by spare diet, and his general drink was water, in which hay had been boiled.[1] He always, however, took the first taste of the wine, and then gave it to those who sat at the table with him: he ate a portion of the meat that was placed before him, but fed chiefly on bread. All things, however, are clean to the clean, and fault lies not in the food but in the appetite. He often exposed his naked back to the lash of the discipline. Immediately over the sackcloth he wore a monk's habit, as being abbat of the monks of Canterbury; above this he wore the dress of a canon, that he might be in conformity with the clerks. But the stole, that sweet yoke of Christ, was ever, day and night, around his neck. His countenance externally was fashioned like that of the multitude, but in his inward soul he was very different. In these respects he took for his pattern S. Sebastian and S. Cecilia; the former of whom, beneath the covering of a military cloak, bore the

[1] Was this for ascetic reasons, or a sort of toast and water? Robertson calls it fennel-water.

spirit of a soldier of Christ, whilst the latter, subduing the flesh with sackcloth, appeared outwardly adorned in vestments wrought with gold. In his table and his dress he studied to be really religious, rather than to seem so. Intent on prayer, he endeavoured to reconcile, and in a manner to unite his created spirit to the Creator Spirit. As the interpreter between God and men, he in his prayers commended man to God, whilst in his preaching he commended God to man. He was zealous in reading the Scriptures, and had by him one learned in the sacred page. Sometimes after dinner he conferred with his clerks, hearing them and asking them questions. His companions at meals were religious and clerks virtuous and learned. He had, in the same way, a household chosen, with whom all good men were hospitably entertained, and treated with every respect. In almsgiving he was most munificent, for he sometimes sent four or five marks to the hospitals and poor colleges; sometimes he sent meat and provisions.

"His predecessor, Theobald, of blessed memory, had doubled the regular alms of the bishops, his predecessors: and now Thomas, in the spirit of pious rivalry, doubled all Theobald's donations. In order to fulfil his holy purpose, he set aside the tenth part of everything he received, from whatever source it was derived. In his secret cell he every day, kneeling on his knees, washed the feet of thirteen beggars, in memory of Christ: he then, and after a full refection, gave four shillings to each of them. If he was on any occasion, though seldom, prevented from doing this in his own person, he took care to have the duty discharged by deputy. In his solitary hours, it was marvellous how plentifully he overflowed with tears, and when he was serving at the altar, you would fancy that he had before him our Lord's passion bodily in the flesh. He handled the holy sacraments with awe and reverence, so that his very manner confirmed the faith and conduct of the beholders.

"Further: he received into his house the wandering and needy: he clothed many against the severities of winter. At Canterbury he often betook himself to the cloisters, where he sat, like one of the monks who generally sit there, studying in some useful book: afterwards he went to visit the sick monks, and to learn their wishes, that he might gratify them. He was the comforter of the oppressed, the husband of the widowed, the friend of orphans. He was, moreover, humble and affable to the mild, but severe to the proud. Against the injustice and insolence of the powerful he was lifted up like a strong tower against Damascus; nor could the prayers or letters of the king himself or any other person in favour of anyone prevail unless according to righteousness.

"The purity of his life was now perfect, he who even when chancellor had never passed the bounds of purity and honour. He was a second Moses, often entering and going out from the tabernacle of the Lord: entering it at the accepted time for the contemplation of God, and going out from it in order to perform some work of piety towards his neighbours. He was a second Jacob, at one time paying his visits to the more prolific Leah, at another, to the more beautiful

Rachel.[1] He was like one of God's angels on the ladder, whose top reached to heaven, now descending to lighten the wants of man, now ascending to the gate of Divine Majesty, and the heavenly splendour. Aloof from the transitory things of this world, he gazed with ardour on the things that are above. His mind was bent on those virtues which render happy this present life, and earn for us the life which is to come. His prime counsellor was Reason, which ever ruled his evil passions and mental impulses, as a mistress rules her servants. Under her guidance he was conducted to virtue, which, wrapped up in itself, spurns everything that opposes it, and deriving its origin from itself, again returns to itself, and embracing everything within itself, never looks abroad for anything additional. He possessed virtue of four kinds. Prudence, which gave him discernment in the notice of things, in the estimate of persons, time, and place, in the avoidance of evil, and the choice of good. He possessed Justice (Righteousness), whereby he studied to preserve to God and his neighbour that which belonged to each. Fortitude, which vindicates in adversity, and protects the mind from the pain of present evils, and the fear of future ones. Temperance, which in prosperity checked all tendency to immoderate indulgence and recalled him from all licentiousness and desire of the things of this world, as well as from indecent mirth. These four virtues form the true four-horse chariot of Aminadab; the first of Diatessarons! the true harmony of man's life! This is that

[1] This is a common medieval form of expression for the active and the contemplative life.

sweet and delectable concert among men, which fills
the ears of God, and brings us to that happy state of
being, where apart from every evil, we shall enjoy this
accumulation of everything that is good.

"This state of being was the archbishop's, and by
it was he supremely blessed: he studied to do all things
firmly, finely, weightily, and honourably, to refer all
things to the test of wisdom, to govern himself; to
listen to the voice of wisdom, not of the mob; to fear
no snare of fortune; to show himself strongly guarded
and impregnable against adversity; to believe himself
born not for himself, but for all who needed his assistance, and especially for his own church, the government of which was on his shoulders; to contemplate
divine things, even whilst he was on earth; to imitate
Jesus Christ, Who was born and came down from
heaven to suffer; to love Him and to keep His commands, and to seek the salvation of himself and the
souls committed to his charge. From this it came to
pass that Thomas obtained grace in the sight of God,
and solid and open glory among men; all the good
bearing testimony in his praise, and passing an un-
bought judgment upon his worth. This is that which
responds to virtue, as the echo answers to the voice,
as the image corresponds to its model. Glory is the
companion of those who live well, and as it is not to be
sought, so is it not to be rejected, but to be ascribed
to God. The apostle says, 'For if I shall wish to glory,
I shall be foolish, but I will speak the truth.' Thomas
feared this glory and rejected it: lest pride should
creep in; seeing that it is written, 'however righteous,
yet you never can be secure.' There is also another

vain and false glory, which the proud and vain, rich men and hypocrites, seek; a specious likeness of true glory, but with no recommendation such as is derived from solid virtue. To the eye, indeed, it appears like it, but it is not so in reality. As the good fear the approach of true glory, so do the evil court that which is spurious; or, if they do a work of praise, by their seeking to derive from it glory or reward, they lose both the name and the merit.

"The glorious archbishop, Thomas, contrary to the expectations of the king and of all his men, so abandoned the world, and so suddenly felt that change which is the handwork of the Most High, that it filled all with astonishment."

A strange mingling, this long eulogy of his chaplain's, of sincerity with the curious, medieval, theological affectation. Thomas himself could set before his soul a new ideal; but his disciples could only express that ideal in conventional pomposities.

Further details of the archbishop's life are added by many another of the biographers, and there are few which we have any reason to distrust. Herbert of Bosham, who was most constantly at his side, gives some which are perhaps the most interesting. He tells how he would attend his master quite early in the morning when he studied the Holy Scriptures, how continually, even when he was riding (an exercise which he saw no ascetic reason to abandon), he would talk of them—he carried a manuscript often in his loose sleeves—and how often he would sigh to "lay aside the cares of the world and in peace and quietness attend to sacred studies." "How carefully," he would say, "would I atone, if I might, for the time I have lost!" His day was ruled by monastic hours. At midnight he would rise to give thanks unto God in the choir; then he would wash the feet of thirteen poor men and give alms, before dawn; so hereafter should the light reveal his humility and charity. At daybreak he went to bed, but rested only a short time. At nine he came out from his room to say mass or be present at it; "for he said not mass every day; and this was not through neglect, as he himself said, but through reverence." When he put on the vestments his eyes were often full of tears, so deeply did he feel the sacred work he was to set about. When he was not celebrating himself, he would read devotional books during the preparation, often the prayers of S. Anselm. He said mass very quickly—not like Roger of Salisbury, famous for his "hunting mass," but to avoid the chance of distraction. Accustomed, like all busy men, to concentration of mind, he yet knew the danger of concentration for too long. "Ye shall eat in haste, for it is the Lord's Passover."

After his mass he would hear suits in his court, if such there were, refusing all presents that it was possible to decline.

At his meals, as has been said, there was every appearance of profusion and delicacy, but he himself ate but little—often only a little partridge or some other dainty thing. Herbert of Bosham tells that a monk who was a guest at his table one day smiled at this, and Becket saw it and said: "If I err not, brother, there is more greediness in your eating beans than in my eating pheasant," which was true, for the man cared only for quantity, not quality. At the dinner in his hall he sat in the middle of the table, looking down the hall. On his left sat monks; on his right those whom Herbert calls the "eruditi S. Thomae," who included John of Salisbury (philosopher, theologian and man of letters), Robert Foliot, Ralph of Sar, Lombard of Piacenza (afterwards archbishop of Benevento—many passed from England to Sicily in those days, and back, as Becket's letters show, his own kindred among them), Reginald the Lombard (son of the bishop of Salisbury, and himself afterwards archbishop of Canterbury for less than a month), Gerard la Pucelle, Hugh of Nunant, and Gilbert Glanville—all of whom became English bishops, and the last the preacher of the Third Crusade. In the hall at other tables sat the knights and other attendants, so placed that they might not be wearied by the pious book that was read, for the clergy's hearing, during the meal.

After dinner the archbishop and his friends talked together, and sometimes he would take a much-needed nap. The rest of the day would be devoted to study, often (as Fitz-Stephen says) in the cloisters, to visiting the sick and other acts of charity. Becket's generosity is reported to have far exceeded that of his predecessors. He had, it may be inferred, a much larger private income, for he most probably saved a good deal, lavish though he was, as chancellor.

Details of all his life at this time, replenished no doubt by memories of his exile, are very full. It might be wearisome to reproduce more. It may suffice to say that they all point to two things—a real change in manner of life and an eager attention to the duties of the episcopal office.

His semi-monastic dress, as has been said, marked his renunciation. He wore it, the black *cappa* reaching to his feet, all his life: at critical times the biographers record the fact. It was his memorial of his school days at Merton, whence Robert the Prior had come to be with him as his constant companion. His stole he wore continually, perhaps that he might be ready (it has rather fancifully been suggested—for it was not difficult to get a stole quickly or even to carry it in a pocket) to give confirmation at any moment. Benedict of Peterborough tells that, unlike other bishops, he would always get off his horse to confer that sacrament; and at places where this happened crosses were often set up, and miracles were heard of there in later days. He was careful, indeed, in all the Sacraments: it was especially noted in regard to ordination and those whom he admitted to the sacred gift of orders.

Herbert of Bosham gives his charge to those he was to ordain at the September Ember season of 1162—"I beseech you, brethren, by the mercy of God that you suffer not my hands to be laid suddenly upon you except you be ready to minister worthily in the Church of God according to the nature of your office; lest I be partaker in other men's sins, who feel myself too much weighted by the multitude of my own. For sure it is that he who ordains, knowingly and without much probation, an unworthy person, even if the ordained afterwards be reformed, gravely offendeth God; for if the ordained man be not reformed, he who ordains defiles himself with the sins of the ordained, with those especially which he doeth after the day of his ordination. Wherefore the apostle commandeth Timothy, saying: 'Lay hands suddenly on no man, lest you be partaker of other men's sins.' And you, therefore, my brethren, we forbid on behalf of Almighty God and ourselves, that any suffer the yoke of the Lord to be placed on him by us, if he feel himself unfit. Let him abide rather in that which is good, so long as he hath not strength for that which is better." Such words in the midst of his address to the ordinands showed how deeply the archbishop felt the grave responsibility of his office.[1] The record is uncommon in the lives of English medieval prelates.

Such was the life and such the aim of the man who had so lately seemed to live simply as a layman, moral and religious, but still ostentatiously secular. It was not long before the news of the change spread. The little Henry, who was often with the archbishop, his former tutor, would mark it and question his father, it may be, as to what it meant. But Henry the king was still for some time abroad. The erudite and the religious, however, had long tongues, and many of them loved to use the pen. The goodness of the new archbishop could not be hid. Thus, Arnulf of Lisieux, never more than a fair-weather friend, at this time of holiness, popularity and exaltation[2]—probably before the end of 1161—wrote to him with an effusive gratitude for his letters because of the holiness of his life, for in him "a great prophet has arisen among us and God hath visited His people." It was not long before the voice of such friends sounded a different note.

[1] Herbert of Bosham, *Materials*, iii, 239.   [2] *Materials*, v, 20–1.

CHAPTER IV

THE BEGINNING OF TROUBLES

THOMAS, archbishop of Canterbury, was still chancellor. There can be no doubt that the king desired him to retain the office. The Emperor had for chancellor of Italy the archbishop of Köln, for chancellor of Germany the archbishop of Mainz. Such an association of a national Church and State had proved very useful during disputes with the Papacy; and the king foresaw such a dispute in England. It is strange, but it was thoroughly characteristic of Henry, in whom insight was the one qualification of a statesman that was conspicuously lacking, that he should have fancied Becket had no similar prevision. It might well have been, for the archbishop's letters in the following years show him a singularly candid critic of the Papacy, that he would not have hesitated to engage on the king's side in a dispute with the Pope; but the interests of the Church, notably of the Church of England, were another matter and a matter now especially committed to his charge.

One of the first instances of this care is to be found in the pains he took to procure a fit successor to the late bishop of London; and the generosity of his nature is to be seen in this letter to Gilbert Foliot, bishop of Hereford,[1] already his opponent, if not his rival—

"That the City of London surpasses in grandeur

[1] *Materials*, v, 26.

all the other cities of this kingdom is well known to all of us, my brother: for the business of the whole realm is therein transacted; it is the residence of the king, and frequented more than any other by his nobles. For this reason it is important that the Church of London, which has now lost its ruler, should receive for its new bishop a man whose personal merit, attainments in learning, and prudence in managing public business, shall not be unworthy of the dignity of that see. After much deliberation in this matter, it is the unanimous request of the clergy, the will of the king and myself, and the apostolic decision, that the general welfare of the kingdom, and the interests of the Church, will best be promoted, by your being translated to exercise the pastoral care over the diocese of London. To this end I have received the instructions of the lord pope, and I enjoin you, by his authority, to give your assent without delay to the election of the Church of London, passed in presence of our lord the king, and with the consent of the whole clergy and ourself; and to take the government of the aforesaid church into your hands with promptitude corresponding to the necessity which exists for its charge to be committed to the counsel and government of such a person. And I entreat of you, my brother, that whereas you are bound to this by virtue of your obedience to ourself, so you may be led by your own inclinations to undertake the duties of this important trust. Thus, not only sincere affection, but also proximity of place will unite us both in the same good work, to give one another mutual assistance in ministering to the necessities of God's Church.''

This letter, and one from Henry himself, overcame the reluctance of the stern Cluniac, and Gilbert Foliot, bitter to others as severe with himself, and proud in asserting the dignity of his position if not consciously ambitious for his own advancement, came to London, to prove the ablest and most relentless of the primate's enemies.

Soon after his consecration Becket resigned the chancellorship. The date cannot certainly be fixed. The signature of the archbishop does not contain the word chancellor after his consecration, but this would in any case hardly have been given. There is nothing to show when the office was actually abandoned. Henry and his queen Eleanor returned to England on January 25th, 1163, and were met by their son and the archbishop at Southampton. In February king and archbishop were at Oxford together, in March at Westminster. On the 17th of March Henry spent Palm Sunday with the archbishop at Canterbury, and two days later they were together at Windsor, urging Gilbert Foliot to accept the bishopric of London. During the months that had passed since Henry's return a second cause of disagreement had arisen. Not only was Henry angry that his friend should have given up his personal service but he resented the delay made by Becket before he surrendered the arch-deaconry. There has been much dispute as to this. The explanation that may be suggested is that Becket wished to settle all the matters as to the respective rights of archbishop and archdeacon before a new arch-deacon was appointed. He did not succeed in doing so, and Geoffrey Ridel, whom the king appointed, proved to be one of his most bitter foes.

Already men were bringing tales against him to the king. He had begun to reclaim for the Church of Canterbury possessions which had been taken from her: "and[1] although mighty folk or even the king's own men now hold these properties, already they must give them up, for in this matter the archbishop maketh all men equal. All properties which have lately fallen off by want of power in the bailiffs of the Church or by reason of indulgence shown to mighty men, such, whereof he knoweth for sure the Church is the owner, he draweth with a strong hand, and without any proof at all, back to the arch-see, saying that he will have no litigation about such properties and privileges which he knoweth, without any doubt to be in the rightful possession of the Church, if she is to be left unrobbed. But everywhere, where the property has lapsed for a length of time, he bringeth forth the testimony of men or of trustworthy documents, and thus taketh them again under the Church." This proceeding, says the Saga, though laudable, was not liked any the more for that.

Among the properties thus reclaimed were the tower of Rochester, Gundulf's splendid work, and the castle of Tunbridge, and, among benefices, the church of Eynesford. The patronage of this last had been seized by William of Eynesford, who expelled the clerk nominated by the archbishop, was excommunicated, and applied to the king. At his intercession he was absolved, but Henry at Windsor—this must have been about March 31st—was heard to say of Becket, "now he has my favour no more." Those who sought to

---

[1] *Saga*, i. 119.

make ill-blood between king and archbishop had hitherto tried in vain. Some of them had crossed to Normandy and told their complaints in the king's ear, but he had put them aside; and when they met at Southampton, the young Henry and the archbishop walking hand in hand, "the king showeth himself right blithe, rising up from his seat to meet the archbishop, and they kiss each other lovingly." Still in the early months of 1163 king and archbishop talked, "as was their wont," of matters of government and policy. It was not till the resignation of the chancellorship and the case of William of Eynesford that the first signs of dissension appeared. To this was added, Grim says, the stern way in which Thomas looked upon the clergy of the Court, lax as such men are tempted to be. And this brings us to the summer of 1163.

During the late spring for about a month the archbishop, with Roger of Pont l'Evêque, archbishop of York, had been absent from England, attending the Council at Tours held by Alexander III, the Pope, who, in the Schism, was accepted by those who were not of the Emperor's party. It was at Tours that he spent the anniversary of his consecration, the octave of Whit Sunday, 1163. The Council itself was of no particular importance, but to it Thomas submitted the claim of Anselm, his great predecessor, for canonisation, a claim which was never granted till 1494 and then by Alexander VI. A letter of Alexander III refers it to a provincial council of bishops. But at the Council, as more than one writer suggests, Becket may well have received an additional stimulus to resist the claims of the king against the Church.

The date of the excommunication of William of Eynesford is uncertain. The seemingly trivial dispute with Clarembald, abbat of S. Augustine's, Canterbury, which ended not with S. Thomas's life, as to where he should receive the primate's blessing, and whether he should make profession of obedience, began about this time; and the king was the abbat's patron. But the first open breach was at Woodstock about July 1st, 1163, and the dispute concerned money.

The sheriff's aid, "a customary charge, varying in amount, paid over locally to the sheriffs,"[1] had long been paid from the shires. It was, says Edward Grim,[2] a sum of two shillings from each hide, and no doubt was supposed to be used for the defence of the shires. Henry wished to take it simply as revenue, to be paid into the Exchequer. Becket, a constitutionalist to the core, declared that it should not thus be paid, but that if the sheriffs did their duty they should receive the payment as of old. Henry swore by God's eyes that it should be as he willed; Becket, "by the reverence of those eyes by which you have sworn," that it should not be thus paid from his lands or those of the Church. The opposition was that of a statesman to an arbitrary innovation, rather than that of an ecclesiastic. Henry—so Grim says—yielded, but his anger was not set at rest. And almost immediately there arose the real matter of permanent division, the constitutional question of the relation of the Church courts to those of the State.

---

[1] Mr Round, *Feudal England*, p. 501, was the first to make this clear. Dr Stubbs had spoken of the sum in question as probably Danegeld.   [2] *Materials*, ii, 374.

For some time, the biographers tell us, Henry had been considering the position of the clergy in regard to the law of the State. During the reign of Stephen the independence of the Church as an Estate, and of its individual members, had grown visibly. Monasteries, enjoying exemption from many of the claims of ordinary life, had spread widely over England: during the nineteen years of king Stephen, under the influence of the Cistercian revival, more religious houses had been built than were founded at any other period of the same length in English history. The clergy had exercised almost a commanding influence on the decision of questions of national concern: first Henry of Winchester, then Theobald of Canterbury, was the arbiter at times of crisis. The very Charters of Stephen bore witness to the exceptional position of the clergy. As the civil courts, central and local, ceased to work regularly during the wars, the Church courts naturally stepped into their place. Men brought suits where they could procure a rapid and probably a just decision, and where, on the whole, the forms were less complicated and the proceedings more intelligible. When Henry began to restore the working of the lay courts, and designed to make the supremacy of the Crown uniformly effective everywhere throughout the land, over all persons and in all causes, the position of the Church, coherent and fixed in its isolation, confronted him. And it seemed that a theory of independence involved practical results of scandal and wrong.

The matter came to a crisis, no doubt by the king's arrangement, about July, 1163, when Henry and Becket were both in London. Simon Fitz-Peter, a man of some

DISPUTE BETWEEN BECKET AND HENRY II

importance, with lands in Somerset, Wiltshire, and Northamptonshire, who was sheriff of Bedfordshire and Buckinghamshire 1156–60, and of Northamptonshire 1155–61 and again 1163–70, and recently had been one of the king's justices in eyre in Bedfordshire, complained that he had been insolently treated by a clerk, Philip de Brois. And then, says Edward Grim, he proceeded to revive a charge long forgotten. Philip had been accused of murder, tried in the court of the bishop of Lincoln and acquitted. But Henry, or "one of the king's officers, wishing, from an old grudge he bore him, that the clerk should be ruined," brought up the charge again and insisted that it should be heard in the lay court. The clerk refused to be tried again and poured abuse upon the justice. The justice formally complained to the king. Henry insisted that the man should be tried again for murder and anew for his insulting language. Becket claimed the trial for his own court at Canterbury, and there the accusation which had already been heard and judged was of course dismissed, while for the abuse a sentence of scourging was given, with a heavy pecuniary punishment. Henry was dissatisfied and declared that the bishops who had judged the case had had more respect for the archbishop than for him. "By God's eyes," he said, "you shall make oath to me that you gave a just judgment and spared the man not because he was a clerk."

Two other cases were brought up to increase the dissension. A clerk in the diocese of Salisbury had mortally wounded a man: he was brought before the bishop in his court. Jocelin of Salisbury, old and timid, applied to the archbishop for his advice. Becket "writeth back awarding in a full and formal sentence, that the priest be degraded from all his honours, and move not his foot out of a house of penitence for ever."[1] There was the case also of a certain clerk of Worcestershire who was said to have seduced the daughter of a certain worthy man, and on her account to have killed the father himself. This clerk the king wished to be tried and judged in the lay court. The archbishop was for refusing and gave the clerk to be kept in custody by the bishop, to prevent his being handed over to the king's justice. Another case was on behalf of a clerk who stole a chalice from the Church of S. Mary-le-Bow, and whom the king, when he was caught, wished to be judged in the secular court. Thomas had him tried in his own court and sentenced him to degradation and branding.[2] It may be that in thus going beyond what canon law allowed the archbishop hoped to mitigate the king's wrath, as Fitz-Stephen suggests. If he did, he was much deceived.

A Council at Westminster on October 1st, 1163, brought matters to an issue. It was alleged that the cause of summons was to secure the recognition of the archbishop of Canterbury as "primate of all England," a title which the archbishop of York refused to allow. But the real object was very different. It was the whole question of the right of jurisdiction over criminous clerks. Henry complained of the venality and the exactions of the archdeacons. But their excesses were only the symptoms of a deeper disease. Thus

---

[1] *Thomas Saga*, i, 143.
[2] These last two cases are from Fitz-Stephen, *Materials*, iii, 45–6.

the king spoke to the assembled bishops and abbats, canons and clerks, to "all the barons and a multitude of mighty folk." The speech as given by the Icelandic Saga[1] is found in no other authority but bears the stamp of truth, bitter irony veiling a determined purpose—

"We have been silent awhile," he said, "and meekly listened how you bishops are willing to dispose yourselves towards our royal rights and rule here in England. Now that we have been watching your doings we have been thinking and peacefully searching our mind, as to what kind of fault ye might happen to have found in us, that we must needs be deemed less worthy than other kings, who have been before us, to wear an untottering crown, in virtue of such law-enactments and royal prerogatives, as each one has had and enjoyed in due succession, and no learned men before you listed to withdraw from royal honour. Now although matters of this kind multiply daily, according as your boldness waxeth more and more, we yet desire, as at this time, to turn our speech chiefly towards those men of forfeited lives whom you name clerks, but whom we call so much the worse than lay-folk, in that they have had the foolhardiness to push themselves into the honours and ordinations of Holy Church, turning her dignity and liberty into mockery and fell thraldom; for they may by rights be far rather called the doers of the works of the devil, than consecrated clerks, who forbear doing any kind of mischief much less even than lay-folk who lead all the days of their life in honouring and obeying the law. Now ye, the

[1] *Thomas Saga*, i, 146–8.

bishops, maintain, that it is written in your canons, that such dishonourable things should be protected, and withdrawn from rightful punishment, in that ye think that none beside yourselves alone are able to understand the laws of the emperor or those of the Church; but with greater truth we know, that there are with us men so wise in either law, as to be well fit to root out your own misunderstandings or utterly to refute them. These men have testified such to be a true interpretation of the law, that evil-doers, even such as are ordained, shall be delivered unto rightful punishment by kingly power. We therefore demand of you, the bishops, by the honour and the obedience you owe the Crown, that ye deliver all such clerks as you let wrongfully slip away from our power into sundry places inland as well as abroad, into our hand for rightful punishment, and as to this matter we desire to have clear answers from you."

Before making answer to this Becket consulted with the bishops, and they (according to the Saga) left the answer to him, promising fidelity to his judgment; and he, warning them to be steadfast, answered that it was the desire of all the bishops to heed the king's will in all things, save only when it should set "itself up thwartingly against the will of God, and the laws and dignity of the Holy Church." And the claim he made was that where Christian law was rightly kept a Christian person was not judged as an unconsecrated one, and "the ancient decrees of the holy fathers ordain even thus: If clerks shall be taken in such unseemly deeds as manslaughter, theft, or robbery, they shall for a beginning be suspended from all offices, and be deprived of all good coming from the Church; then be excommunicated and degraded from all orders; and, thus degraded and dishonoured, they are amenable to lay-folk law, but not till then." And he added that so long as he could hold it up the law of the Church should not fall. There are different versions of the speech, but they all have an unyielding note. Some mention the "two swords," Church and State, jurisdictions separate, and the clergy not amenable to lay courts.

Henry, in great anger, demanded the bishops' assent to the customs of his grandfather—the "avitae consuetudines" which became the catchword of his claim. Becket replied that this should be given to all that was right, "saving our consecration and the unimpaired rights of God." So the Council was broken up in anger.

Henry was already endeavouring to win the bishops over to his side. Arnulf of Lisieux had his clever plan to turn the Church against the archbishop, his friend. Roger of Pont l'Evêque was easy to convince. A case of clerical crime in his diocese had been brought to the king's knowledge in 1158, while Becket was still chancellor, and he had then asserted clerical privilege. At Westminster he had spoken up for the Church. But now with the bishops of Lincoln and Chichester—the latter had already been sharply chidden by Becket—he agreed to accept the royal customs, if nothing were exacted contrary to the rights of their order. To Becket Roger appeared as "the incentor and head of all evils."

Henry had withdrawn from London without asking

leave of the bishops and without their blessing. He had, the morning after the Council, demanded from the archbishop the surrender of the manors of Berkhamsted and Eye, which he still held, and of the tutorship of his boy Henry. There was then, perhaps, a pause.

The next act of archiepiscopal ceremonial performed by Becket was the translation of the body of S. Edward Confessor to a dignified shrine in the Abbey of Westminster.[1] At the end of the year (December 22nd)

[1] There is some difficulty about this date. The Westminster authorities are not in themselves conclusive on the point. Flete (MS. No. 29, in the chapter library), whose date is c. 1421–65, quoting from Richard of Cirencester, also a monk of Westminster (whose date of death the dean of Westminster gives as 1400), says that the body of S. Edward was translated in the presence of the king and the archbishop of Canterbury on October 13th, 1163, being a Sunday. But Herbert of Bosham (*Materials*, iii, 261) places the translation, at which he states that both king and archbishop were present, in the same year as the consecration of the conventual church at Reading, which was undoubtedly in 1164. Bishop Stubbs (preface to *Benedictus Abbas*, ii, p. cxxxiv, note) endeavoured to reconcile the authorities by the suggestion that the date of October 13th had been falsely given by inference from the later translation. The dean of Wells (Dr J. Armitage Robinson, formerly dean of Westminster), to whose kindness in showing me a learned note of his on the question I am deeply indebted, however, states that a MS. calendar (c. 1210) in the British Museum proves that the Feast was observed on that date at the beginning of the thirteenth century, and is supported by the Westminster Cartulary called Domesday (the date of which is the beginning of the fourteenth century). We may from this regard October 13th as practically certain for the date of the translation. The only difficulty about the year is the statement of the chroniclers that Henry left Westminster (after the Council) early on October 2nd, and there is no proof of his returning there soon. But on the other hand the next date—that of the meeting near Northampton—which is also given as October, does not make it impossible that both king and archbishop were in Westminster on the 13th. Herbert of Bosham, however, is at this point extremely uncertain in his dates. While he

Thomas consecrated the first of the only two bishops on whom the grace of episcopacy was conferred by his hands, Robert of Melun, who succeeded Gilbert Foliot at Hereford. Becket and John of Salisbury had both attended his lectures at Paris. His only other consecration, it may be added here, was that of Roger, son of Robert, earl of Gloucester, to the see of Worcester, on August 23rd, 1164. Both consecrations were at Canterbury. Before either of them the disputes between king and archbishop had broken out. Becket had pressed upon the king the need of filling the vacant sees, warning him gravely: it was another cause of irritation to the autocratic monarch.

Henry had broken finally with his old friend. But he gave the archbishop another chance of personal submission. They met in a field near Northampton, and Henry reproached him for his ingratitude and reminded him that he was the son of one of his villeins —which was rather an insult than an accurate statement of fact. Becket replied by a quotation from Horace, of which he was rather fond—he was not, he admitted "atavis editus regibus," but nor was S. Peter to whom were given the keys of the kingdom of heaven and the rule of the whole Church. "Yes," said Henry sharply, "but he died for his Lord." "And I will die for my Lord when the time is come," was the answer.

certainly gives the Reading and Westminster ceremonials as of the same year, he seems to give the consecrations to Worcester and Hereford also to one year when they were really the one in 1163 and the other in 1164. I am on the whole inclined to accept 1163 as the date of the translation, but the matter cannot be considered at all certain. It is quite possible, as the dean suggests, that the date, October 1st, may antedate the Council.

"You lean too much on the ladder you rose on." "I lean on the Lord: cursed is he who putteth his trust in man." So they parted, Becket still clinging to the phrase on which the bishops had agreed, "salvo ordine."

Day by day, as Henry pressed his claim and asserted it by intrigue and by authority, opposition rose against the hardy primate. Gilbert Foliot claimed for his see an independence of Canterbury: he had delayed and he now refused to profess obedience to the primate: he declared that London had exceptional privileges. John of Salisbury mockingly said that to win them he would be willing to go back to Roman times, make S. Paul's a heathen temple, and himself an archflamen. Mockery did not mend matters. Some wit to satirise this weakness of Foliot's said that he once was awoke in the night by a demon who said to him—

"O Gilberte Foliot
Dum revolvis tot et tot
Deus tuus est Astaroth,"

to whom he, with a "Tace, demon," replied by a deserved but not so happily expressed rebuke. And close at home Clarembald asserted his independence, just outside the precincts of the cathedral church.

Becket invoked aid from without. If England, in the person of king and prelates, was turning against him, he was confident that he could fall back on the support of the Pope, who though in exile at Sens and accepted by even less than half Christendom, could still say words that might avail. In a letter written in September, 1163, about the time of the Westminster Council, the archbishop thanked Alexander for a "letter of consolation" he had received, and bewailed the storms that were breaking over the Church. The iniquity of men waxed strong since they saw the weakness of the Roman Church. Secret matters he would communicate through a sure messenger for safety "when almost all things that are said either in the ear or in company are repeated to the king." A month later John des Belles-Mains, a Canterbury man and companion of Becket in Theobald's household, who in this year had become bishop of Poitiers, wrote to represent the state of the Pope's opinions. The miserable weakness on the part of the Papacy, which prevented a settlement of the matters in dispute for ten years and was ultimately responsible for the murder of the archbishop, had begun. "You must expect nothing from the Curia in any matter that might offend the king." Exile seemed only too probable, but John would share it with his friend. Becket's envoy, Master Henry, reported to the same effect. While Louis VII offered "the reception of a companion on the throne" if the archbishop should be driven from England, and the count of Soissons was equally sympathetic, the papal Court, though it praised his fortitude, was wholly influenced by worldly motives. The papal party were terrified at the thought of desertion by Henry. In all matters Alexander was temporising and feeble. So indeed it proved. He tried to propitiate the bishop of London and the archbishop of York, and only after some pressure did he even forbid the latter the aggression of carrying his cross in the province of Canterbury.

The desire of Alexander III to propitiate Henry was no doubt mingled with an honest wish to end the

ecclesiastical troubles of England. He wrote to
Gilbert Foliot, urging him to mediate between king
and archbishop. He sent Philip, abbat of l'Aumône
(Blois), to represent him in England and to press
Becket to yield, with the assurance that it was only
a formal assent to the ancient customs that Henry
desired. With the abbat was the bishop elect of Hereford, Robert of Melun, and John, count of Vendôme.
They found Becket at Harrow manor, where he had
first joined the household of Theobald; he submitted,
and went to Henry at Oxford in December, 1163.
He saw the king in the strong castle of Robert d'Oilli,
whence his mother, the Empress-queen, had made her
romantic escape one snowy night not many winters
before, and there, with the Pope's envoys around him,
the archbishop promised to obey the ancient customs
of the realm and to submit to the king "in bono."
This was a practical omission of the saving clause,
"salvo ordine suo."

Peace, it might be fancied, was made. But the very
reverse was the case. Henry regarded the concession
as a triumph to himself and determined to fix it once
for all. He sent envoys—the servile Arnulf of Lisieux,
and Richard of Ilchester, archdeacon of Poitiers, soon
to become conspicuous among Becket's foes—to Sens,
to demand that Roger of York should be made papal
legate for all England and the archbishop of Canterbury and all his suffragans be required, by the Pope,
to observe the "ancient customs" of the realm. And
he summoned a Council to meet at Clarendon to
receive the submission.

CHAPTER V

THE CONSTITUTIONS OF CLARENDON

To Becket the demand for a public assent to the "customs" put the matter in a wholly new light.[1] He came to the Council with a mind hesitating and undecided. What were the "customs" to which he would be required to give this formal consent? The Council sat at Clarendon, a royal hunting-lodge, near Salisbury, for a fortnight in January, 1164, from the 13th to the 28th.[2] At first it seemed only as if what the king demanded was a formal promise of obedience. For three days the matter was argued, the bishops urging the primate to give way. Thomas hesitated: Henry was furious. At last two Templars swore to him, as it appeared, on the king's behalf, that only a formal and verbal promise to obey the customs was needed to bring peace to the Church. Foliot declared in later years that Becket said, "It is my lord's will that I forswear myself: I must run the risk of

---

[1] This was admitted by Canon J. C. Robertson, not a very favourable critic of the archbishop, who says that as his compliance "had been obtained by the assurance that the king had no thought of pressing the matter beyond a mere formal submission—nay, that he had sworn this to certain cardinals—the demand that an acknowledgment should be publicly made took him wholly by surprise." (*Becket*, p. 96.)

[2] As to the dates see Eyton's *Itinerary of Henry II*, and Norgate, *Angevin Kings*, ii, 44 *sqq*. Stubbs's *Select Charters* gives the day as "quarta die ante Purif. B.V.M.": but if that feast is recognised as beginning on its eve, Feb. 1st, Jan. 28th would be the fourth day before it, which seems to reconcile the different accounts, perhaps, better than Miss Norgate's note.

perjury now, and then do penance as best I may." The words are unlikely enough: if they were said, no doubt "my lord" meant the Pope, who had put such pressure on him to repudiate his former bold attitude, a return to which, the archbishop saw, would be inevitable. However this may be, it seemed now too late to go back: surely he could trust the king's word: surely he might follow the Pope's advice. He promised, in public, to obey the laws and customs of the king in good faith, and by his advice the other bishops did the same.

But this was not the end: it was only the beginning of new strife.

Next morning the king ordered the customs of the realm in his grandfather's time to be put in writing by the oldest of the barons. The duty was discharged, it seems probable, by Richard de Lucy, the justiciar, and Jocelin de Balliol. When the document appeared it was far from being what Becket or the bishops expected. It was a coherent and definite attempt to codify the main customs which regulated the relations between Church and State, in the interest of a centralising and unifying power which should place all law and government under the control of the Crown. This was Henry's definite policy: it was to this that he devoted his working life. Already he had begun to put it into action in his foreign dominions, and he never lost an opportunity, whether the case affected a church or a priest, a castle or a baron, of carrying it out in England itself. This policy was visibly embodied in the Constitutions of Clarendon.

The document professed to be a record or recognition of all the customs and liberties and dignities of the king's predecessors, particularly of Henry I. Briefly, the clauses were as follows.

The first ordered that any dispute as to advowsons and the right of presentation to ecclesiastical benefices should be decided in the king's court. This was contrary to the Church's claim to have jurisdiction over her own concerns, because it manifestly did concern, to some extent, the "cure of souls"; which, it may be noted, had been especially reserved to the Church courts by edict of William the Conqueror. And during the reign of Stephen, as the letters of John of Salisbury show, the right of presentation had been treated in Church courts. On the other hand, such rights were undoubtedly matters of patronage, and as such capable of transfer without reference to the Church. If there had been no other cause of dispute it is not likely that this would have been a bar to a compromise between king and archbishop.

The second clause, which was uncontested by the Church, aimed at preserving the royal rights and feudal services in regard to churches on the king's estates.

The third was the real point at issue between king and archbishop: it shall be reserved for discussion till the less important clauses have been mentioned.

The fourth dealt with a subject already important and soon to be of still greater import—the right of the king to prevent anyone leaving the kingdom without his licence. It specifically stated that no clergy-folk, from archbishop to beneficed priests, should go abroad without licence and giving security to procure no ill to the kingdom. The kings had certainly demanded this constantly if not invariably; only so recently as Alexander III's Council at Tours Becket and Roger of York had received such licence. But the aim of the formal repetition of the order on this occasion undoubtedly was designed to prevent appeals to Rome without the king's assent. With it clause 8 ordered that no appeal should go beyond the archbishop's court—to which the king might remit a suit for re-trial if the archbishop should "fail in showing justice"— without the king's assent. It was at once seen what these clauses meant, and they more than any other caused the Pope to support Becket in rejection of the Constitutions. The meaning was expressed by Robert of Gloucester, in the time of Henry III, as being that the king should be "in the Pope's stead." It was that which the papal Curia naturally regarded as fatal; the other clauses against which it protested so loudly in England it yielded to without reluctance in France, when Philip Augustus demanded them. But to this it could not, without suicide, consent.

The fifth clause entered upon a delicate branch of the Church's law. Excommunicates, it ordered, should not be required to give security for the future, before they were absolved, but only security to abide the judgment of the Church. It was an endeavour to free the excommunicated person from an absolute submission; and the position became of very grave importance at the end of Becket's dispute with the court.

The sixth declared that fixed legal witness was required in accusation of laymen in the Church courts, with a provision to enable the sheriff, in the case of a criminal of high rank, whom men might fear to accuse, to swear a jury to give evidence on their knowledge.

The seventh was a repetition of an order of William the Conqueror forbidding the excommunication of a tenant in chief without the king's knowledge, and it extended the rule to an interdict on the land. It had already been a matter of dispute in the case of Eynesford. It seemed practically to place it in the power of the king to decide whom the Church should admit to communion—a claim that it was impossible a spiritual society with the slightest vestige of logic or self-respect could admit.

The ninth was a complicated one as regards the trial of suits concerning ecclesiastical tenure. If there were dispute as to the tenure on which a particular piece of land were held it should be decided in the king's court. The ecclesiastical lawyers opposed this because it seemed to allow to the State courts a right of decision in regard to Church possessions, but their claim was surely hypercritical. It was, however, one of the many comparatively subsidiary points which became important when all were accumulated. Alexander III ordered that disputes between clerk and layman as to the "title to English land, or at least the possessory title to English lands, should be subject to ecclesiastical decision. But the king's claim was certainly not extravagant, and may be regarded as a concession."[1] The

---

[1] See Pollock and Maitland, *History of English Law*, i, 246–7, "If as regards criminous clerks the Constitutions of Clarendon are the high-water mark of the claims of the secular judges, as regards the title to lands they are the low-water mark." The history of frank-almoign is explained in i, 126, 240–51; ii, 148.

clause shows also the custom of Assize (the Assize *Utrum*), substituted by Henry II for wager of battle, in suits concerning property.

This was perhaps the most important of all the legal novelties of Henry II's reign.[1]

The tenth was contingent on the seventh. The eleventh, to which the Church made no objection, declared that clerks, from archbishops downwards, who held of the king in chief held according to the ordinary law of fiefs.

The twelfth declared a custom which had certainly been observed under the Norman kings. Vacant bishoprics and benefices should be in the king's hands: Becket's chancellorship had shown many examples. When an election should be made it should be in the king's chapel, under the influence, that is, of the king. Though Fitz-Stephen claims for the chancellorship of Becket that elections were free then, and vacancies not prolonged, the case of his own election and the vacancy which preceded it is a very clear example of the custom which Henry's lawyers here set down.

Other clauses dealt with the help of Church and lay courts to each other; and the restriction of the right of sanctuary to persons, not goods; with pleas about debts, of which the king claimed the jurisdiction, but the Church declared that as a moral matter they fell to her; and with the security for feudal services, forbidding the ordination of villeins without their lord's leave. To this last the Pope agreed; the Curia cared little for the service of poor men. But Guernes, the French biographer of Becket, indignantly protests

---

[1] See Holdsworth, *History of English Law*, 3rd ed. i, 329.

against it as restricting the claim of God on the service of all.[1]

Points of considerable interest and importance, constitutionally and historically, are involved in many of the clauses. But none so decidedly touched the vital question, as it seemed to medieval lawyers, as the question of jurisdiction over criminous clerks. It is well to see at first what Henry really claimed. He demanded that clerks, if they were accused of a crime at common law, should be tried in his courts; if the crime was against Church law only, the Church might have jurisdiction. The clerk, in the first place, must appear in the lay court and plead to the charge there, though it might be heard, by clerical privilege, in the Church courts. When the case was being heard a royal officer should always be present; and if the Church court found the man guilty "the Church ought no longer to protect him."[2] The Church, that is, might degrade him if she would—though the clause makes no reference to this—but the State should have the punishing in more

[1] Guernes, ed. Walberg, p. 86:
  Fiz a vilain ne fust en nul liu ordenez
  Sens l'asens sun seignur, de qui terre il fust nez
  — E Deus a sun servise nus ad tuz apelez!
  Mielz valt fiz a vilain qui est prouz e sencz,
  Que ne fait gentilz hum failliz e debutez.

[2] I adopt the explanation, which is, indeed, as regards the meaning of the clause, convincing, of the late Professor Maitland, *Roman Canon Law in the English Church*, pp. 132 *sqq.* But I do not think the facts warrant some of the inferences that he draws. Henry *does* "propose that a clerk should be punished by a temporal court"—which Professor Maitland denies—or at least he says nothing whatever about degradation: he merely says that if the clerk confess or be convicted the lay court shall punish him: he does not even imply that it shall wait for his degradation from orders.

material ways, and might, indeed, if she would, "betake herself to his limbs," in the phrase of another of Henry's legal enactments. Over the clause hot debate arose. The bishops on Henry's side urged Becket to consent; he, it seems, consistently declared that to allow it would be to let a man be punished twice for the same offence, contrary to the elementary principles of justice. More than that he may have said: so much he certainly did say.

When we disentangle the issues, which in the contemporary accounts, written by indignant partisans, are generally confused or prejudiced, or both, we may arrive at three questions. They are these: the claim of the Church to jurisdiction over its own officials or those under its special protection; the question of double punishment for one offence; and the nature of the punishments which ecclesiastical courts imposed, as distinct from those of lay courts.

As regards the first point, there seems to be little doubt that Henry did not claim the right, for the lay courts, of trying clerks accused of crime. It may matter very little—it probably did matter very little to Becket and those of his mind—that this claim was not made when the claim to punish such criminals, after they had been found guilty in their own courts, was pressed. But that it was not made showed at least that Henry was satisfied with the way trials were conducted in the Church courts: though he would send his "minister" to be present, he would accept the trial as a fair one. On the other hand, Becket did explicitly assert,[1] and the literature of the time asserted

---

[1] e.g. Materials, v, 388.

again and again, that the king sought to "draw clerks to secular judgments." The concession on the king's part that the trial itself should be held in a Church court was a concession to legal theory: it did not affect practical fact. And the clergy have always been more practical, and less satisfied with theoretical concession, than their critics have asserted or their enemies desired. If a man were accused in the temporal court, and sentenced there to a layman's punishment, what did it matter, the Church might fairly say, where he was tried? The accusation and the sentence were the work of the State, not of the Church. This was quite plainly to "draw clerks to secular judgments," whether it was to draw them to secular trial or not.

But Henry's claim had a considerable force of law behind it. It was at least arguable—it has indeed been argued with the masterly skill of one of the first of modern medievalists[1] that he was justified by canon law: that Gratian might be read in his favour, and so justified him already, and that Pope Innocent III unquestionably did, in the future, decide in the same way. Degradation by the Church should result in the delivery of the clerk as a layman for a lay court for a lay punishment. This view has the sanction of the great civil legist of the sixth century. Justinian, in his 83rd Novel, orders that a clerk on being found guilty shall be degraded by the bishop and then sentenced by the secular power.[2]

[1] F. W. Maitland, *op. cit.* pp. 141 *sqq.*

[2] *Corpus Juris Civilis*, iii, ed. Schoell and Kroll, iii, 409–10. "Ut clerici apud proprios episcopos primum conveniantur et post haec apud civiles judices." This might have been quoted by Professor Maitland, if he had noticed it, as showing that Henry

The point at issue here seems then to have been a practical, not a theoretical one. Henry's theory was undoubtedly contrary to that of Becket, and he had support in civil law for it: there is no reason to suppose that he ever actually admitted the right of the Church exclusively to judge its own officials. Becket undoubtedly did assert that the civil courts had no right to judge clerks. And when it came to the constitution drawn up at Clarendon he must have seen that this really made that claim on behalf of the State. The Church's claim, it should be remembered, was, rather vaguely, pressed to include not only all officials of the Church, from sextons to priests, from sub-deacons to monastic servants, and even, it seemed, those who were under, in old English phrase, the *mund* of the Church, widows and orphan children, and those over whom the protection of the Church was shed. Such a claim is found constantly in early laws, and seems to have been admitted.

The question of double punishment is again a practical one. If a man was not in holy orders it does not, of course, enter into the dispute; it would not, that is to say, concern the large class of which we have last spoken. But for those who had received ordination merely claimed what Justinian had claimed and what had not when claimed been resisted by the Church. Canon Robertson had noted this novel as illustrating the king's claim. The note on the subject in Pollock and Maitland (2nd ed. i, 455–6), does not seem to come to any definite decision or to quote any definite early authority save Stephanus; but "in later times the canonists admitted that there were various cases in which the degraded clerk was to be delivered to the lay power for further punishment." The note ends "we dare not speak confidently of such a matter but have grave doubts about the assumption" [viz. "that all Becket's claims were justified by the law of the Church"].

from the Church the solemn and terrible act of degradation was a distinct, and, to all but desperate criminals, must have been a truly awful punishment. Chosen by the Lord to be His ministers upon earth, to declare, so far as poor humanity could, His will, and be the unworthy channels of His divine gifts, hideous indeed was the fall which could bring men to such acts of sin as should merit the deprivation of that commission so solemnly given. In the intense solemnity of medieval religion, dwelling far more than modern teaching, whether in Rome or England, on the tremendous issues of life, on death and judgment, on the *quatuor novissima*, the four last things, the sentence of degradation from the ministry might well seem the expression of the divine sentence, "Depart from Me, ye cursed." It would be difficult, indeed, to exaggerate the awfulness, to the medieval mind, of a degradation from holy orders. At the least, then, there can be no doubt that it was a punishment, a very distinct punishment. And when the king claimed to add to it some other sentence, given by a lay court, he was in plain fact giving a second punishment: richly deserved, it may have been, but a second punishment it undoubtedly was. A clergyman had been tried for crime and found guilty and degraded from his orders. No one doubted that the degradation was a punishment; if it were not, why was it given? To add to it the chopping off a hand or a foot was, obviously to all men, to give a second punishment. This was the opinion of eminent crown lawyers. The great Bracton, a century later, held that as a rule degradation is sufficient punishment for a clerk.

So much may be admitted. But it was argued, by the eminent medievalist to whom we owe so much of the elucidation of the question of Henry II and the criminous clerks, that[1] "the judgment of the ecclesiastical court must put an end to the whole case. It condemns a clerk to degradation. If that is correct it must also be a complete judgment. It ought not to be followed by another sentence."[2] There is a little ambiguity here which it may be well to elucidate. Degradation was not "a complete judgment." With it the Church gave, as without it she gave, when the case required it, a sentence which affected the body, as well as that sentence which affected the status and the soul. A man degraded from holy orders might be punished, we have already seen,[3] with imprisonment for life, with scourging, with heavy fines, with branding: not only he might be, but such punishments actually had been given by Church courts in England within the last two years. And a letter of Alexander III to Gilbert Foliot[4] shows that such an amplification of the sentence of degradation was regarded not as a second punishment

[1] Maitland, *op. cit.* p. 138.

[2] When I wrote this in 1910 Mr H. A. L. Fisher (now Rt. Hon., and Warden of New College, Oxford), in a letter to me made this very fair criticism, "Surely when Maitland speaks of a 'complete judgment' he means a final judgment which 'cannot' as he says 'be *followed* by any other sentence.' It can, of course, be *preceded* by another sentence, but after degradation the clerk is no longer a clerk and can therefore not receive further spiritual penalties. Isn't this so?" I hardly think it is: I think the degradation was part of one sentence with the imprisonment, or whatever it was, that was ordered at the same time by the spiritual court. To-day when a man is imprisoned and fined (as sometimes happens) no one regards this as two sentences.

[3] See above, pp. 77–8..

[4] *Epp. Gilb. Foliot.* ii, 67.

but as part of the punishment for the one offence. A clerk who has forged is to be deprived of every ecclesiastical office or benefice for ever, and banished the country: if he should return he is to be confined in a monastery as a prisoner for the rest of his life.

But when we speak of the punishments imposed by the ecclesiastical courts, while we are careful to remember that they were not contrasted with the punishments of lay courts, as modern critics of Becket seem to imagine, by being what such critics would consider to be purely sentimental penalties as opposed to severe physical ones, we must recall also the real distinction there was between them. The Church courts could not sentence to death or mutilation. The punishments of the lay courts in Henry II's time were largely of that nature. Lay courts knew no such thing as penal imprisonment; pecuniary penalties they inflicted for criminal offences for the most only as part or consequence of a physical punishment. The Church's penalties were no doubt the expression of a blind revolt against the cruelty of the age and of an attempt at amelioration rather than mere punishment. The State set before itself the ideas of vengeance and of example: the Church those of castigation for the benefit of the offender's soul and without closing the door to amendment upon earth.

This then must be understood. There was a deep cleavage between the claims of Church and State. However far this may have been a theoretical matter it was most certainly a practical one. And Becket was not contending for the immunity of clerical offenders from any real punishment. If he had so contended,

most certainly public opinion would not have been, to
the extent that it was, on his side. One may not wonder
that a wise thinker in seclusion, such as William of
Newburgh by Bridlington in Yorkshire, should see
that both Henry and Becket were striving after their
fashion for the right, but be unable to decide with
which the right really lay.

Such was the position when the Constitutions were
brought before the Council at Clarendon. Becket protested that if clerks were to be brought before secular
courts Christ was again to be before Pilate.[1] The freedom of canonical elections he could not abandon without the sanction of the Pope and the whole Church.
He could not but remember that though the Charter
of Henry I had sought to control it, the freedom had
been allowed by the Charter of Stephen.[2]

So the moment of decision came. Armed men beset
the deliberating bishops, and great earls declared their
dread lest bloody deeds should be done. "No new or
unheard-of thing would it be," said the archbishop,
"if it should be our lot to die for the Church's rights.
The Company of the Saints have taught us by word
and by example. But may the will of God be done."
So it was that he and the bishops gave their promise.

But a new demand followed. He must set his seal
to the document. What did this involve? For the
Constitutions ended with the words, significant or

---

[1] The parallel is interesting, and its exactness does not seem
to have been observed by modern writers. As Pilate said, so Henry,
"Take ye...and judge...according to your law": the trial was
ecclesiastical, the State claimed to punish. So at least Becket
would naturally interpret the Gospels.

[2] "Canonice substituatur" is the phrase it uses.

mysterious, that there were many other customs and dignities of Holy Mother Church and of the lord king and the barons which were not there set down but which are to be preserved to the Church and king and barons and inviolably observed for ever. Becket refused to seal: "Never," he cried, "while life is in this earthly vessel." He took away the document, for he knew not what might happen in regard to it. And so he went towards Winchester.

As he went his people murmured. Their babble— of iniquity, and the synagogue of Satan, of tempests, and of the flight of the shepherd—reached his ears. "What strength has he left who has betrayed his conscience and his honour?" said the ready-tongued Welshman, Alexander Llewelyn, faithful in perils, cautious yet bold, who bore his cross and read aloud at meals, standing close to the archbishop's chair. The archbishop caught the words and asked bitterly of whom he spoke. Llewelyn did not hesitate to answer. "Of thee. Thou hast to-day betrayed conscience and good fame, left to posterity an example odious to God and contrary to righteousness, and hast stretched out thine hands to keep customs of impiety and with Satan's ministers hast united to the destruction of the Church's freedom." Becket instantly declared his repentance, groaning bitterly, and vowed that he would do no priestly act till he should be absolved. He had fallen, said his friends, like David and like Peter, but like them he should be lifted up.

But for the present everything seemed against him. His oldest friend and best adviser had been separated from him and was forced into exile. Among the bishops he had no steadfast support where he had not open hostility. Within a month of the Council of Clarendon the Pope granted to Roger of York the office of legate. He wrote, on February 27th, to Becket, that Henry had urgently desired the confirmation of the Constitutions, that he would not give this but thought it wise to humour the king about the legation. A letter, quickly following this, has a curiously shuffling air. We did not grant the legation, says the Pope, till the king's messengers had promised, and offered to swear, that the letters should not be given to Roger without your consent. We will never make your Church subject to anyone save ourselves alone.[1] Cold comfort, when all seemed lost. So the spring passed.

In April Alexander wrote again. He had heard that Becket had suspended himself from saying mass, and he deplored the scandal. He reminded the archbishop that there was great difference between evil things done voluntarily and done under compulsion. The intention it is that gives its mark to the act: for, as Gratian says, quoting Augustine, "Inasmuch as voluntary evil is sin, so if it be not voluntary it is not sin." But confession and penance should bring peace. And the Pope

[1] "Let not your heart fail you, my brother, because the legation has been granted: for the ambassadors gave us beforehand an assurance from the king, and offered themselves to confirm it on oath, that the letters should not be delivered to the archbishop without your knowledge and consent. You cannot believe that it is our wish to humble you or your church, by subjecting it to any other than to the Roman pontiff. Wherefore we advise your prudence, as soon as ever the king shall be known to have delivered the letters, which we cannot easily believe he will do without your knowledge, to inform us at once of it by letter, that we may, without delay, declare you and your Church and city to be exempt from all legatine jurisdiction." *Materials*, v, 87.

absolved him from his act of consent to the Constitutions and commanded him not to cease from saying mass.

During March, 1164, it seems that Becket had an interview with the king at Woodstock, but nothing came of it. On Sunday, April 19th, they met again at Reading, where the archbishop, attended by ten of his suffragans, consecrated the church of the abbey founded by Henry I. A month later, on S. Alban's Day, John of Poitiers wrote to Becket[1] from Sens, where Alexander III was in exile, reporting the Pope's desires. He evidently foresaw that flight, if it was not already contemplated, would soon be the archbishop's only safe course: he rejoiced that no full consent by signature and seal had been given to those detestable and profane Constitutions. Matters were bad enough about the legations and the atrocious Clarembald. The Pope could not be depended upon, evidently. So he ended, "I further advise you that either in your own person, should you come into Gaul on account of your case, or by letter, if you should receive leave to depart you should make more intimate acquaintance with the abbat of Pontigny, though I and our common friend, Isaac, abbat of Stella,[2] will procure that that most holy house of Pontigny should have perpetual memory of you in their prayers; you will also find that the same house is ready, if need be, to serve your temporal necessities; for in labours and in holiness the said abbat is more powerful than all the abbats of the Cistercian order. And there—I speak to safe ears—

[1] *Materials*, v, 110.
[2] That is of l'Etoile, or the Blessed Virgin of Poitiers.

I have chosen my place of exile when I can no longer support the tortures of our tormentor."

And it was not long before the messengers of the tormentor began to harry the good bishop to some purpose. One was his own archdeacon, Richard of Ilchester. He hurried to the Pope at Sens. And Becket at home in vain attempted to see Henry at Woodstock. Then, going to his manor of Aldington, he made two attempts to escape, from Romney. The first time the wind was contrary and he was obliged to return; the second the sailors put back, recognising him and dreading the king's wrath, and he went back to Canterbury.

One of his servants was audaciously going to sleep in the archbishop's own chamber. After supper he began to think sadly of his master's evil case; then when night was half over he wished to sleep and told a boy to go and shut the outer door. There on the doorstep sat the archbishop himself alone. The lad in terror fled in, thinking he had seen a vision, but the clerk would not believe him and went to see for himself. There was the archbishop, who then entered the house, and, sending for some of the monks, told them of what had happened to him, and so after a brief supper went to bed. Next morning came some of the king's men to seize his goods, but when they saw him they retired in silent confusion. Henry, indeed, knew of his attempt at flight, and, in another meeting at Woodstock, half laughingly reproached him for it. He did not give him all the ceremony that was the due of the primate of all England. He asked him whether he did not think the kingdom big enough to hold them both. He had already prepared a further scourge for his back, in "the case of John the Marshal."

CHAPTER VI

THE COUNCIL OF NORTHAMPTON

IT was clear to Henry that he would not secure the supremacy of the civil power over all estates of the realm so long as Becket was archbishop to uphold the privileges and separatism of the Church. It was dangerous to attack him directly; and it might be much easier to secure his defeat by a side blow. Enemies were gathering round him, like bees, as the faithful Herbert says: a sting from one of them might be fatal. And so there appeared the case of John the Marshal.

John Fitz-Gilbert, marshal to Henry II's mother and brother of her chancellor, who held his office hereditarily, had been with the Queen Empress at Oxford in her famous adventure, and bore an evil record among the oppressors of England.[1] But he was a great baron and a man of proved strength and loyalty to the Angevins. He had brought an action in the archbishop's court concerning the manor of Pageham, Sussex, a property of the archbishopric. When the suit seemed to be going against him he made oath that he could not get justice in his lord's court, for the purpose of having the suit transferred to the royal court, the Curia Regis at Westminster. Becket was summoned thither for September 14th. He did not come; but he sent four knights with letters from himself and the sheriff of Kent, declaring that John had departed from his court because he was failing in his evidence and had taken

[1] See Round, *Geoffrey de Mandeville*, p. 416.

oath on a tropary (a book of the versicles sung before
the introit at mass), "which he took from under his
cloak, though the judges of the archbishop's court declared that he ought not to have brought with him a
book for the purpose of making oath nor have made
oath on such a book." Pride and illness kept Becket
from Westminster. Henry angrily dismissed his messengers and ordered another day for the suit. He
accompanied this by the insult of sending a summons
to the Council which was to be held at Northampton
on Tuesday, October 6th, 1164, addressed not to the
archbishop,—though he should have had a writ "solemn
and to him first of all," since by custom all the greater
barons were summoned by special writ individually
addressed, a writ which has the historical importance
of being the foundation of the House of Lords as constituted by Henry II's grandson,—but in the general
writ sent out to the sheriff of Kent to summon all
the lesser tenants-in-chief in his shire.

When Becket arrived at Northampton with his train,
the faithful Herbert among them and the admiring
remembrancer, William Fitz-Stephen, both of whom
left their records of this crisis of the strife, he found his
lodgings taken by William de Courcy, another of the
Angevin special servants. He waited, angry no doubt
at heart at the two insults, till the king came. It was
not till the day after that appointed that Henry was
ready for the Council: he had hawked along every
river and brook as he came and did not enter Northampton till nightfall. Next morning Becket said mass
and his hours and went to the castle. There he was
kept waiting in the ante-room till the king had heard

mass. As Henry came into the room on his way from chapel the archbishop rose, made his reverence and stood ready with a calm countenance for the kiss of salutation, but Henry would not give it.

In spite of the rebuff he boldly named his two causes of grievance. Henry said William de Courcy should give up the rooms, but that John the Marshal was in London on his business—"at the quadrangular table which is called the Exchequer from its chequered squares," says Fitz-Stephen—and would return next day, when the suit should be heard.

So on Thursday, October 8th, the case came on, many barons of England and Normandy, and all the bishops, save Walter of Rochester and one or perhaps two others, being present. It was much more than the case of John the Marshal. It was now contempt of the Crown's Majesty; for Becket, though summoned by the king to Westminster at John's suit, had neither come nor sent valid excuse: so the charge ran, and the king demanded the judgment of his barons on his archbishop.

The barons were in a huge majority, whatever might have been the bishops' vote, and English barons were never sorry for an opportunity to abate the pride of an ecclesiastic: they declared Becket guilty and placed him *ad misericordiam regis*. To be at the king's mercy meant liability to an arbitrary fine, and the fine was fixed at £300.[1] The barons were eager to fix the sentence, but

---

[1] I am inclined to think that Guernes is right, who gives this sum. Grim, Ralph of Dissay, and the Anonymous (?Roger of Pontigny) say £500, a huge sum. William of Canterbury says £50. M. Walberg in his edition of Guernes, p. 244, also accepts the figures given by Guernes.

not to pronounce it: surely that must be the bishops' business. They were equally reluctant. At last the king made old Henry of Winchester, who had consecrated the primate, deliver it. Becket did not receive it without protest. "If I were silent at such a sentence future ages would not be dumb. This is a new form of sentence: perhaps it belongs to the new rules made at Clarendon," he said ironically. "Never has it been heard of that an archbishop of Canterbury should be tried in the king's court for such a cause: the Church's dignity forbids it, and the dignity of his own person, for he is the spiritual father of the king and of all in the realm." So Herbert expands the protest. Much more did Becket resent the action of his suffragans than even that of the barons; it was indeed unheard of that an archbishop should be judged by his suffragans, he said.

But he submitted, as the bishops advised, "because it was not lawful to gainsay the sentence and record of the court of the king of England." All the bishops were his sureties, save only Gilbert of London, who refused. But this was not the end.

Henry now demanded £300 received by the archbishop from the wardenship of Eye and Berkhamsted. This in spite of the fact that the *Pipe Roll* of Michaelmas, 1163, the year before, marks him as discharged of all dues from the latter manor: as to the former a sum of £150. 3s. 7d. had been paid in that year but without account. Whatever may have been the cause, or the justice of this demand, Becket, while declaring himself not liable, said now that he had spent far more on those castles and on the Tower of London.[1] Henry said that

[1] See above, p. 35.

this was not by his order, and the archbishop then agreed to give the money: he would not let money be a cause of dispute between them. It is a remarkable example of the way in which feeling was turning in his favour that William of Eynesford[1] became one of the sureties for his paying.

But there was still more. On Friday, October 9th, the king demanded 500 marks, which he said had been lent by him during the Toulouse war, and another 500 which he said had been borrowed from the Jews on the royal security. And more, before the day was over. Already the archbishop was finding it difficult to get sureties for such large sums. Now he was required to give account of all the revenues of the archbishopric during the vacancy and of all other bishoprics and abbeys which had been vacant while he was chancellor. Becket threw himself at the king's feet, and the bishops with him; and Henry swore by God's eyes that he would have an account of every penny. From that moment the courtiers regarded the primate's doom as sealed; the barons and knights no longer came to visit him, says Fitz-Stephen significantly, "for they understood the king's mind."

On Saturday, October 10th, the bishops all came to the primate's lodging, for he had demanded their advice before he gave answer to the king. Henry of Winchester promised his help towards providing the money, and advised that an attempt should be made to pacify the king with a large sum. Becket offered 2000 marks. Henry refused them. Then the bishops advised that he should plead the quittance he received when he

[1] See above, pp. 73 *sqq.*

was made archbishop. Henry replied that he had not authorised it.

The bishops met together again; some reproached their primate, others gave half-hearted support: all evidently feared the lion's wrath. Hilary of Chichester expressed the candid wish that the archbishop should become plain Thomas again, and behind his back he quoted the text, "Every plant which my Heavenly Father hath not planted shall be rooted up," while he counselled resignation. One bold man said: "Be it far from him that he should think of his own safety and dishonour the Church that chose him." And so one after another gave contrary advice. Thus the Sunday passed in consultation so deep that, as Fitz-Stephen says, one could scarce breathe at meal time.

On Monday morning the body failed the stout spirit of the archbishop. The familiar signs of a nervous breakdown appeared: shivering and the acute pain of neuritis. When Henry heard of the primate's illness, he only sent to demand his answer, and the archbishop replied that if his strength allowed he would come to the king and do as duty bade. He was up on Tuesday morning early, and said mass at the altar of S. Stephen, using the collect for that saint and having the introit "Princes sat and spake against me," and wearing the pallium. He had been told that this mass would protect him, say some; but if he had ever shown a sign of fear he showed none now, though men had told him that Henry was swearing to take his life or tear out his eyes and tongue.[1]

---

[1] Robertson, *Life of Becket*, p. 118, with an unconscious humour considers the report "greatly exaggerated," reminding one of "Mark Twain."

He had already seen some of the bishops, charged them to reject the Constitutions and, on their obedience, not to join in judging him but if any evil should befall him to excommunicate those who caused it. Foliot instantly replied that he would appeal to Rome.

Becket had meant to go to the king barefoot and in his mass vestments, but some of his clerks and the Templars dissuaded him. Some (but not those who might best have known) say that he carried with him the Host concealed in his raiment. He rode into the hall, got off his horse, and took his primatial cross from the Welshman's hand. There Gilbert Foliot met him. Hugh of Nunant, archdeacon of Lisieux, who was with him, said: "Lord bishop of London, will you suffer him to carry his own cross?" "He always was a fool, and he always will be, my good man," said the bishop. And so the archbishop, bearing his cross, went into the Council chamber and took his seat, and the bishop of London sat near him, and told him that it needed only now for the king to take his sword and they would be a match. "Nay," answered Becket, "for the cross is the sign of peace; and would I might always carry mine."

Then came Roger of York, who had loitered that he might not seem to be advising the king. He had his cross borne before him, in spite of Canterbury and Rome, and angrily bade Becket lay his aside. So they were summoned to the king, who, when he heard of how the archbishop of Canterbury had come, had withdrawn himself into an inner room: bishops and barons went to him, and Becket with his own clerks was left alone in the great hall. Silently they sat awhile. Then Herbert told him he might excommunicate his foes, for already there were cries that Henry had proclaimed him traitor, and men passing through the hall uttered loud threats. William Fitz-Stephen spoke loud that he might hear and gently counselled meekness and a suffering for righteousness, and quoted Gratian and S. Gregory. And around them the tears flowed from men's eyes. Becket sat in silent thought, and then Fitz-Stephen lifted up his finger and pointed to the Sacred Figure on the cross. And so he prayed and took comfort. Years after, says Fitz-Stephen, the archbishop reminded him of that moment.

At last came the king's command: to withdraw all appeals to Rome and all commands to the bishops, and to stand to the judgment of the king's court upon the accounts of the chancellorship. Becket heard, still seated, and then clearly and boldly he made his refusal, halting not in one word, says Fitz-Stephen. He had not been summoned for any cause but that of the marshal: to no other would he answer. He had been given free to the Church of Canterbury. Yet it were not lawful to produce witness against the king, nor would he do it. He had given himself to the Church's work and God had brought his work to nought. No more sureties could he bring. And still he appealed against those bishops who had judged him. He appealed, for himself and the Church of Canterbury, to God and the Pope.

When they heard this, some of the barons, calling out that William the Conqueror knew how to tame clerks, went to the king, and with them went the bishops. Long the timid prelates argued with Henry and then came back, some weeping, to declare that they appealed against their primate, and, having by his advice sworn to the Constitutions, they would observe them. The bitter enemies, York, London and Chichester, declared that they charged him with perjury in their appeal to Rome.

Still Thomas made answer. He would meet the appeal. No one had sworn at Clarendon except "saving the Church's honour and law." The Pope had rather condemned than approved the Constitutions. And if the flesh failed at Clarendon, yet was no one bound to do what was unlawful.

The bishops went back to the king: then was the barons' turn. What their judgment was no one heard, for when Robert Beaumont, earl of Leicester, the aged justiciar, came to deliver it, Becket at last rose, cross in hand, and forbade him to speak. No judgment would he hear, for there had been no trial. "Now will I depart, for the hour is past," said he, and bearing his cross he walked to the closed door, which someone silently unfastened for him. Voices called after him "traitor" and "perjurer." As he passed through the crowded hall he stumbled over a bundle of faggots, and he turned to Hamelin, the king's bastard brother, and said, "Were I a knight, my own hands should prove thee false." Some say he called him "bastard," some that he taunted Ranulf de Broc with the hanging of one of his kindred. But Herbert of Bosham, who says he alone was with his master when they left the inner room till they came to the outer hall, says only that he turned a stern face to those who taunted him, and said that were it not for his priesthood he would defend himself in arms.

The outer gate was locked, but one of his squires found the key, and he rode forth alone—for Herbert could not at first find his horse. A great crowd surrounded him and begged his blessing; scarce could he control his horse and carry his cross. When they reached S. Andrew's monastery, he brought the crowd into the refectory and supped with them. The passage read while they ate named a bishop who in persecution had quoted "When they persecute you in one city flee to another," and his eye caught the faithful Herbert's. It seemed a divine intimation. Already many of his own household had fled.

He sent a last message to Henry demanding a safe conduct to Canterbury. He was answered that he must wait till the morrow. Then he had his bed laid in the church, and before cock-crow, when the monks (says Guernes, in whose mind lingered picturesque and vivid details which men told him) sang matins softly for fear they should wake him, he had fled with one squire and two canons of Sempringham, the one English order, whose founder was his faithful and admiring friend. Through a storm of pitiless rain he rode away towards Lincoln; there he rested in the house of a fuller named Jacob.[1] Then on he went to the Sempringham house at Haverholme, and down the Witham by boat. At first he wore monastic garb, then the

---

[1] It would be interesting indeed, if, this man, a citizen known to the brethren, as Grim tells, were a Jew, as his name suggests, and even lived in the famous "Jew's house" of stone which stands to-day.

dress of a lay brother; sometimes he was called Brother Derman, sometimes Brother Christian.[1]

From Haverholme he travelled by night into Kent, stopping at another Gilbertine house, Chicksand in Bedfordshire. So he came at last to Eastry, near Sandwich, one of his own manors, where he dwelt in a little chamber looking on the church, hearing mass without any man knowing his presence. Thence on All Souls' Day, Monday, November 2nd, 1164, before daybreak, he took an open boat and with two priests put out from Sandwich. These good men knew how to row, no unusual accomplishment for clerks, but there were others in the boat who gave rather hindrance than any comfort or help.[2] That night they landed at Oye, in the county of Boulogne.

[1] This seems the best way to reconcile the different accounts.
[2] John of Salisbury, *Materials*, ii, 313: "in fragili cymbula a duobus sacerdotibus trajectus est in Flandriam, paucis aliis navigium potius impedientibus quam aliquam solatii vel auxilii ferentibus opem."

CHAPTER VII

IN EXILE

O N the very day when the archbishop crossed the channel there went also an embassy from Henry: Roger of York, Gilbert of London, Hilary of Chichester, Bartholomew of Exeter, and the newly consecrated Roger of Worcester. With them were two priests, Richard of Ilchester and John of Oxford, the primate's bitter foes, the earl of Arundel and other laymen. They bore Henry's complaint to the Pope. Already he had sent a letter to Louis VII denouncing the wicked and perjured traitor, his archbishop: now he adjured him to send back the outlaw to England.

When Becket landed, his troubles were not over. Flanders was not safe: there was an old enemy there [1]: he must keep away from frequented towns. And he who when once he had crossed the channel had so fine a train of knights and splendid horses must now go afoot and almost alone. Wearied, and encumbered by his monastic garb, he slipped and stumbled on the sand, and he tore his hands on the rocks. At last they found a boy whom they made bring a steed: it proved but a sorry ass, with a straw rope for bridle. On this poor beast they threw a cloak and sate their archbishop thereon. So he rode for two miles, till he found it "more bearable and more respectable" to walk. So they came to a village, where an old woman, struck half with pity, half with respect, for a form so noble

[1] See above, p. 47.

and so sad, ran into her house to get him a stick to walk with—and all she could find was a spit; it was dirty and covered with the grease of fish. For even this he gave gentle thanks.

Even now he could not repress the tastes of his youth: he gave a keen glance of pleasure as he saw a knight ride by with hawk on wrist. Someone, as he passed with his three companions, said, "Surely that is the archbishop of Canterbury, or he is very like him." Brother Scailman, the Gilbertine, heard it and said, "You never saw the archbishop travel like this." In an inn the landlord noticed him for his dignified manners and his long white hands, and his wife paid special reverence to "Brother Christian." So they made their way to the Cistercian abbey of Clairmarais, near S. Omer, where they arrived about November 4th. After two days' delay they passed through S. Omer—the very day that the king's envoys did the same—and went to the great house of S. Bertin. With them now were Herbert of Bosham and some clerks and servants who had brought from England money and silver plate.

While they were at Clairmarais Becket had seen Richard de Lucy, joint justiciar, an old friend, who strongly begged him to return to England, adding threats to his requests, and at last telling him he must no longer rely on him. "You are my man," said Becket, "and must not speak to me thus." "I give you back my homage," said Lucy, and the archbishop answered, "I never lent it you."

To prepare the Pope for his coming Becket now wrote to tell of his flight and his hopes.[1]

[1] *Materials*, v, 138 *sqq.*; Nov. 1164.

"In your presence, holy father, is my refuge; that you, who have redeemed the Church's liberties at your own peril, may give ear to me who have followed your example, and suffered equally for the same. The cause of the Church would have sunk before the rapacity of princes if I had not faced the coming evil. The more I loved the king, the more I opposed his injustice, until his brow fell lowering upon me. He heaped calumny after calumny on my head, and I chose to be driven out rather than to subscribe. I was called before the king's tribunal like a layman, and was deserted in the quarter where I had looked for support. My brethren, the bishops, sided with the court, and were ready to pronounce judgment against me. Thus, almost crushed by the multitude of my foes, I have fled to your presence, which is the last refuge of the distressed. Under your protection will I prove that I was not amenable to that tribunal, nor to their judgment. Your privileges, holy father, are at stake: by this pernicious precedent the spiritual power would yield to the temporal. Thus I resisted, for fear that to yield would be a confession of weakness, and bring on me more extensive aggression. But, one may say that those things which are Cæsar's should be rendered to Cæsar. Be it so; the king must, indeed, be obeyed in many things, but not so that he shall cease to be a king: that would make him no longer Cæsar but a tyrant, and those who resisted him would contend for themselves and not for me. The last judgment is admitted to be His Who can kill both body and soul: is not then the spiritual judgment final on earth? Why have I been attacked for appealing to him, who cannot,

must not judge falsely? They have assailed me unjustly, or else they doubt your impartiality. I wonder
not that laymen should thus attack the Church, but I
wonder much more that bishops should have led them
on. Could I anticipate the enmity of those for whom I
encountered such opposition? If they had been willing,
I should have gained the victory. But the head faints
when it is abandoned by the other members. If they
had been wise they would have seen that in attacking
me they were attacking their own privileges, and
serving princes to their own servitude. They left
spiritual things for temporal, and so have been stripped
of both. They judged me, their father, though I
protested and appealed to your holy presence. If they
had conspired in the same way with the king against
the whole Church, what would your holiness then have
said? They plead that they were fulfilling their duty
to the king. I reply that their obligation to him is of a
temporal nature, to me they are bound in spirituals.
What obligations can be stronger than that which binds
them to themselves, and the spiritual concerns of their
souls? They say that this is not a favourable moment
for provoking the king to anger. Alas! this refined
sophistry leads to their perpetual servitude! they are
even accelerating that catastrophe by lending the king's
arrogance wings to fly! Had they paused, he would have
paused also. But further, when is constancy required,
except under persecution? Are not friends then proved?
If they always yield how can they ever succeed? They
must one time or other make a stand.

"Look down then, with condescension, holy father,
on my exiled and persecuted condition: remember

that I was once in a place of pride, from which I have been driven by injustice—and in your cause. Put forth your severity, and coerce those who have stirred up this persecution, but lay it not at the king's door; he is the instrument rather than the author of these machinations."

Becket was ready to follow up his letter by a personal appeal. But meanwhile the king's envoys had been beforehand with him and had had very poor welcome. Louis VII interrupted one of them, in the most clericalist spirit, when he spoke of "the late archbishop." "Late! who deposed him? I am myself a king as well as the king of the English, and I have no power to depose the meanest clerk in my realm." When the earl of Arundel was audacious enough to remind him of the gallant exploits of the exile in the war of Toulouse, and hint at the danger in which he himself had stood, Louis, who must well have known the part Becket had played, replied in the spirit of a true and chivalrous knight that the chancellor had but served his master loyally, who had requited him ill indeed. With the Pope they had no better fortune. Before they were received Herbert of Bosham had also arrived at Sens: he had followed them to Compiègne on his master's behalf and there had a very different reception. Louis had given them cordial sympathy. Henry, he said, should have remembered the verse, "Be ye angry and sin not." Herbert's companion spoke up with no fear of the king: "My lord, maybe he would have remembered that versicle if he had heard it as often as we do in the canonical hours." Louis promised all help; if Henry made much of his *dignitates* (prerogatives) the king of the Franks remembered that among those that belonged anciently to his house was the defence and protection of exiles, especially those who suffered for the Church.

At Sens the Pope saw Herbert before he saw the king's men, and he received the recital of the archbishop's suffering with tears. "While still living he can claim the martyr's privilege," he said. A more formal reception, with cardinals and curia, was given to the king's envoys. Gilbert Foliot spoke bitterly: the occasion of dispute was trivial: Becket had pushed matters to an extreme, and he had entangled himself and his brethren. The wicked fleeth when no man pursueth. "Spare," interjected Alexander. "I will spare him," said the bishop. "Nay, it is yourself that I would have you spare; plainly you hate and persecute an innocent man." And Foliot was silent from confusion. Hilary of Chichester, the eloquent one, fared no better, for he made a bad slip in his Latin, unfortunately saying "*Oportuebat*," whereat the Italians, "hearing him run from *port* to *port*, laughed aloud, and one said, "You have got into port ill." Roger of York spoke with more skill. He reminded the Pope that he had known Becket from his youth, and assured him that his pride could only be abated by a papal rebuke. Alexander talked and temporised: then he said he would send two legates, but they should not have final power: the right of hearing appeals was his own glory which he would not give to another.

Fitz-Stephen, who was not present, tells that a bribe of Peter's pence "from every house whence smoke arises " in England was offered in vain. So the embassy returned, and reported their ill-success to Henry at Marlborough on Christmas Eve. The king waited for the festival, and next day—did he remember Becket's mass of S. Stephen?—he seized all the property of the archbishopric, giving it in charge to Ranulf de Broc, Becket's bitter foe, and the property of all his clerks, and he ordered all his kindred to depart the realm instantly, old and young, even babes in arms. By writs to the sheriffs and bishops he ordered that anyone who appealed to Rome should be imprisoned, and forbade that any of the archbishop's clerks should receive any benefice or money. The archbishop of York required all his clergy to take oath that they would not obey the Pope's commands in the matter of Becket.

The archbishop himself had only the comfort of the Pope's warm sympathy. He had begun the weary years of exile in which he wandered so far over the fair fields of France, where one may follow him and see many a memorial to-day. Some places stand out in the records, and still preserve something of a memory, of the English archbishop.

To follow all his wanderings would perhaps be tedious. At any rate, there is little memory of him that can be recalled at S. Omer or at Montmirail, or Fréteval, the scenes of crisis as the exile drew to an end. The greater interests belong to greater places. At Soissons, a town so famous in the time of Cæsar and in the time of Chlodowech, there is little remaining that the eyes of Becket may have looked upon. The abbey of S. Jean des Vignes, once fortified and castellated like the palace of a great *seigneur*, has long ago been destroyed; the towers and gateway that remain were built a century or so after the archbishop's exile. At Soissons Louis VII welcomed him with pious zest. Thus strengthened by the support of one of Alexander's strong supporters, Becket went on to see the Pope.

At Sens it is not in the abbey of S. Colombe (which, I think, has left us no memorials of its dignity) that his memory is to be sought, but in the stately and beautiful Cathedral and in the clean, fresh streets, where here and there an ancient archway or sculptured portal reminds us that the municipal life goes back to a far past. In the great Cathedral of S. Étienne abides the remembrance of the saint who once worshipped there. Nave and aisles have been trodden by his steps; they were completed while he was still an exile, in 1168, and William of Sens, the architect who designed them, went on to introduce into England that "Pointed" style of exquisite grace and purity, so conspicuous in the building that he had designed, in the great memorial that arose in England to the memory of the saint who had watched the work in the fragrant city on the banks of the Yonne. The choir of Canterbury Cathedral itself, the great memorial to the martyr, and the special ending of that glory of what we call Early English architecture which is known as "Becket's crown," were, it may be, all designed, as the beginning of them was certainly made, by that William of Sens whom the archbishop had seen at work in his own city. The fire that destroyed the ancient choir at Canterbury in 1174 proved a blessing in disguise. It arose again more beautiful, in a new style of severe restraint which was to influence English art for centuries, from the hand of the French architect who came from the city that had sheltered the greatest of the medieval primates, to whom it became, in some sort, a national tribute.

So the memories of Becket pass from Sens to Canterbury. But at Sens they still abide. At the north side of the north choir-aisle of the Cathedral is a little chapel that is called by his name, and though all the decorations there are glaringly modern, the ancient *mensa* (which has been moved from the south side of the same aisle, at the back of the choir) is said—though the tradition is disputed—to be one at which he often said mass. Hard by, on the wall, is a stone figure, in vestments, with the pallium, which has been removed from a house in the city where he is said to have dwelt.[1] It is rough, and it has suffered injury, but it must be very nearly contemporary. It is naturally concluded to be an effigy of Becket. Many think, and I among them, that it has good claim to be the best and most authentic portrait that remains. And there is in the Treasury, almost the most wonderful of all the famous French collections of ecclesiastical art, a chasuble, once dark red and now faded almost into black, with alb, maniple, and stole, which an invincible tradition says that he wore, and a mitre—of later workmanship— that later tales wished to associate with his name. Sens is a beautiful town, fresh and bright, as with something of the river's fresh brightness which girdles the ancient city of S. Savinien. It bears its antiquity— the fine Roman walls, the remains of past glories, ecclesiastical and civil—with an air of perpetual youth.

[1] See frontispiece.

It is a town where banished Pope and exiled primate might well forget some of the sorrows of their lot. And hard by stands the exquisite Auxerre.

Becket would think, when he came before Alexander, of how he had seen the fair district of the Yonne in the days when he was an English scholar at the French schools. Since then he had been the greatest minister, and the greatest friend, of the strongest European sovereign. Then he had been the primate of his realm, and when he had last seen Alexander he had come to him almost as an equal in dignity, and as his superior in worldly state, like Anselm, in the words of another pontiff, the "Pope of another world." Now he came as an exile to an exile; and, weary of wandering, says Guernes, went to the hostelry. A blight had fallen on him which even his faithful clerks felt: not one of them would plead his cause before the Pope. He must do it himself, and perhaps he had not even—so Guernes seems to mean—any silver or gold, any rich plate or jewel, such as the custom is to give the Pope when men go to see him. Only he had the manuscript of those Constitutions which had brought him to this pass.

They were read out, and Becket expounded. There was an *advocatus diaboli*, it seems, in the Cardinal William of Pavia, who tried to trip him up, but he was not to be confused, and so in his "fair Latin" he proved the case as it seemed to him, taking quite half a day in his speech. Alexander listened, pondered, and then in full consistory condemned. Only six out of the sixteen articles could be tolerated: the second, sixth, eleventh, thirteenth, fourteenth and sixteenth (Alexander listened not to the complaint of the poor, who would serve

Christ in His Church) are marked in the ancient copy "toleravit." The rest he utterly condemned.

Meanwhile John of Poitiers had found a refuge for his friend in Burgundy. Sens he was to return to, driven forth from that new place of rest, and turning back to the city where the fair cathedral church was rising towards heaven. In that valley he could be at peace he knew. Those towns on the Yonne have indeed an age-long charm of quietude. But for the time he turned aside.

Far different was the refuge where Becket rested in the two years that followed the first sojourn at Sens, the great Cistercian abbey of Pontigny. Thither he went on November 30th, 1164. The year ended in silence and retirement and something of peace, in the shelter of the noble abbey.

To-day the monastic buildings have been swept away, and there stands only the great church, said to be the only Cistercian church remaining in completeness. It looks, as you draw near, almost as if it were some huge barn—like that grand one at Great Coxwell in Berkshire—so plain is it and unadorned. It has no towers, nothing to break the long line of regular roof, no ornaments or decorations at all; only lancet windows in aisles and clerestory, a rose window at the transepts, flying buttresses, ugly like wooden props, at the east. It is severe in its lowly simplicity, and it is all of one age and one design.[1] In the freshness of its restoration, with white walls and columns unchipped and smooth, it looks in the twentieth century as it must have looked

---

[1] The choir is a little later, but does not differ very greatly from the nave.

when Becket entered its walls to worship for the first time. Thibault of Champagne had begun it in 1150, and it was finished, it would seem, while the English archbishop was a guest of the house. Long, high, severe, the church within is a fit expression of the Cistercian protest for strict simplicity of worship. S. Bernard might have built it for himself to worship in. Of later days are the graceful chevet with seven small chapels, and the oppressive shrine over the eighteenth-century altar holding the body, brown and grisly, in its modern episcopal vestments, of S. Edmund, the successor, seventy years later, of S. Thomas, who died in exile where S. Thomas had sojourned eighty years before. The note of severity was, in the time of Becket, toned only by the strange, appealing pathos of the narrow aisles, where the pointed arches rise sharply from the high, undecorated columns, a long vista of religious light that is not dim. The S. Thomas chapel has gone, the altar at which the exile ministered is forgotten; only the solemn peace of the great village church—such now it is—treasures the memory of his name. There he rested, and the biographers tell us how kindly he took to the monastic life. He put on the Cistercian dress. The Pope sent him a rough woollen habit which he had himself blessed, and the abbat put it on him privately, so he became affiliated to the Cistercians.

"He taketh up," says the Saga,[1] compressing the records of those who were with him, "a new manner of life as it were, reading books and praying in calm quietude, and fervid striving after heavenly things.

[1] i, 316.

Therewithal he exerciseth such temperance as to take no food but according to the rule of Grey-Friars, that being dry and without savour. But this hard way of living his nature may no wise endure, for he had alway fed sumptuously on goodly fare, and therefore he falleth into such hard sickness, that he taketh to his bed. Now when his familiar friends know from himself what causeth his illness, they pray and counsel him, in the name of God, to nourish his body with such food as may be wholesome for his life. This counsel he taketh in a good part, though unwilling, and improveth into a fully restored health after a few days. But how high his virtues were, and acceptable to God Almighty, is now revealed through a heavenly vision, which he had while staying at Pontigny.

"On a certain day, when the blessed Thomas has sung mass, as he falleth down before the altar to pray weeping and sighing, thinking that he was left alone in the church, there cometh over him a voice saying:

"'O Thomas, O Thomas, my Church shall be glorified in thy blood!'

"The archbishop answereth:

"'Who art thou, Lord?'

"The voice speaketh:

"'I am Jesus Christ, thy brother.'

"The blessed Thomas says:

"'May the bliss befall me, O my Lord, that thy Church be glorified in my blood!'

"The Son of God speaketh still:

"'Verily my Church shall be glorified in thy blood; but when she is glorified through thee, thou shalt be honoured by me.'

"From this vision the holy Thomas was filled with such exceeding joy, that in no words may it be interpreted; and such fervour of godly love shot forthwith through his soul, that he yearned above all things else for the privilege of giving his life for the name of God." The Saga says that the abbat of Pontigny, who was in the chapel at the time, knew of the vision, but was adjured by the archbishop to keep silence about it.

Such visions came naturally to the mind of one who spent much time in prayer, and much, it may well be, in brooding on his misfortunes. He stayed himself on study of Holy Writ and on meditation. But still his old tastes remained, and he gratified two of them at least. He could not give up the old habits of an out-of-door man: he took his bath in the little stream which ran through the abbey grounds.[1] All over Gaul he sent his agents to hunt up rare and famous books to have them copied, or bought, for Canterbury: he was still a *virtuoso*, though now it was books he bought, not horses and arms and rich stuffs. But also he made his clerks collect out of all these books, and any others he could hear of, all records of privileges granted at any time to his cathedral church. In the neighbourhood of Auxerre his thoughts turned back naturally to the law he had studied there. John of Salisbury,[2] most faithful of friends, writing in May, 1165, besought him to give his whole mind to God: "Profitable indeed are laws and canons, but now there is not need of them." He can quote the Æneid to the scholar prelate.

"Non hoc ista sibi tempus spectacula poscit," he

[1] See Guernes, 3626, and (Walberg) p. 274.
[2] *Materials*, v, 163.

says, for laws and canons excite curiosity more than devotion. Rather should the priest stand between the porch and the altar, crying "Spare, spare." Not philosophy, but Psalms and the Morals of S. Gregory, would be his best reading.

It was honest advice, and John gave it with some little timidity. And indeed Becket's thoughts could not be weaned from the consideration of his wrongs. The Pope, in June, sent him a formal document annulling—inasmuch as to him, he said, it belonged to correct things evil and prevent their becoming a precedent—the sentence of Northampton presumptuously passed by the bishops and barons of England—annulling it, be it understood, because of its obvious injustice. And he adjured the archbishop to forbear any spiritual censures against the king or kingdom till Easter, 1166. An agent of Becket's described him as very cautious. He was soon to be stirred from his hesitation.

The Schism was still unhealed, and the Emperor Frederick was eagerly seeking for new supporters for his anti-pope, Guy of Crema, called Paschal III. In a Council at Würzburg on Whit Sunday, 1165, he confirmed the election and many bishops took oaths to the Pope. Reginald, archbishop-elect of Köln, declared that he had won over the English bishops, and John of Oxford who at this time had been made dean of Salisbury, and Richard of Ilchester, archdeacon of Poitiers, took oaths to the anti-pope, it was said on behalf of the king and barons. This was very soon felt to be an error. Henry ordered Rotrou of Beaumont, archbishop of Rouen, to write that no such oath had been made for him, and John of Oxford was told to go and assure

Alexander that he had not made it. The Holy Roman Emperor, in a letter "to all peoples, over whom our imperial clemency rules," had declared that he had. So John of Oxford got the name of perjurer (*jurator*) from Becket's party for the rest of his life. It was not so easy to change popes as Henry may have thought. Alexander was not to be led at this moment by his fears. Indeed, he wrote—when he may just have heard of the doings at Würzburg—to Gilbert Foliot in no uncertain language.[1]

Thus runs his letter, in June, 1165—

"It will not have escaped your memory, that our beloved son in Christ, Henry, the illustrious king of England, requested of us formerly, with much earnestness, to permit your translation from the see of Hereford, which you then occupied, to that of London. And, moreover, that to secure our assent he dwelt on the advantages likely to result from your promotion, alleging that London was the seat of the government, and that he wished to have you near his person for the benefit of your counsels, as well in temporal matters as in those that concern his soul. We, therefore, looking to the interest of the king and nation, and above all, of God's holy Church, consented to your promotion. A time has now arrived when we expect to reap the benefits we then proposed to ourselves, and to experience the reality of the hopes which were then held out to us.

"Doubtless you are not ignorant that the aforesaid king has of late fallen off much from his devotion to the holy Church; he has forbidden appeals, has entered into communication with schismatics and persons

---

[1] *Materials*, v, 175.

excommunicated, and exiled from his dominions our venerable brother the archbishop of Canterbury, by which acts he has become even a persecutor of the Church. Wherefore we command you, in conjunction with the bishop of Hereford, to warn the king that he desist without delay from these evil practices and make satisfaction for what he has done amiss; admonish him to love his God with singleness of heart; to respect as he was wont his holy mother the Roman Church; to withdraw his prohibition on all visits and appeals to it; to recall and reinstate our brother aforesaid, the archbishop, in his diocese; to stand fast in his reverence towards the blessed S. Peter and ourself; to attend on works of piety and religion; no longer to oppress, as he is said to do, or permit others to oppress, the churches and clergy of his kingdom or his other territories; but to love, maintain, and by his royal protection support them; that by these means he may obtain from Him by whom kings reign, both a continuance of his temporal kingdom here, and the gift of an eternal one hereafter.

"Furthermore, although we ourself, in consideration of his former devotion and his service shown to us in time of need, still love him with abundant charity, as a noble prince and renowned king, and still labour for the advancement of his glory (though he himself seems to think otherwise of us) with a fervent zeal; nevertheless, it is fit you should recall to his mind that unless he repents of his evil deeds, and that speedily, God will most surely visit him with heavy vengeance, and the time must at last come when our patience can no longer endure.

"These things we desire to lay before him, not for

our own good but for his safety, in return for those many and signal services which he has before now rendered to us as a most Christian king. His greatness is our delight; his welfare, and that of his kingdom, is the object of our most earnest wish."

The reply was that the king had no desire to do more than observe the ancient customs of his land: he did not really intend to stop appeals, or if such a course was contrary to the Church's interests he would submit it to the judgment of a council of his realm. It would be much wiser to treat him mildly. And at the same moment John of Poitiers, thinking that Becket's pride was reviving, was bidding him restrain his ostentation.

"It will be necessary for your lordship, as far as one can judge from the present aspect of your affairs, to husband your resources in every possible way; to let your enemies see that you are prepared for any sufferings to which your exile may reduce you. For this reason I have often warned your discretion, and must still anxiously press you to get rid of your superfluous incumbrances, and to consider the badness of the times, which promises you neither a speedy return nor a safe one. Your wisdom ought to know, that no one will think the less of you, if, in conformity to your circumstances, and in condescension to the religious house which entertains you, you content yourself with a moderate establishment of horses and men such as your necessities require."[1]

The advice was hardly needed. Already the archbishop had fallen sick from his fasts and vigils, from the blows of the discipline administered by his old

[1] *Materials*, v, 197.

chaplain, Robert of Merton, and from his long hours of prayer.

So the year passed on. In England everything was quiet. "Not the least curious part in the Pipe Roll of 1165–66," says Dr Stubbs, "is the almost entire absence of any sign that the continued exile of the archbishop, a leading feature of the history in the writings of the chroniclers, and in the development of national senti- ment, was at all affecting the working of the Govern- ment. His property is in the king's hands, and his name occurs now and then in reference to sureties, but, considering the position which he had occupied four years earlier, he seems to be little missed."[1] Henry held England in his hand. Men held their breath, fearing what might come. Some, like John of Salisbury, could honestly swear that they were loyal both to pri- mate and king. The exiles longed to return. But no way was open. Still the archbishop kept up the appear- ance of his authority. He wrote letters to the Church in Bangor, giving orders about elections; he wrote advice to the old English saint, Gilbert of Sempringham, who had done so much to regenerate the religion of the Midlands. Then at last, as the time grew towards the Easter of 1166, he prepared to speak and to act.

His determination may well have been aroused by the interview which some of his clerks had with king Henry at Angers on Low Sunday, May 1st, 1166. The scene is thus vigorously described by William Fitz- Stephen—[2]

"As Henry sat among his courtiers the first who came

[1] Preface to *Pipe Roll*, 1165–66.
[2] *Materials*, iii, 98.

before him was John of Salisbury, who on entering the room saluted the king, and asked to be allowed to return to England in peace, and be restored to his ecclesiastical preferments, because he had never knowingly done anything to offend the king, and was ready to serve him as his earthly master with all devotion and fidelity, saving his own order. To this it was replied on the part of the king, that John was born in his dominions, and all his relations obtained their subsistence there, and that he had risen under his majesty's protection to riches and honour, and he ought, therefore, to be faithful to the king in everything, not only against the archbishop but against everybody in the world; and when this was said, they put before him a form of oath, binding him to be faithful to the king in life and limb, and to defend the earthly honour of his majesty against all persons whatsoever, and in particular that he would observe the royal Constitutions and dignities as they had been reduced to writing, notwithstanding all that the Pope or his archbishop or bishop might do. John assented to all this until he got to the Constitutions, but here he stuck, saying that the Church of Canterbury had nurtured him from his youth, and that he had sworn obedience to the Pope and to the archbishop, nor would he undertake to observe any of the Constitutions without their authority, but he was prepared to conform to all which met with their approval, and to reject all that they rejected. This answer did not satisfy the king, and John of Salisbury was ordered to withdraw.

"Herbert of Bosham was then called in. 'Now,' said king Henry to his attendants, 'you will see a proud fellow appear.' Herbert was of a great stature and good-looking, and had on a handsome dress of green cloth of Auxerre, consisting of a coat and cloak, which hung over his shoulders in the German fashion, down to his heels, with every other appurtenance corresponding. Having first saluted the king, he sat down. He was questioned in the same manner as John, and made for the most part the same answers. On the mention of loyalty, and the archbishop, he said that the archbishop above all men was most especially loyal, for that he had not suffered the king to go astray unwarned. Of the usages he spoke as John had done, and added, that he wondered the king had put them in writing. 'For,' said he, 'in other kingdoms likewise there are evil usages against the Church; but they are not written, and for this reason there is hope, by God's grace, that they may become disused.' The king, wishing to catch him in his words, asked, 'And what are the ill usages in the kingdom of our lord the king of the Franks?'

"Herbert. 'The exactions of toll and passage money from the clergy and strangers. Again, when a bishop dies, all his moveables, even the doors and windows of his house, become the king's. Again, these and similar ill usages, though they exist, are still not written in the realm of the king of the Germans.'

"The king. 'Why do you not call him by his proper title, the emperor of the Germans?'

"Herbert. 'He is king of the Germans, but when he writes it is written *Imperator Romanorum, semper Augustus.*'

"The king. 'This is abominable. Is this son of a priest to disturb my kingdom and disquiet my peace?'

"Herbert. 'It is not I that do it; nor, again, am I

the son of a priest, for I was born before my father entered orders; nor is he a king's son, whose father was not king when he was born.'

"Here Jordan Tarsun, one of the barons sitting by, said to his neighbour, 'Whosoever son he is, I would give half my land that he were mine.'

"The king was angry and said nothing; Herbert was dismissed and withdrew.

"Philip de Calve was then called in; he was by birth a Londoner, and had studied at Tours two years before the archbishop went into exile: he was very well-informed in the Scriptures, and a most eloquent man, but from ill-health he did not accompany his patron into exile, nor did he go to Rome, or mix himself up at all in the quarrel with the king. All this was now explained to the king; and his cause was supported by some influential advocates, who told the king that when he had heard of his having been deprived of his property in England on the archbishop's account, he exclaimed, 'Good God, what can our good king expect to get from me?' The king was persuaded in his favour, and remitted the oath, together with a free-pardon and the restitution of all his possessions; rising up, turned his attention to other matters."

Herbert of Bosham, one may be sure, told his master of his bold speech with the king, though in later days he did not set it down in his book. He was no more a priest's son, he would say, than Henry was a king's son, for their fathers were not priest or king when they were born. And the experience of John of Salisbury and Herbert at Angers may well have stirred their archbishop to show a similar spirit.

CHAPTER VIII

VÉZELAY

IN the spring of 1166 Becket's patience—a strange
word, some might say, to use of him—had given way.
He thought that only a decisive blow would mend all
that had gone wrong. His authority was despised:
England was oppressed and neglected; the king worked
his will uncontrolled and the bishops cared not for the
flock. He had written to beseech support from every
side, and he had not been without success; even the
king's mother, Matilda, "though she was of the race
of the tyrants"—the phrase of a worthy monk who
went to see her on Becket's part—said not a little in
his favour. The Pope had written on his behalf to the
kings of the Franks and the Scots and the count of
Flanders. The archbishop now, after more than a
year's silence, wrote directly to the king.

He sent three letters, in an ascending scale of severity
and vehemence as he received no answer. The first
was in a sad note of tribulation. The Church was oppressed. He must warn the wicked from his ways. If
Henry would amend them God would bless him greatly
and give glory to his sons; if not he dreaded lest the
sword should not depart from his house.

Again, when no answer came, *exspectans exspectavi*:
"I have waited for the day when God should turn you
from crooked ways and evil counsels; but I have waited
in vain. Yet I have not ceased to pray God for a happy
ending to the strife. Now the care of the Church of

Canterbury forces me to address you warnings and
even worse, for fear I should be an abettor of your
counsellors' crimes; for consent is participation in
evil. Remember that your royal power must not be
concerned with the Church's own matters: priestly
matters are always dealt with in priestly councils."
Then comes the result of those law studies that John
of Salisbury deprecated: "The Decretals have proved
an armoury. Constantine tells the priesthood, 'You
can be judged by no man, who are reserved for the
judgment seat of God,' and Gratian that two powers
rule the world, the sacred authority of prelates and the
royal power, of which the former is so much the
greater that it has to give account of kings. God has
raised you up, but how many kings has God abased?
Remember the excommunication of Arcadius and of
Theodosius. Do you bow before the Church's rebuke
as David before Nathan, and cast away the evil counsellors and all will go well. Repent and 'remember the
last things, so shalt thou never sin.'"

Still no answer. And then came the letter without
superscription save "'These are the words of the lord
of Canterbury to the king of the English': With desire
I have desired to see your face and to speak with you,
for my own sake and for yours. For mine, that I might
recall to your mind how faithfully I served you of old,
and your affection for me might be moved by seeing
me a mendicant among strangers; for yours, as my
master to whom I owe counsel, my king to whom I
owe reverence and warning, my son whom I ought to
castigate and coerce."

So then the archbishop sets before the king what he

thinks are the true relations between Church and State. "The Church of Christ is constituted in two orders, the clergy and the people, the one having the care of the Church that all may be ruled for the salvation of souls, the other contains kings, princes and nobles who have to carry on secular government that all things may lead to the peace and unity of the Church. As it is certain that kings get this power from the Church, the Church not from them but from Christ, so you, king, have no right to judge ecclesiastical causes, matters of tithes, oaths and such like. Err not, therefore, nor consort with schismatics. Remember the promise, which you laid in writing on the altar at your coronation by my predecessor, that you would preserve the liberties of the Church. Restore then the possessions of the Church of Canterbury, and let us her ministers return in safety. Or know for certain that you shall feel the severity and vengeance of God."

Such was the theory which Becket had accepted during the months of seclusion and study at Pontigny. That it had guided his earlier life as chancellor or even as archbishop there is nothing to prove. It was a theory which no doubt he had studied at Bologna and Auxerre, but which had been confronted by very different views for which the civil rather than the canon law was responsible. When he first came into conflict with Henry the matter was one of practical disagreement, and though theory lay to some extent at the back of his disagreement with the Constitutions, it was not brought forward or elaborated till the primate had considered the relations of Church and State in all their bearings, and under the heating influence of ecclesiastical doctrinaires.

The theory which he now set out, in his three letters to Henry, was one for which no warrant could be found in the New Testament; it is hardly too much to say that there was no support for it in the writings of the early Christian centuries: there is no question that it owed its strength to the false Decretals, which had now permeated ecclesiastical law. It appeared full blown in the vehement letters of Hildebrand, and it was gradually accepted, not without reluctance, by other champions of the Church during the struggle concerning investitures. Becket, with his legal training, had now clearly come to see that it was impossible to fight a great king by merely practical considerations, when the strength of the English episcopate and baronage was thrown largely on the king's side. He must have the support of a theory that had great names behind it. When he began to consider whether his own course had been right, and whether he would be justified in yielding to the king's wishes—and there are unmistakable signs during the period when the Constitutions were being considered that he had grave hesitation—he found a theory waiting to his hand, which had been advocated by the greatest Churchmen of the previous generation, and which dissolved his doubts. There can be no doubt that Henry's letter to Reginald of Köln in which he had declared his intention to desert "Alexander and his perfidious cardinals," the contents of which seem soon to have become known, had convinced Becket that his own difficulties were only part of a larger dispute, and were indeed an offshoot of the secular strife between Church and State in which the genius of Hildebrand and the holiness of Anselm seemed to supply convincing argument that the cause of righteousness was involved. Seeing his own misfortunes in that light, and having before his eyes the oppression which his friends and kindred suffered, he determined to take up the cause as one of eternal justice and to press it to a conclusion with all his spiritual powers. Already indeed he may have seen that the question would eventually merge itself in that contest against what later ages called Erastianism, the domination of temporal power over spiritual interests, which eventually brought about his own death. Meanwhile he had convinced himself that he was right, and he would act.

He had sent his last letter by a bare-footed monk, who was charged with still plainer words than were written down. Henry in vain endeavoured to meet the danger by an appeal to the Pope, thus throwing aside his own Constitutions, which had been understood to abolish such a resort. Becket had warned the king's mother that in a very short time he would "unsheath the sword of the Spirit," though even now if her son would listen to her counsels and the voice of God he should be spared: meanwhile the primate waited, "mourning with eagerness as over a dying son." It was to no purpose that the crafty Arnulf of Lisieux wrote to beg him to let the king have the appearance of triumph while he himself could glory before God in the consciousness of right. It was no satisfaction to Becket to be assured that he was offered up as a sweet sacrifice to God for his brethren, or that there was no one who had not bowed the knee to Baal.[1] The unctuous

[1] See *Materials*, v, Letters 162 and 163.

commonplaces of clericalism were never to his mind. His hour of triumph seemed at hand.

The party of Emperor and anti-pope were for the time defeated. The exiled Pope had returned in triumph to Rome, and the first signs of his new confidence in himself were a series of letters in which he threw himself decisively on the archbishop's side. Documents which it is impossible precisely to date belong most probably to this period and form a series of definite meaning. Alexander authorises Becket to issue censures against the invaders of Church property, and he informs the suffragans of Canterbury that he has done so. He requires Foliot and all the English bishops to see that the property taken from the archbishop's clerks is restored: he forbids Roger of York, should occasion ever arise, to interfere with the privilege of Canterbury in crowning kings: by bull he confirms to Becket all the privileges of the metropolitan see. On Easter Day, April 24th, 1166, from the Lateran, he appointed the archbishop of Canterbury legate over the whole of England except the diocese of York, with full powers, which powers in a letter to the bishops he ordered them all implicitly to observe.[1]

Becket, in a letter to Robert of Hereford and Roger of Worcester, announced his legation and instructed them to tell the bishops. He now was ready to act. The notice of appeal sent to Pontigny had arrived when he was gone.[2] Already the abbat had received warning

---

[1] *Materials*, v, Letters 164, 165, 166, 169, 170, 171, and 159.

[2] "An appeal against a sentence of excommunication, in order to be valid, must be made before the sentence is passed; after the sentence, the person excommunicated, being no longer a member of the Church, cannot be acknowledged in the character of an

that if the Order supported the archbishop more the king would no longer endure the injury but find a remedy, language none the less alarming for its ambiguity. Thus, the archbishop might now feel that a whole order of innocent monks was involved in his cause and would suffer if he suffered. An English king with vast foreign possessions was able to execute his threats with terrifying force, as medieval history shows again and again. Becket, who never avoided a conflict, was ready to show how the Church could guard herself against the secular arm. Spiritual censures afforded a weapon that perhaps might even ward off the threatened blow. And spiritual censures were already deserved and already prepared. The archbishop left Pontigny, and a period of peaceful repose was ended.

Pontigny speaks of seclusion and patience, Vézelay of stern protest and command. It is a long journey from the pasture-land of the Cistercian house—and Becket made it longer by a pilgrimage to Soissons, "girding himself for the battle," as says John of Salisbury, before the famous shrines of the Virgin, of S. Drausius, the Frankish saint "to whom men go when they are set to fight," and S. Gregory the Great. It is a splendid church of the Benedictines at the height of their power. Striking is the contrast to the traveller to-day. Pontigny is a perfect example of the "Pointed" style, which in England we have come to call Early English: Vézelay is what we call "Norman."

appellant, but only as a penitent. This is not the case with any other appeals except that against excommunication."—R. H. Froude, *History of the Contest between Thomas Becket and Henry II.* (*Remains*, part ii, vol. ii, 1839.) Becket did not excommunicate Henry, it will be seen, or any of the bishops.

The church of the abbey, dedicated to S. Mary Magdalen, stands on a long, narrow hill which overlooks the valleys of the Yonne and the Cure, and looks across them to wooded heights, almost mountains, whence the forests descend into the valleys and fringe the closely cultivated fields, and where ten miles away is the exquisite little town of Avallon, protected in the Middle Ages on all sides by the hands of Nature and of man.[1]

By devious ways, across winding streams, first over that *pons insignis* of Pontigny that spans the river a few yards from the abbey gate and hard by the old abbey mill, and last over that fine medieval bridge which crossed the Cure, in the valley between precipitous rocks, at the entrance to the domains of the great abbat, whose fortified gate marked the beginning of the lands he ruled, the exiled primate of England drew near to the church where he had determined to vindicate his claim to justice and restoration. Slowly would the little procession of his followers toil up the hill which dominates the country for many miles around. At length they stood in solemn awe before the Judgment depicted over the great west door. "Man's judgment is tolerable only when he speaks for God," some of them would say; "Is it not then least tolerable of all?" would be the question in others' hearts. To-day we can realise the grandeur of that scene when, on Whit Sunday, 1166,[2] before a concourse of "divers nations,"

[1] Avalon, in the department of Isère, is carefully to be distinguished from Avallon (Yonne). The former was the birthplace of S. Hugh.

[2] There is a slight doubt about the date. Herbert of Bosham and Gervase of Canterbury say it was on S. Mary Magdalen's

the archbishop pronounced his sentence of excommunication against the chief offenders, read the Pope's condemnation of the Constitutions of Clarendon, and warned his sovereign and his old friend of the sentence that awaited him, in a voice choked by sobs.

When he had arrived at Vézelay he had heard of the king's illness at Chinon, and by John of Salisbury's advice,[1] he delayed the sentence against him. The offenders he dealt with by excommunication were John of Oxford, because he had fallen into heresy by taking the sacrilegious oath at Würzburg and communicating with the schismatic Reginald of Köln, and because he had "usurped" the deanery of Salisbury, and Richard of Ilchester who had done the like; Joceline de Balliol and Richard de Lucy, the true authors, as his party said, of the Constitutions; Ranulf de Broc, Hugh de S. Clare, Thomas Fitz-Bernard, and all who had laid hands on the revenues and property of the see of Canterbury.

He then denounced the customs, as condemned by the Pope, and chiefly the seventh, as to excommunication of tenants in chief; the fifteenth, giving to lay courts jurisdiction over perjury and bad faith; the third, that clerks should be brought before secular tribunals—the statement is precise, "quod ad saecularia judicia trahantur clerici," not that they should be tried by lay courts but brought into them to plead their

Day; but John of Salisbury, who was probably present, gives Pentecost (June 12th), and Nicholas of Mont S. Jacques, Rouen, confirms the date by indisputable evidence.

[1] John is our original authority for the scene. Letter to Bartholomew of Exeter, in *Materials*, v, 376. Herbert of Bosham adds some details, but he wrote years afterwards.

privilege of clergy, and back again, if found guilty, to be sentenced there; the first, that layfolk, whether king's men or others, should deal with cases concerning churches and tithes; and the fourth and eighth, as to appeals and the right to leave the country freely.

So Becket took his stand clearly on the Pope's side. The Pope's enemies were his enemies. What the Pope condemned he condemned. It was part of that long strife between Empire and Papacy of which men had not yet seen the end. The voice rang through the aisles of Vézelay denouncing the enemies of Pope and archbishop as the enemies of God.

Twenty years before, S. Bernard had preached Crusade on the rock outside, for the great church could not contain the crowd which pressed to take the cross. Fourteen years later, when Becket and his king had passed away, Richard of England, called Lion Heart, and Philip of France, called Augustus, met in the plain below to take the oath of faithfulness in the Holy Cause, having war in their hearts. But never, since that Whit Sunday in 1166, have the very walls of that great church itself, among the finest in the whole world of all the buildings which the French architects call "Romanesque" and we "Norman," echoed to a voice more powerful at a time of greater stress. Becket celebrated high mass, and then he mounted the pulpit, looking down the long nave to where, it may well be, the great doors were open into the wonderful narthex beyond. If Vézelay was not the grandest of all the Cluniac churches, it is, as Walter Pater said, "certainly the grandest of them which remains."

It is typically monastic, typically Romanesque. The

narthex is strangely Byzantine in the decoration of the capitals and the sculptures of the tympanum; there are details which might have come from S. Sophia, as in the grim crypt below there are details which recall the elaborate carving of the capitals in the sixth-century underground cistern (Yeri Batan Serai), at Constantinople. But the general effect is one of immense strength, reserve, and power. The arches of the nave are high up, spanned by stones which are alternately white and a sort of dark green, and above those at the side is no triforium, but a plain, unbroken surface, which has an effect of great severity and above which there is but one small window, a kind of clerestory, to each bay. The decoration, which leaves the walls untouched, is lavished on the capitals, where all sorts of strange stories are depicted, legends of saints and scenes which look like the very life in Le Morvan itself. But the extraordinary minuteness of this decoration, which extends from the west door itself, through the narthex, with its gallery (perhaps for women, as in the Eastern churches which it strangely resembles, on the great days of feasts, when the monks' church was invaded by masses of all nations from afar) and its own splendid portals, up the nave to the later and most beautiful Pointed choir, yet does not diminish the power of the chief note of severity, simplicity, awe. The choir itself, a most exquisite example of the style of the twelfth and thirteenth centuries, may not have been begun when Becket preached his famous sermon. But as he looked westward and faced the massed multitude before him all of the building that his eyes rested on our eyes can see to-day. Magnificent it is, instinct with reverence, almost stupendous in its solemnity. Even here there is a link with his own Canterbury. Already something of the Pointed arch is beginning to appear, in the wonderful narthex, the work of the first half of the twelfth century. But not till the metropolitan Cathedral rose in its new glory as a monument to the martyr was there—it may almost without hesitation be said—anything in England so dignified, so impressive, as the great church of the Cistercians at Vézelay.

And it is at Vézelay, stern and cold, that the memory of the archbishop, in his most unyielding mood, seems most fitly to linger. At Pontigny, the place of his fasts and vigils, dwells rather the spirit of the gentle Edmund, where his body rests.

The archbishop of Canterbury had acted on his own responsibility. Now he wrote to the Pope to tell him what he had done and to ask him to support his actions. Alexander confirmed them. The archbishop notified his action to the bishops of his province, wrote to the chapter of Salisbury annulling the election of John as dean, and to the archbishop of Rouen and the bishop of Chichester, especially advising them of his acts.

The letter to the bishops of his province was as follows—

"My beloved brethren, why do you not rise together with me against the malignants? Why do you not stand up with me to oppose those who work iniquity? Do you not know how that God will scatter the bones of those who strive to oppress Him? They shall be confounded, because the Lord hath despised them. Your discretion knows well that evil, when not resisted, is approved, and truth, when not defended, is crushed:

and, as Gregory says, he is consenting unto wrong, who does not step forward to correct that which requires amendment. For this cause it is that we have too long borne with our lord the king, and the Church of God has gained no alleviation from our sufferance. For the rest, it is dangerous any longer to tolerate the excesses which he commits in his treatment of the Church and of ecclesiastics, particularly as we have endeavoured, by messengers and by letters, to turn him from the error of his ways. And since he has heard, but not listened to us, we have invoked God's Holy Spirit, and condemned and annulled that charter which contains his constitutions, or rather depravities, by which the peace of the Church has been so much disturbed. Moreover, we have excommunicated all who advised them, or have observed them, or aided in their promulgation, and by God's authority, and our own, we have absolved all the bishops from the promise which bound them unlawfully to their observance. 'For who can doubt that Christ's priests are the fathers and masters of kings and princes and of all the faithful? Is it not pitiable folly for the son to exercise power over the father, or the scholar over his master, by whom he believes that he may be bound and loosed both in earth below and in heaven above?' [Here he is quoting Gregory VII, through Gratian.] Wherefore, that we may not fall into this error, we have condemned that writing, and the depravities which it contains."[1]

He gives the clauses as John of Salisbury gave them, and continues—

"Furthermore, we denounce as excommunicate, and

---

[1] *Materials*, v, 392 *sqq.*

do hereby excommunicate by name, John of Oxford, because he has fallen into a damnable heresy, by making oaths to schismatics, whereby the schism in Germany, that had well nigh expired, has revived, and because he has communicated with Reginald the schismatical bishop of Köln, and because he has usurped the deanery of Salisbury contrary to the mandate of the Pope and of ourself. And as this deed is unlawful and detrimental to the Church, we have utterly annulled it, and have commanded the bishop of Salisbury, as soon as he sees our letters, to hold him no longer as dean.

"Also, we have excommunicated, and do hereby excommunicate, Richard of Ilchester, because he has fallen into the same damnable heresy, by communicating with the same Reginald, the schismatic of Cologne, and by contriving evil against God's Church, in conjunction with the schismatical Germans, and particularly against the Church of Rome, by the treaty which he has contracted between those Germans and the king.

"We excommunicate also Richard de Lucy and Joceline de Balliol, who were the authors and fabricators of those depravities aforesaid.

"Also Ranulf de Broc, who has seized, and holds in his possession, the goods of the Church of Canterbury, which are the inheritance of the poor, and because he detains in custody our men, both clerks and laymen.

"Also Hugh de Saint Clare and Thomas Fitz-Bernard, who also seized and holds possession of the goods and possessions of the Church of Canterbury without our consent.

"We have, moreover, pronounced the same sentence

of excommunication against all who shall hereafter lay hands upon the possessions of our Church, according to that sentence of Pope Lucius: 'All plunderers of the Church, and alienators of sacred property, we do anathematize and condemn, and pronounce to be guilty of sacrilege: and not only themselves, but all who abet them; for the same punishment awaits the agents and their abettors: and Scripture says in another place, 'He who consents unto sinners, or defends another in his sins, shall be accursed before God and man, and shall be corrected with the most severe correction.' And again: 'If anyone defends a sinner, let him be punished worse than he who sinned.'

"In truth, we have delayed to pass sentence on the person of our lord the king, waiting, if perhaps he may, by God's grace, repent: but we will pass it ere long, unless he does repent. For this cause it is, that we command your fraternity, and enjoin you in virtue of your obedience, that whereas we have excommunicated the aforesaid persons, you also, as is your duty, shall also hold them as excommunicated, and denounce them as such, according to that decree of Pope Honorius: 'Let all bishops certify to the neighbouring bishops, as well as to their own clergy, the names of those whom they have excommunicated, that they may be fixed publicly upon the doors of the church, and all who come may see them, and thus they may be excluded from entering in, and all men may be without excuse.'

"Moreover, we commend you, my brother of London, in virtue of your obedience, to certify these our letters to all our brethren, the bishops of our province. Farewell in Christ, and pray for us without ceasing!"

CHAPTER IX

APPEALS AND COUNTERBLASTS

SOMETHING like terror was felt in England when the news of the Vézelay censures arrived. The bishops and abbats met to consult as to what should be done. On the feast of the Commemoration of S. Paul, June 30, 1166, as Foliot was at the altar of his cathedral church, the official notice of Becket's appointment was handed to him.[1] But before this the bishop had addressed joint letters to the Pope and the primate.

The first was practically a vindication of Henry. The bishops of London and Hereford had reproved him and he had borne it well. The peace of the realm had been disturbed by certain clerks, and the king's desire was only for justice, while the bishops had clung to clerical immunities. It was thus that the king had had the ancient liberties of his realm defined, and that was the whole of his cruelty, perversity and malignity, with which the world was ringing. Then came the fierce letters of Becket reopening strife which had been healed. Here the bishops showed themselves partisans. And so they appealed to the Pope, lest worse should befall them.

To Becket they said—and the letter was sent in June, 1166, under the name of the Clerus Angliae—that they had heard with gladness that he was spending his time

[1] On the whole, though I see the difficulty as to date, I think Canon Robertson's view, *Materials*, v, 417, is correct. But see Miss Norgate, *Angevin Kings*, ii, 68, note.

abroad in poverty and prayer: while this could be said of him his friends could use their influence with the king without hesitation. But now he had written fiercely and with threats of excommunication. This was obvious ingratitude. Let him look back to the time when he was raised from so low a state to be the king's friend and high in rule of all his dominions from the Pyrenees to the North Sea: and then Henry went further and against the advice of his mother and the groans of the kingdom and the whole Church, raised you high in the things of God. Spare yourself! —it was an unhappy return to Foliot's phrase which the Pope had rebuked, and marks the real author of the letter. For in his exasperation the king may well desert to the anti-pope, he who hitherto has stood firm as a rock—this was a bold statement indeed. Much more to this effect; and an appeal, which the king supported.

To Becket, who loved argument, and had an undoubting belief in the strength of his cause, this letter seemed to have delivered his foes and his critics into his hand. Thus he replied—[1]

"Thomas, by the Grace of God humble minister of the Church of Canterbury, to his reverend brethren in general, by God's grace bishops of the province of Canterbury, if indeed the letter be their joint production, health and grace to act as they have not yet acted. Your joint letter, my brethren, which has just reached us, but which we cannot easily believe to have proceeded from your joint wisdom, has filled us with astonishment. Its contents seem to convey more of

[1] Dr Giles's translation, *Materials*, v, pp. 490 *sqq.*

irony than of consolation; and I would that it had been
dictated by pious zeal and feeling of charity rather than
the suggestions of the will....

"Would to God, my beloved brethren, that you had
the same zeal in defending the liberty of the Church
as you have shown towards its confusion in your letters
of appeal falsely, as we believe, so called. But her
foundations are upon a rock, nor is any man able to
up-turn, though he may shake, them. Why do you
endeavour to confound me, and in me to confound
yourselves and me together? I have taken the whole
danger upon myself, I have borne so many reproaches,
so many injuries, and have suffered proscription in
behalf of all of you. It was expedient that one man
shall be afflicted for the Church, that so she might be
released from slavery. Consider the matter in single-
mindedness, examine it well, and weigh well the result,
that you may set aside the majesty of royalty and regard
to persons of whom God is no accepter, and that you
may be brought to understand the true nature of what
you have done and of what you are about to do. May
God remove the veil from your hearts that you may
perceive your duty. If there be anyone among you who
can say that since my promotion I have taken away
from him an ox or an ass, or his money; if I have
judged unjustly the cause of anyone, or to the injury
of anyone among you have procured advantage to
myself, let him now speak and I will restore four-
fold. But if I have offended no one, why do you leave
me to fight alone in the cause of God? You are fighting
against yourselves in that cause so vital to the interests
of the Church. Do not so, my brethren, do not, as far

as lies in your power, confound both yourselves and
God's Church, but turn to me and you will be safe.
For the Lord hath said 'I will not the death of the
unrighteous, but rather that he should be converted
and live.' Stand manfully with me in the battle, with
shield and sword, rise up to aid me. Gird yourselves
with the sword of God's word, which is all powerful,
that we may be the better able to strive in the discharge
of our duty against those who work iniquity and assail
that liberty which is the existence of the Church, without which she cannot flourish nor keep down those
who would possess as their inheritance the sanctuary
of the Lord.

"Let us make haste then lest the anger of God
descend upon us as upon negligent and slothful shep-
herds. Let us not be taken for dumb dogs, that cannot
bark; let it not be said of us by those who pass by,
'From the elders of Babylon iniquity hath gone forth.'
If in truth you listen to me, know that the Lord will
be with you, and with all of you, in all your ways to
give peace to his Church and to defend her liberties.
If you will not listen to me, let God judge between me
and you, and at your hands will be required the troubles
and confusion of his Church. For whether the world
will or no, she must stand firm in the word of the Lord,
whereon she is built, until the hour come when she
shall pass from this world to the Father. God will
judge why you have left me alone in the battle, with no
one of all those who were dear to me to go up with me
to the fight; insomuch that each of you may think or
say, Woe to him alone, for if he falls he has no one to
raise him up. But my hopes are laid up within my own

bosom, for he is not alone with whom the Lord is; when he falls he shall not be dashed to pieces, for the Lord sustains him in his hand.

"But let us come to the point, my brethren; has it escaped your memory how I and the Church were dealt with when I was still in England? what was done at the time of my departure, after my departure and in these latter days, and especially at Northampton, when Christ was judged in my person before the tribunal of the prince? when the archbishop of Canterbury was constrained by the injuries done indiscriminately to himself and the Church of God to appeal to the Roman see, and to place under the protection of God and the Roman Church all the possessions which belonged to him, or rather which belonged to the poor, for they are the patrimony of our crucified Saviour, not given for our use but entrusted to our stewardship? Although the Divine mercy has sometimes allowed the archbishop of Canterbury to be exiled unjustly, yet who ever heard of his being tried and condemned, compelled to give bail in the king's court, above all by his own suffragans? Where did they find this adverse authority, or rather perversity of the law and of the canons? Does not this act of enormity produce shame in all of you— shame leading to confusion—confusion to repentance and repentance to retribution, both before God and man? To these great injuries wrought against God and His Church, and against me fighting in God's cause, I was unable to submit with a safe conscience to remedy them without danger of my life, or to dissemble them without risk of my soul's salvation: wherefore I chose rather to turn aside for a while that I might dwell with greater benefit in the house of the Lord than in the tents of sinners, until their iniquity should be complete, the breasts of the wicked laid open, and the thoughts of their hearts be revealed. Thus the injuries that were done to me were the cause of my appeal. This was the occasion of my departure, which you say was so un-expected; and if you, who know what was intended against me, and how I was dealt with, would but speak the truth, you will admit that I was to keep my depar-ture secret, if I wished it not to be prevented altogether. But the Lord rules our misfortunes and turns them to good. He had regard to the honour of the king and his party, that nothing might be done against me which would redound to his dishonour, or to the dishonour of his family. And it turned out well for those who were eager for my death, and who thirsted for my blood, who aimed at the eminence of the see of Canterbury, and at my destruction, with an avidity which, I grieve to speak it, is said to have surpassed even their ambition. We have appealed against them, and whilst the possessions of the see of Canterbury, of myself and of my adherents, remain as they ought in safety, we have been engaged in prosecuting our appeal.

"If, as you say, things have been disturbed by my departure and in consequence of my departure, let him take the blame who gave occasion for this disturb-ance; the fault lies with him who does the deed, not with him that retreats from it; with him who inflicts, not with him who shuns an injury. The author of mischief is he who has given cause for it. What more can I say? We presented ourselves before the court and explained the injuries done to the Church and to ourselves, the cause of our coming, and the motive of our appeal: there was no one to answer us in anything; we waited, but no one brought anything against us: no judgment was reported against us until we came before the king. Whilst we were still waiting, as is usual, in the court, if by chance anything should be objected to us, our officials were forbidden to obey us in anything of a temporal nature, or to minister to us in any way against the command or without the knowledge of the king. It was you, they say, my brother of London, with Richard of Ilchester and the archbishop of York, who advised this sentence. After this they hurried to our lord the king, and the advice which they gave him will recoil on the head of the adviser. Without a trial, and for no reason, after we had already appealed, and whilst we were still remaining at the [papal] court, the Church was plundered and proscribed, clerks as well as laics, men and women, women with infants in the cradle. The goods of the Church, which are the patrimony of our crucified Saviour, were added to the exchequer; part of the money was converted to the king's use, part to your use and to the use of your church, my brother of London, if we have truly been informed. We now claim it, if you have had it, at your hands, enjoining you by virtue of your obedience that within forty days after the receipt of this letter whatever you have received from thence, or have converted to the use of your church, you restore the whole thereof within the period above-named without excuse and without delay. For it is unjust and contrary to all right that one church should be enriched out of the spoils of another. You must well know that of things taken from churches that man is ill qualified to exercise lawful authority who practises violence and injustice.

"Under what perverse code of laws or preposterous canons shall those who commit sacrilege and invade the goods of the church, shelter themselves, unless they restore what they have taken away? Shall they have recourse to an appeal? This would be introducing novelties, contrary to all justice, into the churches. Consider the consequences of your proceedings. Unless you take good heed they will be turned against yourselves and your churches. The Church of God would be hardly dealt with if a sacrilegious robber, invading its possessions and the possessions of his neighbours, should be able to protect himself by an appeal. It is in vain to implore the aid of justice when you have yourself neglected her and outraged her commands. Is it adding toil to toil, injuries to injuries, if we have been unable to bear such enormities as these and others which have been brought and still are wrought in the Church, because when aggrieved we appealed and left the court, because we ventured to complain of the injuries done to the Church and to ourselves, because we do not hold our peace on all these subjects, because we are preparing to correct them? Sore, indeed, is a man's distress when he is denied the consolation even of complaining. You, my friends, whose minds are more elevated and endowed with greater prudence than the rest, since the children of light, why do you deceive your brethren and those who are placed under you? Why do you lead them into error? What authority of Scripture has conferred on princes this prerogative in spiritual matters which you are seeking to confer on them? Do not, my brethren, confound the rights of the monarchy and the Church. Their powers are distinct, and one of them derives its authority from the other. Read the Scriptures and you will find how many kings have perished for usurping to themselves the sacerdotal office. Take heed to yourselves in your discretion lest the weight of the Divine arm fall on you for such a crime. If it so fall you will not easily escape.

"Consider, too, our lord the king; you are courting his favour at the expense of the Church: take care lest he perish (which God forbid!) with his whole house, as those have perished who have been detected in such iniquity. Unless he desist from his attempts with what conscience can we withhold punishment or dissemble his misdeeds? Let him do so who has the power to cast a veil over sin, not I, lest such dissimulation recoil upon my own soul.

"You hint in your letters, or rather you say openly, that I was raised to this dignity amid the clamours of the whole kingdom and the groans and the sorrow of the Church. Know you what saith the Truth? The mouth that knowingly speaks falsehood slayeth the soul. But the words of a priest ought ever to be accompanied by truth. Good God! would not one of the common people blush to say what you have said? Consult your own consciences, look at the form of election, the consent of all who were concerned therein, the consent of the king expressed through his son and through his emissaries, the consent of his son himself and of all the nobility of the kingdom. If anyone of them spoke against it, or opposed it in the least, let

him speak who knows, let him proclaim it who is conscious of it. But if any individual thereby had a downfall let him not say that his private molestation was an
injury done to the whole kingdom and to the Church.
Remember, moreover, the letters of the king and your
own letters how you all, with much urgency, demanded
the pall and obtained it for me. This is the truth of
the matter. But if anyone has felt envy, or been actu-
ated by ambition if so peaceful, so lawful, and so
unanimous an election hath grieved anyone's mind and
led him to practise machinations by which things have
become disturbed, may God induce him, as He would,
to confess his error, may he not be ashamed to acknowledge the disquietude of his mind in the face of all
men.

"You say that the king raised me to honour from
a mean estate. I am not indeed sprung from royal ancestors, but I would rather be the man to whom nobility
of mind gives the advantages of birth than one in whom
a noble ancestry degenerates. I was, perhaps, born
beneath a humble roof; but by God's mercy, that
knoweth how to deal graciously with his servants, and
chooses the humble to confound the brave, even in my
humble condition before I entered into God's service
my way of life was sufficiently easy, sufficiently honourable, as you yourselves know, even as that of the best
among my neighbours and acquaintances, whosoever
they might be. David also was taken from the goats
to become the ruler of God's people, and was exalted
by his courage and glory because he walked in the ways
of the Lord. Peter was taken from fishing to become
the head of the Church, and, by shedding his blood

for Christ, he was thought worthy to receive a crown in heaven, a name of honour upon earth. I pray that we also may do likewise; for we are the successors of S. Peter, not of Augustus. God knows with what eagerness the king himself wished my promotion. Let him consult his own intentions; they will best answer him; and we, too, will respond to the requirements of our duty, more faithfully by God's mercy, in our severity than is done by those who flatter him with falsehoods. For better are the stripes of a friend than the deceitful embraces of an enemy.

"You throw out against us an imputation of ingratitude. But there is no mortal sin which entails infamy on a man, unless it has proceeded from the intention. Thus, if one commit homicide unwillingly, though he is called a homicide, and is one, yet he does not incur the guilt of homicide. We apply the principle in this way: Though we owe obedience by the divine law to our lord the king, if we are bound to pay him respect by the royal prerogative, if we have checked him or warned him as a son with paternal love, if after warning we have grieved that he did not listen to us, and by the force of duty exercise towards him censure and severity, we believe that we are acting rather on his behalf and for his good, than in opposition to him; that we deserve praise at his hands rather than blame or the reproach of ingratitude. Certainly, benefits are often conferred on men against their will, and that man's safety is better regarded who is deterred from the perpetration of a crime by force even if he cannot in any other way. Besides, our Father and patron, Christ Himself, exonerates us from the stamp of ingratitude. By His Father's prerogative we are bound to obey Him, and if we neglect this we shall be justly punished by being disinherited. A father can disinherit his son for a just cause: for He says, 'If you do not tell the wicked of his iniquity, and he die in his sin, I will require his blood at your hand.' If, therefore, we do not convene him who sins, if we do not reprove him when he will not listen to us, and coerce him when he is pertinacious, we offend against the precept and are justly disinherited as guilty of disobedience. By his prerogative of being our patron we are held to revere and to obey Him, because we are his freed men, for whereas we were slaves of sin we are become freed unto righteousness through His grace. As therefore we are bound to no other, but saving our allegiance to Him, if aught be done vexatiously against Him to the injury of his Church, if we do not punish the crime by exerting in His cause that solicitude which is incumbent on us, He will deservedly withdraw from us the benefits which He has heaped upon us, and thus we indeed show ourselves ungrateful.

"You name to us the danger which will accrue to the Roman Church, the loss of her temporalities. This danger falls on us and on ours, but nothing is said of the danger to the soul. You hold over us a threat that our lord the king will withdraw (God forbid it!) from his allegiance and devotion to the Roman Church. God forbid, I say, that temporal gain or loss should ever cause our lord the king to fall back from his allegiance or devotion to the Church! This would be criminal and damnable even in a private man; how much more so in a prince who draws so many after him. God forbid that any of the faithful should ever entertain this thought, much less speak it, however humble he may be, not to say a bishop.

"Consider in your discretion, lest the words of your mouth should tempt anyone, or even several, to the risk and damnation of their souls, like the golden cup of Babylon, smeared within and without with poison, of which he that drinks fears not the poison when he sees the gold; thus a desire to do this deed may spread abroad, and yours will be the deed. For He who is not deceived, brings the secret deed to light, and unveils wicked machinations.

"The Church hath ever increased and multiplied under tribulation and blood-shedding. It is her peculiarity to conquer whilst she is injured, to possess understanding when she is refuted, to succeed when she is deserted. Do not mourn for her, my brethren, but for yourselves, who are earning for yourselves a name, but not a great one, by such words and deeds, in the mouths of men. You provoke against you the anger of God and of all mankind: you are preparing a halter for the innocent, and inventing new and ingenious arguments, to subvert the liberty of the Church. My brethren, by God's mercy, you are labouring in vain. The Church will stand, though often shaken, in that firmness and solidity wherein she was founded, until the general consummation of all things, when that son of perdition shall arise, who will not, we think, arise from the west, unless the order of things as spoken of in the Scripture shall be perversely changed.

"If, however, it be a question of temporal matters, we should rather fear the loss of souls than of temporalities.

Scripture says, 'What doth it profit a man to gain the whole world and lose his own soul?' We, therefore, utterly cast from us the danger to us and to ours: for he is not to be feared who kills the body, but He who kills both body and soul.

"You reprove us for suspending our venerable brother, the bishop of Salisbury, and excommunicating John, the schismatic ex-dean; for inflicting punishment, as you say, before hearing the cause, or following the usual course of canonical judgments. We answer that the sentence of both was just, the suspension of the one and the excommunication of the other. If you knew the whole course of the matter or rightly attended to the order of the judgments we think you would alter your opinion. Such is the extent of authority, as you ought to know, that in manifest and notorious crimes a hearing is not required. Consider diligently what was done by the bishop of Salisbury about the deanery after the prohibition, which our lord the Pope and ourselves made under pain of excommunication; you will then be able to judge whether the suspension did not ensue after an act of manifest disobedience. Wherefore the blessed Clement says, 'If all of every degree, whether princes of inferior or superior rank and all the rest of the people, do not obey their bishops, they shall not only be branded with infamy, but cast out from God's kingdom and the company of the faithful, and banished from the threshold of God's holy Church.'

"As regards John of Oxford, we reply that different persons become excommunicated in different ways; some by the law which denounces them as excommunicated, others marked by a sentence, and others again by communicating with those who are excommunicated. Now John of Oxford fell into a damnable heresy by communicating with schismatics and with those whom our lord the Pope had excommunicated, and so contracted in himself the taint of excommunication, which pollutes like a leprosy and involves the guilty and those who consent with them in the same punishment. And whereas John, thus excommunicate, usurped the deanery of Salisbury contrary to the commands both of our lord the Pope and of ourselves, expressed under pain of anathema, we have denounced him and excommunicated him, and hold him as utterly excommunicate.

"We have, moreover, annulled, and do hold as null, whatever has been done during his deanship, and connected with his deanship, as also our lord the Pope has already annulled it by authority of the eighth synod, of which this is the import: 'If anyone openly or secretly shall converse with one who is excommunicated, or join in communion with him, he at once contracts in himself the pain of excommunication.' The Council of Carthage also says: 'Whosoever communicates with one who is excommunicated, if he is a clerk, shall be deposed. Take care, therefore, in your discretion, that none of you communicate with him.' For Pope Calixtus says: 'Let no one receive any that have been excommunicated by their priests, before he has made full enquiry on both sides, nor communicate with them in prayer, or in meat or drink, or with a kiss, or with words of salutation.' For whosoever shall communicate knowingly with the excommunicated, in these and other particulars which are forbidden, shall, according to the institution of the Apostles, lie under similar excommunication. This is the canonical regulation, not repugnant, as we believe, to the canons, but supported by their authority....

"To the fear of censure from us you oppose an appeal, not of remedy but of impediment. We know that everyone who appeals does so in his own name or in the name of another. If in his own name, it is either against a censure already passed or one which he fears will be passed upon him. We are certain that no censure has been passed on you by us, thank God, which requires that you should have recourse to an appeal, nor do we believe that there is any cause between us at present which especially concerns you. If you have appealed from fear that censure will be passed upon you or your churches, consider whether your fears are such as ought to be entertained by men of courage and fortitude, whether it be an appeal which ought to suspend the authority and power which we have over you and your churches. It is thought by the well-informed, and we also think the same, that it is of no weight, both because it is destitute of form and because it is inconsistent with reason and utterly unsupported by all justice.

"If you have appealed in the name of another it must be in the name of the king or of some third party. If not of a third, it must be in the king's name. Wherefore you ought to have known in your discretion that appeals were introduced to repel injuries, not to inflict them, to relieve the oppressed, not to oppress them more. If then a man appeals, not from confidence in the justice of his cause but for the sake of creating delay and that sentence may not pass against him, his appeal should not be listened to.

"For what will be the condition of the Church, if, when her liberty is subverted, her possessions taken from her, her bishops expelled their sees, or not peacefully reinstated in full possession; the robbers who plunder her and invade her rights, shall appeal against their sentence and find safety in their appeal? What destruction will this be to the Church! Reflect on the consequences of your words and deeds. Are you not Christ's Vicars? Do you not supply His place on earth, to correct and punish malefactors, and cause them to cease from persecuting the Church of God? Is it not more than enough that they should assail the Church, without your standing forward in their behalf, to the destruction of the Church and of yourselves? Who ever heard anything so strange? It will be proclaimed and published in every people and nation, that the suffragans of the Church of Canterbury, who should live and die with their metropolitan in defence of the Church and her liberty, and submit to any sacrifice for the same, are desirous, at the king's command, as much as in them lies, to suspend his power and authority, that he may not exercise the severity of discipline on those who offend against his Church. One thing I know full well: you cannot sustain the part of both sides, both of the appellant and of him against whom you appeal. You are the appellants, and the appeal is against yourselves. Is not the Church one, and are not you part of its body? This is truly a Cadmaean conflict, that the members of the Church are waging against their head, which is Christ. I fear, my brethren, though God forbid that it should be so, lest they say of you, 'These are the priests, who have asked, where is the Lord? and holding the

law, have known me not?' Moreover, we believe that
in your discretion you cannot be ignorant, that appellants are only heard when it is their own interest at
stake, or they are deputed to maintain the cause of
another. Is it to your interest that those who offend
against the Church should not be restrained? Surely
not, but rather the contrary. But if the man who sub-
verts the liberty of the Church, invades and seizes her
goods and converts them to his own use, is not heard in
his own defence when he appeals, surely those cannot
be heard who appeal on his behalf. Neither our lord
the king can derive support, nor you advantage from
the appeal which you have made in his favour. If he
can neither appeal, nor instruct another to do this in
this cause, neither can you receive from him instructions to appeal for him. We add further, that you can
in no way take up the matter for him in this cause. For
no bishop can maintain the part of another against himself, particularly to the injury of the Church, of which
he is the defender, and above all when the Church in
general is assailed. If, therefore, the appeal concerns
you not, and you cannot undertake it by commission,
nor defend the cause of another, your appeal cannot be
heard, nor is it good in law.

"Is this your devotion, is this the consolation and
fraternal charity which you show to your metropolitan,
who is suffering exile in your cause? God forgive you
for such a want of tenderness! Are you ignorant, my
brethren, what a great gulf is established to the destruction of the laws and canons between us, so that none of
you can pass over to us without risking loss of life or
mutilation of limb, though any one of us may, if he

pleases, cross over to you? We wonder, therefore, what order you preserve, when there is no order observed towards us as regards churches or ecclesiastical persons, but wrongs and a state of terror, such as, I pray, may not last for ever. Both ourselves and our adherents are plundered. Some of them have been redeemed, as well clerks as laics, that had been taken since our appeal made at Northampton, and your appeal against ourselves. Moreover, since that appeal, as you term it, a general edict has been issued, that all of us who are found on English ground shall be taken prisoners; that none of you or of our other friends shall dare to receive our letters or our messengers. This then is the respect shown to an appeal, during the continuance of which, if it be a just appeal, no fresh step should be taken. Look ye to this. How can you expect us to receive your letters and messengers, or to listen to what they say? But by this we do not mean, however we and ours may be dealt with, that we have ever done anything irregularly towards the person or the kingdom of our lord the king, or your persons and churches, or by God's mercy will we ever do so.

"We had fancied, if you understood me rightly, that you would have shown your zeal for the Church, by blaming us for our too-long endurance, rather than by praising us for this delay of severity. For delay is dangerous: and too much patience is censurable rather than praiseworthy, having more of vice than virtue. Hence it is that we tell you in few words and affirm it unhesitatingly: our lord the king will have no reason to complain if, after being frequently and duly warned by our lord the Pope and us, both by letter and by messengers, his refusal to make amends should draw down upon him severe censures. He is not wronged whom justice duly punishes; and to sum up all in few words, let it be clearly understood by you, that those who invade and plunder the possessions of the Church are protected by no plea of justice, nor can appeal in any way avail them. If, moreover, my brethren, you desire to be of use to the king, as is right of you, and as we also wish, God who is the searcher of hearts well knoweth, take heed to assist him in such a way as not to offend God, nor the Church, nor your own order; to the end also that he may escape speedily and providentially from the danger to his own soul which is awaiting him. Thus much have I urged, if perchance by the divine grace he may be advised by you to make amends to the Church: she will rejoice at the return of her son, for she has always been and still is ready to receive him with devotion and gratitude, and we, too, shall rejoice.

"But you say that he is willing and ready to make amends to the Church by your judgment, if any contention has arisen between him and us concerning the liberties of the Church, of which there can be no doubt, for it is well known to all the world. This proposition of yours is unreasonable and contrary to justice: how then can we do wrong by not entertaining it? Is that a sufficient reason why we should not feel the Divine wrath for turning a deaf ear to canonical censure, and for adding injury to injury? It is certain that you cannot act as judge between him and us. In the first place, you are his opponents, or you ought to be, in defence of the liberty of the Church, which is committed to your care: look to it if you neglect this duty, for hesitation will bring you into danger. In the next place, we nowhere read of superiors being judged by their inferiors, metropolitans by their suffragans. Thirdly, there are some among you whom the Church and we regard with suspicion; I hope not all of you: the reasons for which are different, but for the present we forbear to mention them.

"I pray, then, that our lord the king may listen to the petition of his faithful servant; and not despise the counsels of his bishops, the admonitions of his father: so may God bless him, and prolong his days and the life of his sons for many years to come. May he permit his own Church to enjoy peace and liberty under him as under a most Christian king, whilst the Roman Church is suffered to exercise in his dominions the same jurisdiction and liberty which she has a right to, and which she possesses in other countries. Let him restore to us and to the Church of Canterbury the rights, liberties, and possessions which have been taken from us, in full security, that so we may serve God in peace and tranquillity, and he may employ our services as shall seem good to him, saving the honour of God, and of the Roman Church, and of our own order. Such are the royal dignities and good laws, which a Christian king ought to demand and to observe: in these he should take delight, and the Church flourish under him. Such laws as these are in accordance, not in opposition to the law of God, and he who observes them not, becomes an enemy to God; for the law of God is pure, converting the soul. For the Lord says of his own laws, 'Keep my laws,' and the prophet says, 'Woe to those who establish unjust laws, and writing, write iniquity, that they may oppress the poor in judgment, and do violence to the cause of the humble ones of God's people.'

"Let not our lord, then, be ashamed to return to a better state of feeling, to humble himself in humility and contrition of heart before the Lord, to make satisfaction to Him and to His Church for the injuries he has done it. For the Lord does not despise the humble and contrite heart, but embraces it in sincerity. Thus also holy David, after he had offended, humbled himself before the Lord, and asked for mercy, and obtained forgiveness. Thus also the king of Nineveh and all his city, when threatened with destruction, humbled themselves before the Lord in sackcloth and ashes, and by contrition of heart obtained a remission of their sentence.

"We write thus to you, my brethren, not that you may be put to confusion, but that when you have read our letter and comprehended its import you may the more boldly and freely do what duty bids you. May you henceforth so act that we may the sooner have peace and the Church more ample liberty. Pray for us that our faith may not fail in tribulation, but that we say with the apostle, 'Neither death, nor life, nor angels, nor any other creature shall separate us from the love of God.'

"Farewell, all of you in the Lord; may the whole English Church remember us daily in their prayers."

So ends the great letter which sums up, a veritable pamphlet, all that the archbishop could say on behalf of the position which he had conscientiously reached. It was a manifesto of the party, small indeed among the higher clergy and nobles, opposed to the measures of

Henry II, behind which they seemed to see the grim figure of a lay power suppressing all personal and class liberty. It can only have been as viewed in this light that such an appeal won the sympathy of the people of England. And win that it certainly did; for that Becket's popularity among the poor was not only that won by a demagogue or a thaumaturge is evidenced by the fact that the cause for which he had contended won, to all outward appearance, a triumphant victory after his death.

It was a magnificent manifesto, but it was very far from being unanswerable. And Gilbert Foliot, bitter always and now goaded to fury, answered it in his sharpest vein of anger and reproach. His method of reply was to recall the whole of Becket's career. Charge after charge was levelled against him. He had bought the chancellorship. He had greedily sought the primacy, and he had been forced on the monks and the bishops by the threats of the king, forced by the sword of the lay power, that sword which he had himself plunged into the bosom of the Church when he had made her pay the huge *donum* for the war of Toulouse. At Clarendon it was he who was the deserter, he who deserted his brethren, ready to perjure himself for the peace: he who having given promise to the Constitution wherein he was forbidden to leave the realm yet fled: he who disobeyed the king's citation to do justice: he who refused to give account of the money he owed. "You say it is an unheard-of thing that an archbishop of Canterbury should answer to such things in the king's court; and you may say that no one ever before heard of an officer of the king's court having so suddenly mounted to so high a dignity—that he should one day be following his hounds and hawks, and the next be bending at the altar and ministering in sacred things before all the bishops of the realm."

If by deceit the kind-hearted Pope was led to take his side, no arguments of his would convince those whom he had urged to suffer martyrdom when his own example was one of flight. The king only cared for the Constitutions because they were his ancestors', and because he would be shamed if he gave them up in answer to violence. Concession should come from him who was the Church's representative: then peace could be made with the religious and beloved king.

It was a bold answer. Yet perhaps the bishops did protest too much: "our religious and gracious king" had hardly yet won its place into conventional usage in spite of a monarch's known characteristics.

And it is only fair to observe that John of Salisbury when he read the letter did not hesitate to say that the bishop of London was a liar. He had been present himself at the election, he said, and he remembered that while Foliot was the only bishop who did not express pleasure at the nomination of Thomas he was one of the first to give his vote for him.

Neither letter, to say the least, made for peace. And Becket would relax none of his claims to obedience. To Geoffrey Ridel, his archdeacon, he wrote in imperious terms commanding his attendance: did he remember how long he had been away from his own archbishop Theobald? To the bishop of London he wrote repeating his orders.[1]

---

[1] *Materials*, vi, 35.

"We remember having ordered you to hold as excommunicate throughout your diocese, and to signify the same to your brethren, certain persons whom for their injuries towards the Holy See and the Church of Canterbury we formerly excommunicated. If you have faithfully discharged this order to the honour and advantage of the Church and your own salvation, we congratulate you for your fraternal obedience. But if not, we mourn for you, not on our account, but for the wrong done to the Pope and the Holy See. And may God avert from you the consequences of disobedience. For though the anger of the sovereign pontiff may be delayed, and his hand seem slow, yet the wound with which he punishes demerit never can be healed: and no one under the sun can save a man out of his hand. No one but an infidel, or what is worse, a heretic or schismatic, can refuse to obey his mandates. But we are addressing one who knows the law, as well as we, who has been nurtured in virtue, in religion, in obedience, and who needs no teaching. A man may cheat his own soul, but cannot cheat the word of God, which says, 'Woe to them who justify the wicked, and call good evil, and darkness light.' At present he is pronouncing that woe! but will soon inflict it bitterly. He punishes the powerful, and exercises the severest judgments on those who neglect the duties of their rank, and refuse to warn the wicked of their wickedness. Hereafter he will crown in triumph those who faithfully obey, and meanwhile consoles those who strive against injustice.

"We beg of you, therefore, and beseech you in the Lord Jesus, that whereas crimes have for our sins multiplied in the world, you do rise up to support the Church, and put forth the sword of the word, which is committed to us, to punish the evil and protect the good, that you may not be found to bear that sword in vain. If you shall see any remiss in doing right, animate and encourage them, and take to yourself what Christ, Who is now again crucified by the wicked, said in the moment of his passion, 'And thou, when thou art converted, strengthen thy brethren.' You will have us to aid you in liberating the Church, and in nothing that concerns God's honour will we fail to give you our support, as far as his mercy shall give us strength. But our lord the Pope will give you the aid that is required; and he has already committed to us to be his representative in England, as you may perceive from the letters which we here forward to you.

"We, therefore, command you, my brother, and in virtue of your obedience, and in peril of your orders, we enjoin you, on the authority of the Pope, to communicate these our letters to the fellow bishops of your province, and to the bishop of Durham, as speedily as possible, and afterwards to have them restored to us.

"Moreover, by the same authority, and under the same perils, we command you to show due respect to the bearers, who are the accredited agents of our lord the Pope, and provide for their full security, as you wish regard to be shown to your own dignity."

But for the present Foliot could safely afford to disregard the primate's injunctions. By his appeal he had prevented the issue of sentence against him till Ascension Day, 1167. And Henry was determined to have vengeance. He now reinforced his threats by a message to the general chapter of the Cistercians held at Citeaux in September, 1166; and the supreme abbat himself went to Pontigny to warn Becket of the consequences of his remaining there still.

In November the archbishop left Pontigny. If he could not tarry in Burgundy, Louis VII was eager to welcome him into his own land of France. The king rode along the valley and came to the Cistercian house, where he courteously thanked the monks for their kindness to the exile and declared that he would now take charge of him himself; so says Guernes of Pont Ste Maxence, who would very well know the story of his king's kindness.[1] A letter of John of Poitiers suggests that the king was thinking to provide for the archbishop by the revenues of some vacant see: perhaps the idea of a translation had already seemed possible.

As Thomas rode towards Sens he went sadly: Herbert, his companion so often, tells that generally he would talk much and brightly as he rode. The abbat of Pontigny, who rode beside him, asked him the reason of his sadness. It was, he said at length, reluctantly, a vision he had seen. He had seen himself in a church, pleading before the Pope, and opposed by cardinals in king Henry's interest; then came four knights, who dragged him forth and slew him by cutting off the crown of his head where he was tonsured. It was not one of the dreams which fulfil themselves, but rather one which might well come to a man who often brooded on his fall. The abbat took it lightly. How should this come to one who eats and drinks?

[1] But Herbert of Bosham, who is perhaps here a better witness, says (*Materials*, iii, 402–3) that he had been sent by Becket to Louis, that he met the king on the way and was charged by him to invite the archbishop to his territory.

(*Non bene conveniunt nec in una sede morantur:* the cup of wine which you drink and the cup of martyrdom.)

The archbishop bore the monastic rebuke meekly, for he answered that though he indulged in such pleasures of the body, yet "He Who justifieth the ungodly hath been gracious to me and revealed this mystery."

At Sens, a city delightful for its situation, generous in its inhabitants, which fascinated Herbert of Bosham as it fascinates English travellers to-day, everyone was polite and gracious; it was a town of good feeling and good company. And so the archbishop was made welcome. The archbishop Hugh was his old friend, and his successor (1168) William of Champagne, whose sister had married Louis VII, was as warm a supporter. Becket withdrew to the abbey of S. Colombe, on a bank of the Yonne to the south of the city. There he settled down again to the quiet regularity of monastic life.

Henry's letters continued to reach the Pope and the cardinals. And thus they read:—The alliance with the Emperor was not schismatic in intent: Becket had banished himself: the king will not suffer the dignities and usages of the realm to be diminished; whosoever shall attempt to diminish them shall be held a public and avowed enemy. A turn of fortune was indeed placing Henry in the ascendant. In dread of the Emperor's army, which was making way in Italy, supported, as men said, by the rich English king's money; influenced by the marquis of Montferrat, whom Henry was bribing by a marriage treaty; startled by the extremity of violence in which Becket seemed to indulge; and anxious, like so many of his predecessors (and successors) to deal with his difficulties with the help of "my lady

Mora," Alexander listened to the soothing words of Henry's envoy, John of Oxford, *jurator*, heard him swear that he had done nothing wrong at Würzburg, absolved him, confirmed him in his deanery, and finally suspended the effect of all the archbishop's acts and, after answering the appeal of the Clerus Angliae on December 1st, wrote to Henry on December 20th, announcing that he had appointed as a legatine commission Cardinals William of Pavia (whom Becket knew of old as hostile to him) and Otto of Ostia, with powers to judge and to absolve. To Becket[1] he explained his action with some timidity. "Si non omnia secundum beneplacitum succedant ad praesens dissimula!" was his advice.

So ended the year 1166, and Becket seemed at the lowest point of fortune.

---

[1] *Materials*, vi, 123.

CHAPTER X

ATTEMPTS AT RECONCILIATION

B ECKET might well feel alarm. The legates left
Rome on January 1st. "One of them," he declared,
"is weak and fickle"—that was Otto: "the other treacherous and crafty: both are avaricious and unjust." John
of Salisbury, more mildly, said that while William had
the good opinion of the king, not the fear of God and
the Church, before his eyes, the other was of good
repute, "but still a Roman and a cardinal." John of
Oxford had bribed the papal officials and procured
copies of all the archbishop's letters; he came home,
says John of Salisbury, with apocalyptic vehemence,
"exalting himself above all that is called God or is to
be worshipped." Henry had "Pope and cardinals in
his purse." Becket could hardly believe the news:
"if it be true," he said, "the Pope has strangled the
Church."[1]

There were still attempts at mediation, apart from
the legation: they might at least gain time for a settlement to be matured; so the old Empress Matilda (who
had only a few more months of life) and Rotrou, archbishop of Rouen, were instructed by the Pope to inter-
vene. Henry, says Rotrou, bore the intervention very
restively. "It is well known how evilly he has wrought

[1] "Quae si vera sunt, tunc procul dubio suffocavit et strangu-
lavit dominus papa non modo personam nostram sed et se et
omnes ecclesiasticas personas utriusque regni, immo etiam utram-
que ecclesiam, tam Gallicanam quam Anglicanam."—*Materials*,
vi, 153.

against me and my kingdom; how proud and rebellious, and seditious against me he has been." So he spoke of Becket. It was not very hopeful. Remonstrances began to flow in to the unhappy Pope. Henry, count of Troyes, and Matthew, praecentor of Sens (Senonensis ecclesiae minimus), told him some home truths, and dissected the character of John of Oxford for his benefit. And Becket himself wrote thus—[1]

"We hereby send to your holiness the bearer of this letter, who for his station in life is very intimate with us, and, for his great talent, a man of fidelity and capacity. We pray your mercy to hear him in our behalf, for our miserable condition is become wearisome, perhaps even loathsome to our friends, and, as some tell us they imagine by your silence, a subject for contempt with your holiness. Even our enemies, cannot but look upon us with compassion. Rise, my lord, I pray you, and make no longer tarrying: let the light of your countenance shine upon us: save us and our wretched companions in exile, for we are perishing. Let us not be put to shame among men: our adversaries insult us and Christ's Church; let us not be brought to contempt among the people, when we have invoked you by name, holy father, to watch over us, but, by the name of the Lord Jesus, earn for yourself a name for ever, and restore your endangered reputation; depressed as it is in France by the return of that excommunicated and false schismatic John of Oxford, and the vaunts which he has promulgated. God knows that I am speaking the truth: if you do not believe me, ask those in France, who are most zealous of your honour, and most desirous

[1] *Materials*, vi, p. 154, Dr Giles's translation.

to promote the advantage of the Church. Your reputation, I say, is at stake; your reputation which has hitherto passed without spot or blemish among mankind, and been preserved harmless through all dangers, when everything else has been polluted. Let your authority resume its force, and go forth, my father, so that that prate-apace may be confounded, and may acknowledge that he has spread what is false, promulgating lies. Let him feel your severity, for he has cut off all hope of forgiveness; let him feel your vengeance, for he has disabused your kindness: let the world be told that he has found Christ's vicar founded on a rock not easy to be moved, that he is not a reed as the malignants whisper, but the upholder of equity and justice; not an acceptor of persons, not a favourer of either party in his judgment, but a dispenser of justice equally to the king and to the peasant. God bless your holiness, that it may be well with us and our wretched companions in exile."

He wrote also to "all the cardinals of the Roman Church" in words of no mild expostulation, "not in anger but in warning."[1] As effective, it may be, was a letter from Master Lombard of Piacenza, afterwards archbishop of Benevento and cardinal. It was certain, he said, that the king had only demanded legates out of subtilty; he was determined never to give up his "dignities"; he was in great fear of excommunication or interdict: his great hope was that the Pope would die. Canonists like Lombard had great influence. More impressive still were two letters from Louis VII, who told him that many were scandalised at his action. Louis,

[1] *Materials*, vi, 156 *sqq.*

who was on the point of one of his small wars with the House of Anjou, was still to be reckoned with, whether as friend or foe.

So Thomas, "by the grace of God archbishop of Canterbury, and legate of the apostolic see," kept up his courage, and again addressed himself to "Gilbert, bishop of London—would that he were brother—that he may depart from evil and obey God rather than man." And thus he wrote—[1]

"Though your aim, which has been all along to effect the downfall of the Church and of ourself, thereby excludes you from the communion of the faithful, and from the way of salvation; yet in regard to your salvation, which, as God knows, we earnestly wish for, and considering that though Christ came to call not the righteous, but sinners to repentance, yet He rejects a feigned repentance, and judges of its sincerity by our deeds; considering also that the tree is known by its fruits, we, therefore, for your disobedience and contumacy, to say nothing of the rest of your conduct, can no longer pass you over with impunity, though in charity we shall rejoice if even now you will repent and produce fruits worthy of repentance: we shall then no longer bear in mind the things which you have done to your prejudice, if your repentance is sincere, and your actions in uniformity therewith. We invite you to this with fatherly solicitude, we exhort you to look thoughtfully unto your ways, to deeds worthy of a bishop, that we may not be obliged, in administering punishment, to have recourse to severe measures. We command you, therefore, in virtue of your obedience, in peril of your

[1] *Materials*, vi, 181, Dr Giles's translation with alterations.

rank and order, to send back to us our lord the Pope's letters concerning our legateship, which we sent to you that you might show them to our brother bishops.

"If you have so shown them, it is well; but if not, know for a certainty that you will have to answer for having suppressed them. May God's mercy inspire into you a penitent heart. If you are wise in time, and hasten to make atonement, God will spare you, and speedily convert you."

Such letters had no effect. Foliot remained determined in resistance. He waited, indeed, as was natural, to see what would happen when the legates arrived. Meanwhile John of Salisbury, ever as indefatigable in friendship as candid in criticism, was writing letter after letter to the notables of Europe, to counts and bishops, and to those in England who could reach the ears of the bishops.

This letter to Reginald, archdeacon of Salisbury, the bishop of Salisbury's son, is characteristic—[1]

"He must be an inhuman and impious man, who is not grieved at the affliction of his father, particularly when so many and great marks of fatherly kindness have been shown, as clear as daylight, towards the son. The Lord condemned the Canaanites to perpetual slavery, because their father, Ham, from whom they derived their name and race, behaved inhumanly towards his parent; for an impious deed entails a taint upon the descendants of the doer. Thus, the hateful yoke of slavery was a warning to all men against such impiety.

"I should consider myself as worse than any of the

[1] *Materials*, vi, 187.

Canaanites, if I did not sympathise with my suffering parent, and feel in my soul the stripes which he receives, even more severely than the sore of my own wounds. My conscience is the best witness of this fact, and God Who searches the heart, and Who, sooner than was believed, will bring to light the hidden things of darkness, and make manifest the counsels of the heart. We are now standing before His tribunal, and await His sentence in our cause, so that it is foolish and rash to lose by deviating from the truth the reward of all our labour, of all our life, if indeed our sufferings have been to our salvation, and our actions conformable to the rule of right. I have laboured with my lord of Canterbury, as he well knows, using language at one time palliative, at another time of rebuke; but all my labour, I grieve to say, has been vain. It would be tedious, and indeed unnecessary, to state the objections which he makes to our arguments and entreaties, for master Gilbert, of whose fidelity to you I have no doubt, will hear all most fully from his own mouth. I call God to witness, and will answer for it with my life, that the archbishop sincerely loves the bishop, and desires that he should stand safe and unharmed. But he insists, that as he has given an example of disobedience to others, he shall now in his own person give an example of salutary and indispensable obedience. If the bishop will do this, for which he has the authority of Scripture, the advice of his friends, and the commands of the Pope, he will find the archbishop, whom he, perhaps, fears unnecessarily, an affectionate father, and more prone to forgive than to punish. For you may well remember the rescript which the bishop of Coutances lately received from the holy see, and of which information was sent, or ought to have been sent, to you. You know also what consolation your own dean brought back from thence. If you do not know, I wish everything which he did at Rome, in other causes as well as this, had been made known, not only to you, but to all the world. Moreover, if it were lawful to punish such things, we could easily state what has been done in the matter of the constitutions, about which the quarrel began between the king and the priesthood, the reconciliation of the archbishop, the liberties of the Church, and the restoration of the exiles. I could also tell of the oath which has been taken, and the articles of agreement between the parties. At present we have orders not to speak of these things, as long as there is hope that the parties will be as good as their word. But there is nothing hidden which shall not be made known, and that soon too by God's good pleasure. For the hour is at hand, when those who are detected in perjury shall be destroyed; the time of visitation and of vengeance is approaching. Meanwhile, if my advice is asked, I answer before God, whom I invoke to witness the truth of my words as on the last day, I answer freely and fully, and with that faith which is due to my father: first, that we should study to follow the precepts of the divine law, but if that is silent, let us turn to the canons and precedents of the saints of old, and if there we find nothing to the point, we must explore the writings and receive the counsel of those who are wise in the fear of the Lord, and especially of those, whether few or many, who prefer God's honour to everything besides. For no one can walk safely, if he neglects the law of God, that unerring rule, which all should follow."

He added a letter to the bishop and father, in a further attempt to pacify enmities. Everyone, it seemed, except irreconcilables like Becket and Foliot, was eager for peace. It remained to see what the legation would do to bring it.

Thomas held on his way unmoved. He called upon his "venerable brother and dearest friend," Roger, bishop of Worcester, whom he had summoned to his side, repeating the order in virtue of obedience; for himself he waited for the coming of the legates.

Early in the spring of 1167 Otto wrote from S. Gilles, in Provence, prattling about his journey and the towns he had seen on the way, and asking for an envoy to explain the archbishop's views; the reply alluded to a hope (attributed politely to the Gallican Church) that he would come by clean and open ways. Events in Italy were not favourable, however, to the archbishop's hopes. Alexander was in great straits. The Emperor's army was advancing, and in the spring he had to fly from Rome. Meanwhile the legates entered France with a bold face. William of Pavia wrote to Becket that he would be no respecter of persons. This then was written—[1]

"We have lately received your highness's letter, wherein we are made to drink wormwood, ill concealed by the honey of its beginning, or the oil of its conclusion. You tell me that you have come down to these parts to decide the questions which lie between our lord the king and us, as shall seem to you most expedient. We do

---

[1] *Materials*, vi, 208

not believe that you are come for this, nor do we admit your intervention, for many reasons, which at a fitting time and place we will state. If, however, any good or chance of peace shall be brought about by your means, I thank God and you for it. May it be well with your eminence, so it may be better with us."

The letter may well be read to show the temper of one of the chief combatants. Happily, milder counsels prevailed and the following letter was substituted for it—[1]

"'Thanks to your excellency's kindness for the letter with which you have at last deigned to visit our insignificance. That insignificance derives its character in the minds of many from our present condition, not from the past; and may be changed, if God pleases, into a much more bright and prosperous future. You say that whereas many think you have been engaged in various ways to our disadvantage, this has proceeded from your wish not to incur the suspicion of the king, or to cause him to become less zealous towards the Church and less disposed to make peace with us. God knows whether this is true, and the event will show. But whereas you say that you are come down into these parts to judge between us, as may seem to you best for the Church; this certainly is not impossible. We believe, however, that we know well what you are come for, and what we have to suspect at your hands. We wish to exhort your discretion in the Lord, to conduct yourself in this business to the honour of God, the re-establishment of the Church, and your own credit among the people. If any good or chance of peace shall result by your

[1] *Materials*, vi, 209.

means, we thank God and you for it. We earnestly hope that you will consider what burdens the English Church and we have endured and are still enduring, and how the same suffering extends from us to the Church at large. The eyes of all men are directed to this matter, and they are waiting to see the end, in what way the pride of kings will plume itself in triumph, or bear up under defeat. We pray God that it may suffer defeat, and not gain a victory by your intervention. Fare— may it be well—with you, and may it for ever be well with you, that it may be better with us also and the Church."

Even this letter was not approved by John of Salisbury: "nec prior nec posterior mihi placet conceptio litterarum quas ad dominum Willelmum mittere decrevistis, qua nimis plenae videntur suspicionibus et supra modum dentosis salibus abundare." It seems probable that neither of them was sent. John of Salisbury himself wrote in a conciliatory way to William of Pavia, and Becket contented himself with some very sharp words to the Pope. It does not seem that he knew that on June 17th Alexander had been guilty of what he would regard as unparalleled treachery. He had granted to Roger of York authority, at the request of "our dearest son Henry, the illustrious king of the English," to crown the king's son, an open affront to the immemorial privileges of the see of Canterbury.

But events had moved rapidly. On August 1st Frederick I had been crowned, and the anti-pope, Paschal III, had been enthroned in S. Peter's. Within the month the plague had broken out among the German troops, Reginald of Köln was dead, and several chiefs of the army, and the troops were in flight. Some of this was known to Becket when he wrote as follows—[1]

"To his much loved lord and most holy father, Alexander, by the grace of God supreme pontiff, Thomas, the humble minister of the Church of Canterbury, a wretched and miserable exile, health and an ever constant mind against the fierceness of princes.

"In our solicitude for your health and well-being, we hoped that we had certain intelligence about you and your brethren, and the marvellous doings of the Lord toward yourself and his Church. For the news reached our ears, and spread through all Gaul, of the humiliation with which God has lately visited the schismatical Frederick, in sight of his people and nation. But since reports are both right and wrong, we earnestly entreat your fatherly goodness to communicate to us by letters and messengers the glad tidings, as soon as possible, if God has done towards you as He generally does towards those who trust in Him, and do not place their reliance on a frail arm of flesh, or in the deceitful aid of princes. If the event is really as it is reported, blessed be God, who knows how to deal mercifully with his servants. How great is his power, how boundless his mercies! Unless He keep the city, he that guards it watches in vain. If we only view rightly what has happened, God has never wrought a more signal act of mercy since time began. He has justified his justice, by crushing the contrivers of this wickedness, the authors of this persecution: He has consumed them by a most signal destruction. I pray also that He may have consigned that prince himself whilst still living to per-

---

[1] *Materials*, vi, 227 (in part paraphrased).

petual infamy before all the people, so that he may be a derision to every passer-by, and that everyone's finger may point at him, whilst they say, 'Look, there is he who did not make the Lord his helper! He trusted in his own power, and has fallen in his vanity. Better would it have been, if he had died gloriously fighting against his foes, than to have lived, and so become the laughing-stock of all men.' Who then that is Christ's vicegerent on earth, will dare to be servile towards princes, and to spare those who sin to the confusion of the Church? Let him who dares do this, not I, lest the sin of the offender be transferred to my own shoulders, lest I become guilty of dissembling guilt, though I have done nothing guilty. But on this subject I have said enough to my lord. Whosoever wisely examines the works of God will speedily discover what is next to be done.

"In the second place, we wish to inform your holiness that our fears have been realised respecting the presumption and arrogance of my lord William of Pavia, as you may see by his letters, which he addressed to us on his first arrival. From the tenour of your holiness's letters to the king of the Franks and to us, we had hoped to receive consolation and peace, and not confusion, from his mediation between the king of England and us. For he is not the man to whose arbitration we ought to bow in this matter: particularly when it was the urgency of the king of England which induced you to send him, rather than your own bidding. We hold it inconsistent with justice to abide the judgment of any man who seeks to make a profit out of our blood, and hopes to obtain reputation and glory from the price of iniquity. We therefore affectionately entreat your fatherly goodness, if you have any regard for us, that the power of this man, if he has any over us and ours, may, by your interference, be revoked. Let this hammer be removed who chooseth rather to be the hammerer of clerks,[1] in compliance with the will of princes, rather than of princes, in accordance with the will of God. On all these points, and others which the bearer will inform you of, we pray you in compassion for our exile to hear us. Have mercy upon our protracted miseries, for all mankind are now looking to see them ended. Let your authority resume its force, and the sword of S. Peter be unsheathed, to avenge the injuries of Christ and of His Church. Let those who have for a while dissembled, and despised the avenging hands of S. Peter, feel at last their weight, that so the Church's liberties may have time to breathe, after their long depression, and that the world may rejoice and glorify God for his mercies towards you, that so the bark of S. Peter, which all thought was sunk, may, by your means, ride triumphant, and the presumption of kings be beaten down, which all thought had been successful. I should have had much to say to your holiness on this subject, but to avoid prolixity, I here make an end, hoping to hear from you what my soul longeth after. One thing, however, I will add, which must not be passed over in silence. My lord William, and his friend the king, thought, perhaps, by protracting the time, to have eluded your authority by some casualty or other. But

---

[1] "Transferatur malleus iste a nobis qui potius elegit esse malleator clericorum, etc." It is amusing to find in this cardinal the forerunner of the English "malleus monachorum."

God will, I hope, cause all casualties to turn out for good, and so he who thought to delude you, will himself be deluded, and, by God's mercy, fall into the snare which he laid for you. May your holiness fare well, and be preserved for long years, that it may be well with all of us."

Matters were by now looking better for Becket. Two letters of Alexander, who had now good hopes of recovering his position, made it clear to the legates that they had no complete power to settle the question.[1] Frederick in September retreated to Pavia, where he remained till March, 1168. Still the whole business dragged on week by week and it was not till November 18th, 1167, the octave of S. Martin, that the archbishop met the legates on the frontier, at the edge of the Norman plain, between Gisors and Trie, by the famous tree of conference whose cutting down forms an important incident in the chronicles of Henry II's day.

Becket himself went, warned, it was said, by visions. Herbert tells that he had seen poison offered to him in a cup of gold; Guernes, that from the cup there crept out two spiders, which he explained after the manner of Joseph, the cup as the king's proposals, the wine that was stirred as the deceitfulness of Henry, and the two large spiders as the two cardinals.

The conference failed on the simple ground that the archbishop demanded as a preliminary the restoration of the property of his see. He wrote his own account of what was said to the Pope.[2] Perhaps John of Salis-

---

[1] *Materials*, vi, 200 and 232: the former written on May 7th, the latter on August 22nd.
[2] *Materials*, vi, 245.

bury's, written in all probability to John, bishop of Poitiers, gives a less prejudiced view.[1]

"I do not doubt that you are anxious about the state of the Church and the issue of the legatine commission. I therefore write to inform you thereof briefly, and to give you and other pious friends as much consolation as is in my power. You must know, then, that our lord of Canterbury and certain of his fellow exiles had a speech with the cardinals on the octave of the blessed Martin, between Gisors and Trie. The legates said much about the kindness of the lord Pope, and the solicitude with which he regards us, about their own labours, and the dangers of their journey; about the king's greatness and the exigencies of the Church; about the badness of the times, about the favours the king had formerly bestowed on his lordship of Canterbury, and the honour he had always rendered him; something too they added, about the injuries the king complained of receiving from his lordship, intimating among other things that he had instigated the king of the Franks to war. Finally, they wished to devise some means for allaying the existing indignation, which they said could not be effected but with much humility, moderation, and deference.

"His lordship of Canterbury, in all humility and sweetness, expressed his sense of their kindness, and that of his holiness the Pope; and proceeded to show the futility of the king's complaints, and the extent of the Church's sufferings. As to the humility and defer-

---

[1] *Materials*, vi, 256. R. H. Froude took it to be by Jocelin of Exeter. It is found in seven sources and is headed "Amicus amico. Verba domini Cantuariensis cum legatis inter Gisortium et Triam."

ence which they recommended, he was most anxious to exhibit it in every possible way, saving only the honour of God, and the liberty of the Church, and the dignity of his own person and the possessions of the Church. If this seemed too little, or too much, or in any way different from their view, he was ready to make any compliance consistent with his oaths, and saving his order.

"They answered, that they were not sent to advise, but to consult him, and, if possible, to contrive some terms of reconciliation; and proceeded to enquire whether, in the presence of the legates, he would pledge himself to observe the usages which had been observed towards former kings by his predecessors; and thus to return to the king's favour, and to the duties of his see, and to procure peace for himself and his.

"The archbishop replied, that no king had ever exacted such a pledge from any of his predecessors, nor would he, by God's grace, pledge himself to observe usages manifestly opposed to the law of God and the rights of the apostolic see, and destructive of the Church's liberty. That these usages had been condemned in the presence of the legates themselves, and of many others, by the Pope at Sens; and that some of them had been anathematized, with other observers, by himself, on the Pope's authority—for which proceedings there were many precedents.

"He was asked if, though he could not confirm, he would at any rate promise to overlook and tolerate them, or, without making any mention of them one way or another to return to his see in peace. He answered with the proverb of our nation, that in such a case 'silence is consent.' For that, if at any time when the usages are actually enforced, and the Church is submitting under compulsion, all collision was to cease, and the subject was to be dropped, under the sanction of the legates; this would be a positive acknowledgment of the king's claims. He added, too, that he would endure exile and proscription for ever, and, if it pleased God, death in a just cause, rather than buy peace at the cost of his own salvation, and of the liberty of the Church. After this the schedule of these abominations was read over, and the cardinals were asked whether they were such as any Christian could observe much less a shepherd of Christ's flock.

" They proceeded to another question, asking whether he would abide by their judgment as to the matters between himself and the king. He said that he relied on the goodness of his cause; and that whenever himself and his should be restored to their possessions which had been confiscated, he would readily let the law take its course, and had neither the power nor the will to decline the arbitration, either of their lordships, or of any others whom his holiness the Pope should appoint in such time, place, and manner as should be right. But that, in the meantime, neither he nor his could be required to enter on litigation, nor indeed had they means wherewith to do so: for that they depended, even for their daily bread, on the munificence of his most Christian majesty.

"He was then asked whether he would consent to their hearing evidence on the appeal of the bishops, for that the appellants were ready. The archbishop, remembering the circumstances under which the pretended appeal had been notified to him, and that it had been conceived in the name of all the bishops, abbats, and dignitaries of his province, whereas he well knew that they had not been assembled at Rouen, and indeed that most of them had known nothing of it, while of those who did, many disapproved it as being rather an evasion than an appeal; answered, that he had received no instructions from the Pope upon the subject, but that on receiving them, he would return such an answer as he might judge reasonable. Finally, that the poverty of himself and his friends disabled them from undertaking lawsuits and expensive journeys —nor would he consent to encroach on the bounty of his most Christian majesty, by asking him to maintain them in hired houses."

John adds how the matter appeared to Louis VII. "The day following, the most Christian king admitted the legates to an interview, and, with the ceremony of an oath, asserted the innocence of his lordship of Canterbury, protesting that he had always counselled peace on such terms as should secure the honour of the two kings, and the tranquillity of their people.

"The archbishop requested the legates to favour him with their advice, and to point out any line of conduct which they might judge to be for the interest of the Church. They expressed their confidence in his zeal, and compassion for his sufferings, and thought his present line of conduct could not be altered for the better. On this they parted with mutual expressions of good will."

Then the legates went on to the English king. They found him at Argentan on November 25th, 1167.

Hardly pleased could he be, and after two hours' talk he sent them away so hastily that they had to take any horses they could find; and Henry said aloud so that they might hear, "I trust to God I may never set eyes on a cardinal again."[1]

That was the first interview; a second followed next day, and on the vigil of S. Andrew the king went off hawking early in the morning so as to avoid seeing them, and the bishop of London took his place as chief spokesman. The king, he said, was quite ready to agree to the cardinals' decision; it was the archbishop who was the obstacle, with his hasty way of striking, and excommunicating people without notice. The king wanted his 44,000 marks of silver for which the chancellor had never given account.

Then, after the manner of some clergymen's merriment, of which Dr Johnson has given the immortal designation, Foliot must needs say in a mighty jocular way that Becket thought consecration washed away debts as baptism did sins. And he himself, Gilbert of London, had weighty grievances, too, against the archbishop. So everybody appealed to Rome.

And so the legates must depart, in an atmosphere of crocodiles' tears, and Henry begged humbly that they would get the Pope to rid him of Becket altogether, and "he shed tears in the presence of the cardinals and others." William of Pavia joined in the weeping, but Otto, good man, could hardly conceal his mirth. And the correspondent ends with the information that Otto

---

[1] The account of this interview is from a letter to Becket from a friend. Canon Robertson has not got the date right.—*Materials*, v, 269.

will never consent to the archbishop's deposition, and the king wants nothing but the archbishop's head in a charger.

Becket, confronted with new appeals, and no nearer to the crossing of the channel than before, could find relief only in very candid expressions of opinion, The legates had told the Pope, and told the archbishop, what they had done and failed to do; they had announced the appeal of the bishops, and had forbidden him to issue excommunication or interdict. To the Pope and to William of Pavia then, he wrote thus.

To the Pope, with the now familiar superscription of "miser ac miserabilis exsul."[1]

"We send to your holiness our faithful clerks the bearers of these letters, two of our wretched fellow-exiles, to inform you what has happened to us in these latter days, and to tell you of our misery and our anguish, which is immense. May your holiness grant to us at length that long-hoped and long-delayed release from the oppressions to which ourself and our Church are exposed. Hold out the right hand of compassion and raise us up, lest we faint beneath tribulation more severe than was ever before felt since tribulation first began. We have been drawn along, as your excellency well knows, no less cruelly than unjustly, from one season to another, so that our soul sinks under its sufferings; we are worn out and almost ground beneath the weight of our miseries, and what is worse, your apostolical authority is meanwhile departing, which, by God's mercy, should have lifted us up out of our anguish before we were entirely spent. Incline thine ear then, my lord,

[1] *Materials*, vi, 293.

and hear us; let thy eyes look upon me, and behold
if there ever was wickedness like this, if there ever was
grief like mine: we are given over to be plundered, unless God's mercy, by your hand, visit us. We are become
a derision to those who are round about us, by the authority of your legates, who have acted no less wickedly
than presumptuously towards us and the Church. If
they have done so to us in the green wood, what will
they do in the dry; what will they do if their legation
lasts, which I wish had never been granted? They have
suspended us, as far as in them lay, from all the authority
which we have possessed over the English Church.
This never could have been done by you towards me
at any prince's or other man's bidding, nor shall it
now, by God's mercy, be done, as your highness has
most surely promised us. Why, my lord, have you given
the legation to that man? My lord should have considered, if he will allow me so to speak, what else could
be expected from one, whose whole soul has been
poured out to sacrifice the dignities of the Church, if
he can but gain the king's favour? My lord, my lord,
it is to you that we look to save us from perishing. Help
us, my lord, and fulfil the promises, which I hope did
not exhilarate our hearts in vain. We waited, as your
highness bade us, we waited for peace and it came not.
We waited for good at the hands of your legates, and
behold greater affliction and more intense tribulation.
Pity us, O lord Pope, pity us, for there is no one next
to God who will fight for us but you and your faithful
ones. Pity us, that God may pity you at the last judgment, when you shall render an account of your stewardship. You are, next to God, our only refuge: for even

those who out of respect for the holy Roman Church ought to have stood by us and fought for us, set themselves against us, that they may gain the favour of men. We have exhausted our means, and have endured vexation upon vexation, nor have we strength left us to endure the least of their annoyances. We pray your highness then to aid us and the Church, and check this wickedness, whilst there is still time. We can scarcely breathe for our anguish; hasten then to bestow your grace upon us, before we perish. May your excellency's life, which next to God's love is so dear to us, be long spared, to bestow upon us your munificence, and recall us from the gates of death. Be it known to your discretion, that three days before these evils came upon us, our messenger set out for your court, bearing our letters, in which we told you we had parted from your legates. The king and queen of the Franks, and some of the princes and bishops of his kingdom, together with some other more humble friends of yours, wrote to you, giving thanks to God and to you, that the lies of John of Oxford and the other ambassadors of the king, about our downfall and deposition, were at last refuted by the arrival of your legates. For it was felt as a scandal by all in the realm of the Franks, and by all everywhere, among whom that report was spread, except among the adversaries of the Church and ourself. But now our harp is turned to mourning, our joy to sadness, and the last error is worse than the first. We pray you, therefore, to apply a speedy remedy to the approaching evils that the truth may be manifest to all, how these things have been done without your knowledge or commands."

To William of Pavia the tone was very different and the matter very direct—[1]

"I did not think that I was to be set up for sale to the buyers, or that you would make gain of my blood, and procure out of the price of iniquity a name and reputation for yourself. You would have looked for another field wherein to reap your harvest, if you had not been perilously forgetful of your station, and weighed the sports of fortune in a very different balance from mine. You were encouraged, perhaps, to do so by the contemplation of my humbled condition; you beheld my adversity, but you should have looked forwards to greater prosperity hereafter. The vicissitudes of things are great, and as the fall from success and triumph is easy, so may we also rise again. I cannot believe your prudence to be ignorant, though you have yet had no personal experience of the truth, that there is nothing so firm that it has not danger lurking near it; nothing humble which good fortune may not shine on! I write thus, that you may for the future more carefully consider these changes of fortune; observe them when considered, and when you have considered, be indulgent. The vessel of S. Peter ought not to have been exposed to these storms; though she cannot be crushed, she may yet be shaken; she cannot sink, but will float again, however the waves may toss her. If then you wish to be a true disciple and good seaman of that Pilot and true fisher of men, as you have often felt the favouring breezes of prosperity, so should you present yourself with courage under every danger to meet the frowns of adversity. If you have received good from the hand of

[1] *Materials*, vi, 296.

fortune, shall you not receive evil also, evil which perhaps will endure but for a moment? Thus our master,
Peter, the chief of the apostles, not by yielding, but by
resisting kings and disturbing the peace of the wicked,
gained for himself by martyrdom a name on earth and
glory in heaven. In this way has the Church gained
strength and renewed vigour, when it was thought that
she was annihilated. In short, this is what I wish you
to do; so act here that you may live in the Lord. Farewell, that thence I, too, may fare better!"

That was the end of the legation: the legates returned whence they came, and no one was the better
for their coming. They were, as John of Salisbury had
said of one of them, Romans and cardinals.

CHAPTER XI

LEGATIONS AND APPEALS

WHEN the failure of the legation was clear, five English bishops renewed their appeal against the action they feared on the part of their primate. Thus what amounted to practically a whole year's delay was secured. Various candid advisers wrote much candid and contradictory advice to the Pope. Becket continued his endeavours to rule his province from Sens; for example, rebuking Geoffrey of Monmouth, bishop of S. Asaph, not for his literary performances as moderns might but for his absence from his diocese and his interference with the diocese of others.

But difficulties were arising about the Church property which had been seized, and the exiled archbishop was by no means satisfied with the action of the legates in absolving some of those who still held ill-gotten gains. He wrote sharply to his agents with the Pope on the point and in the same letter he alluded to a project by which it had been suggested that he should be sent off to Sicily, by exchange with some prelate more amenable to royal reason, in these words—[1]

"In addition to the above, we have been told by somebody, that according to what William of Pavia hinted to the king, and perhaps to others, his majesty would never have adhered so strongly to the scheme of our translation, if he had not foreseen that it would be agreeable to the Pope. But we would have our lord

[1] *Materials*, vi, 316.

the Pope and our other friends to know, and I request you to impress it firmly and constantly upon them, that we would suffer ourself to be put to death, as God, who is the searcher of hearts, well knows, rather than to be torn away alive from our mother, the Church of Canterbury, that has nursed us, and exalted us to our present state. Their attempts, therefore, are of no use, for such is the settled purpose of our mind. You may say, moreover, that if there were no other cause than the spoliation of our Church and of other churches in the land, by the hand of that man, we would rather, God knows, die any kind of death, than live to dishonour, or that he should escape without receiving from us the punishment, which, unless he repent, will be his due."

Meanwhile the Pope was still endeavouring to avoid an entire breach with Henry, and on the return of his legates he wrote to the king a pacifying letter.[1] He had seen Henry's envoys—who included the archbishop's old enemy, Clarembald, abbat of S. Augustine's. The date of the letter is probably May, 1168. It announces that the Pope has forbidden the archbishop to put out any sentence of excommunication against the king or nobles of England,—had this order reached Becket?— and that this letter should be a sufficient exemption if such censure should be issued. Henry had found the Pope and his legates to speak with different voices: he should remember that S. Paul had frequently changed his mind—not that Alexander can remember having changed his. But if he has shown any alteration it is not to be attributed to fickleness and it must be

[1] *Materials*, vi, 377.

remembered as regards popes "that we are men and liable in many things to be deceived and circumvented."

A letter from Becket to the Pope, a little later, is a curious commentary on the Pope's optimism and hesitation—[1]

"We send back to your holiness the bearer of these presents, who will faithfully and accurately explain to you the unfortunate nature of his business, and how he and his brothers have been dealt with in England in consequence of your letters. Unless the Divine clemency stretch forth its hand to raise them up by your agency, it is all over with the fortunes of their order. May it please you then to let him and his brothers experience the benefit of our intercession, for the unjust vexations which they have suffered, render them fitting objects of your commiseration. And I pray you, my lord, to consider attentively into what irremediable confusion the English Church has been thrown, and what evils have resulted to every class of persons living in that kingdom, from that pernicious indulgence which the king boasts he has obtained by the intervention of certain of his friends of the Curia, who show more regard to princes than to their God. Though this indulgence may easily be revoked, yet the pernicious precedent has been set, and will encourage his successors to similar acts of daring, from a certainty of being able, by some means or other, to escape punishment.

"We have one miserable source of consolation in all this, if you will allow me to say so: that the Roman Church takes this mode of rewarding its friends and faithful children. May God comfort her better than

[1] *Materials*, vi, 398.

she provides for herself: may he comfort the Church of England and us, and all our wretched ones. I know what grieves me most: it is this; that crime can never be blotted out or become obsolete by time: there is no forgetfulness for sin, but evil deeds become at last evil examples. May your holiness fare well and flourish: quickly, if it pleases you, relieve our misery, that we may at least live, whereas at present our life is but a death, and God knows how undeservedly!"

Throughout these months the affairs of Becket were complicated by the Pope's difficulties, by the hostility between Henry and Louis, and by many political embarrassments throughout Europe. The letters of John of Salisbury, vivaciously describing events and retailing conversations, throw curious and amusing light on many an ecclesiastical and political passage of arms. Insurrection in Poitou and in Normandy, continual disturbance on the frontiers, the death of great English nobles such as Robert of Leicester, who had attempted to deliver the barons' sentence at Northampton, and whose refusal to communicate with Reginald of Köln had preserved the king from the open error of accepting the anti-pope, and Patrick, earl of Salisbury, killed by the Poitevins, made Henry feel that dangers were surrounding him more and more closely and he was almost isolated in resistance. He talked of going to Jerusalem on a pilgrimage, but people had learned to distrust him. So the months dragged on; and as for the way money was spent at the papal court and the way in which every sort of influence was used to terrify the Pope, why, in John of Salisbury's words, "haec in ecclesiae Romanae scribentur annalibus." On May 19th,

1168, the Pope wrote to Becket from Benevento, expressing his fear lest Henry should ally with the Emperor, and therefore forbidding him to issue any censures. After this there was no peace for the Pope at Benevento: "the threshold of the Apostles was worn by our messengers and by our enemies," says Herbert of Bosham. And meanwhile, as Thomas wrote to Conrad, archbishop of Mainz, "The king boasts of our suspensions as with the voice of a herald in both kingdoms, and declares that the time which is allowed to him to receive me back to his grace is the Greek Kalends," and John of Salisbury told Master Lombard of a similar boast that Henry knew everything that happened at the papal court and could circumvent every move of the exiles. And Alexander continued to write pacifying letters.[1]

A new legation had been appointed in May, 1168: it consisted of Simon, prior of Mont-Dieu, Engelbert, prior of Val S. Pierre, and Bernard de la Coudre, monk of Grammont, the last of whom was by his rule forbidden to use pen and ink. It was a long time before they were able to act. The two former wrote to the Pope at the beginning of 1169, when they had at length had a meeting with both the kings, for they were to combine in an attempt at a political reconciliation with their efforts for the restoration of Becket. On the feast of the Epiphany the meeting took place at Montmirail in Maine. Peace was made between the two kings, homage being done to Louis by the English king's sons, Henry and Richard.

By the advice of all his friends Thomas attended the

[1] *e.g. Materials*, vi, 484.

meeting on January 6th and 7th, 1169.[1] Long was the discussion, and at last the advisers thought that they had induced him to omit the phrase "saving our order," or that alternative to which he now clung, "saving God's honour." Herbert of Bosham tells the story with vivid particularity. Henry and Louis were sitting together, waiting to see what should happen. Herbert edged through the crowd and whispered in the archbishop's ear a warning not to suppress the words. "He turned and looked me in the face, but could not answer, for the crowd that was about him, seeking to have speech with him; and so he was brought into the presence of the kings." With him went William, archbishop of Sens.

He flung himself at the king's feet and said he placed himself at his mercy and at God's, for God's honour and the king's honour. Henry at once burst out into rage, denounced him for his flight. "I ask for nothing," he said, "but that he should keep those customs which his five predecessors kept, themselves saints some of them and workers of miracles." Becket answered that he had sworn fealty saving his order, and would never depart from his oath: no more had been asked from his predecessors, nor would he give more. A few minutes afterwards, when he was further pressed, he said that though none of his predecessors had done so and he was not bound to do it, yet for the sake of the Church's peace and the king's favour he would promise to keep

[1] See the valuable paper of M. Louis Halphen, "Les entrevues des rois Louis VII et Henri II durant l'exil de Thomas Becket en France" in *Mélanges d'histoire offerts à M. Charles Brémont par ses amis et ses élèves*, 1903.

those customs which had been kept by his predecessors, saving his order. "Never will I allow that phrase," said Henry; and so they parted in anger.

Becket was beset by advisers all urging him to yield, till night fell and the kings rode away, Henry swearing that he would be avenged. Hardly one of the archbishop's own men supported him now. When a horse stumbled, as they rode, one of them, Henry of Houghton, called out, "Get up, saving the honour of God, and of Holy Church, and of my order." It was some time before the archbishop replied to the taunt: then he said he would accept the best terms he could get, yet the liberty of the Church, of which the king said nought, was far more important than the return and restoration of the exiles.

As Becket went back to Sens through Chartres, where before long the exquisite sculpture of the splendid Gothic of Northern France in the thirteenth century was to represent him among the martyrs on the south porch of the cathedral church,[1] the people pointed at him and cried out "Here is the archbishop who in yesterday's conference would not deny God for the sake of kings or be silent as to His honour," and Becket was troubled and full of compunction.[2] No man, in-

---

[1] The sculpture is an interesting one. "Il est agenouillé au pied de l'autel de sa cathédrale. Les assassins vont le frapper de leurs épées; l'imagier n'avait de place que pour en figurer deux. Ils ont un costume absolument semblable à celui de saint Théodore sur l'embrasement. Leur tête est coiffée du capuchon en mailles de fer, ce qui leur donne un air étrange. Le saint baisse la tête pour recevoir le coup mortel. Il est devant un autel muni d'une nappe plissée avec soin, une calice est sur l'autel."—Bulteau, *Monographie de la Cathédrale de Chartres*, 2nd ed. 1887, p. 362.

[2] Herbert of Bosham, *Materials*, iii, 436–7.

deed, found it more difficult to know what he should do now to do right than he; only that bold scribe who flaunted his cloak of Auxerre before Henry was ever at his side to urge him to be firm. Old friends such as John of Poitiers urged concessions, and he indeed came to Becket at Étampes on Henry's behalf and endeavoured to arrange a meeting at Tours, where Henry might stay in the city and the archbishop safely in the great abbey of Marmoutier. But he had gone farther than Becket warranted, in making this proposal: he had represented the exile as willing to trust himself entirely to the king, "as a Christian prince to provide for the Church's honour and his own." An answer from the archbishop left no hope that he would consent to use such words—[1]

"Dearest friend, why have you dealt with me thus? Why have you strangled both me and yourself? You have given that man a handle for disparaging both of us and of maligning me. The animal is greedy of glory, and already too prone to destroy the Church; and now he will have it published in the streets and proclaimed in the face of the Church, that we have yielded unconditionally to his wishes, without mentioning God's honour or our own order, though it is less than ever proper to pass these over, when by doing so we bring confusion and ignominy on the Church, which is clear and manifest apostasy.

"If you will only recollect yourself, we parted at Étampes on a very different understanding from this. When we took leave of one another, I told you to insist on this condition only, that the man should restore us

[1] *Materials*, vi, 493.

his favour according to our lord the Pope's instructions, and give us back our Church in free possession. You asked me whether I would have a day appointed for an interview if he should wish to see me, and I replied, that I would have no day fixed till he should obey the Pope's mandate, but that as soon as he had done that, we could meet him on any day that he might appoint, and do all that lay in our power, saving God's honour and our own order. It was on this footing, my dear friend, that we parted. To this understanding you ought to have adhered, for no one knows better than you, that we do not dare to go one step beyond this, consistently with our duty to our God. I would have you to know, therefore, my soul's half, that it is not our intention, nor is it safe, to have a day fixed on, or to go to a conference, until he shall have received the Pope's mandate, and further, if so please him, until he shall have put it in execution; lest perchance, which God forbid, if we give occasion for delay, the failure of our lord the Pope's mandate may be imputed to us, which would clearly be against our interests. Farewell ever!"

John of Salisbury wrote a further letter to the same friend. The archbishop, he said, was desirous of peace, but far more desirous of the glory of God; and there was hope that vengeance would not be long deferred. He wrote also to the legates Simon and Bernard, speaking of Henry's sending of John of Poitiers as a crafty move and expressing his distrust of the ascetic Bernard, who would never use pen or ink: "It is often so that those who are boastfully declared to have nothing yet covet all the more this world's goods or glory," wrote

John, who himself used the pen freely enough. To Bartholomew of Exeter he told the strange words Henry had used—that no Church in the world had such freedom as the English, and that the clergy were the most unclean and atrocious persons, guilty of sacrilege, adultery, theft, murder, and every crime.

Thomas himself did not leave the matter thus. He wrote directly, bitterly,[1] declaring himself ready to place himself at God's mercy and the king's, and as Henry wished it, to promise to observe the customs as his predecessors had observed them, "quatenus possem salvo ordine meo, et si aliquid amplius vel expressius promittere scirem in Domino, paratus fui, et sum adhuc, pro recuperanda gratia vestra." "Never," he said, "have I served you more freely than I am ready now to do; I beg you to remember my services and the benefits you have conferred on me; for I am mindful of my oath to preserve to you life and limb and earthly honour, and whatever I can do for you according to God's will as for a most dear lord I am ready to do."

To the Pope he wrote again, at the same time, it seems—[2]

"If the cause of our exile, holy father, had not been stated to you in dark colours by our enemies, we have no doubt that the king of England would not so long have abused your patience with impunity. But lo! the truth has at last come out, and our persecutor's designs, by God's grace, are revealed. For lately, when we implored his mercy, on our knees, in the presence of his most Christian majesty, his archbishops, bishops,

---

[1] *Materials*, vi, 513.   [2] *Ibid.* 514.

counts and nobles, he declared that he only required of us that we should observe the constitutions of his kingdom, which our ancestors had observed towards his, and that I should promise this on the word of a priest and bishop, as our messengers will faithfully explain to you. May it please your holiness, therefore, to listen to our faithful servants, who have shared with us in our exile, who were present and heard all that passed, for the English Church is now on its last legs, unless the hand of God and your hand apply a speedy remedy. The king of England boasts that you have conferred on him a privilege, by which he is to be freed from all ecclesiastical censure from us until we return to our Church and be reconciled towards him. It is a thing unheard of amongst us, that a bishop should be obliged to bind himself towards a secular prince to observe anything else besides what is contained in the oath of allegiance. We fear, therefore, though, by God's grace, our fears will be groundless, lest an additional obligation exacted from us may be a pernicious example to other princes, involving not only our contemporaries but our successors. Indeed, it is plain, that if the required constitutions shall be conceded, the authority of the holy see in England will become little, or perhaps nothing. This, indeed, as is evident from the writings and accounts of our forefathers, would long ago have happened, if the Church of Canterbury had not interposed itself to resist princes on behalf of the Church and her liberties. For there has seldom been a ruler of that Church who has not drawn the sword for righteousness' sake, and suffered exile or proscription. It is wonderful, therefore, and altogether astonishing that this persecution of the apostolic power even more than of our name should boast that he has found partizans in such a cause even at your own court. Nor need you fear that he will pass over to the schismatics, for Christ has so humbled him by the hand of His faithful servant, the king of the Franks, that he cannot depart from doing what he wishes."

The anticipation of ultimate success on Becket's part seemed, as the days went on, to have more justification. Louis sent for him; and when a timid clerk warned him that this was in order to drive him forth from Sens, the archbishop answered, "Thou art no prophet, nor prophet's son: prophesy no evil." When he came to the king, Louis fell before him to ask his forgiveness, for the wrong thoughts he had of peace-making at Montmirail: Becket alone had been right, he said. And so even the penless Bernard came to say that he would rather have his foot cut off than that the archbishop should have yielded at the conference.

Early in February, 1169, the legates delivered to Henry not only a "commonitory" but a "comminatory" letter from the Pope, but all Henry would answer to the commination was that Becket should never enter his kingdom again till he promised to obey what his predecessors had obeyed and what he himself (doubtless when he assented to the Constitutions) had promised before to obey.

The archbishop's own version of the situation now reached comes in another letter to the Pope—[1]

"The riches of your long-suffering and the abundance of God's goodness, have hitherto been treated

[1] *Materials*, vi, 519.

by the king of England with contempt, whilst he is ignorant, or pretends to be so, that your patience has for its end only to invite him to repentance. He is deaf to entreaties and to admonitions, boasting, to the dishonour of the apostolic see, and to the reproach of your blessed name, that you have granted him a privilege, by which he will be safe from us as long as he pleases, notwithstanding all the persecutions with which he may assail us and the Church of Canterbury. And the better to persuade mankind of so incredible an assertion, he is exhibiting all over Germany, France, and England, rescripts of letters which you have furnished him with against us, and woe is me that I should say so, against your own self. Thus, he requites your favour and kindness, so that his last deeds are worse than the former. But God has at last brought to light what I wish you had believed at first, for the justice of our cause and the real nature of his intentions have been declared in the face of the world.

"For a short time since, at the second conference, in the hearing of his most Christian majesty and of all present on both sides, after receiving your letters comminatory, which he had often rejected, and then scarcely accepted, he owned that what he requires at our hands is nothing else than the observance of his usages, to which, as your holiness has seen and may remember, God's law and the sacred canons are evidently and altogether opposed.

"At the instance of the most Christian king, and of the holy men whom your holiness has sent, he was indeed prevailed on to drop the mention of usages, but he changed the word without changing his meaning;

requiring that we should promise, on the word of truth, simply and absolutely, to act as our predecessors had acted. This, as he said, was the only way for us to obtain our Church and peace in his dominions; but that even then we should not have his favour; which he added, because he conceives that by your holiness's rescript our authority is suspended till such time as his favour is restored us.

"On this proposal being laid before us by the holy men, Simon, prior of Mont-Dieu, and brother Bernard, we answered, 'that we could not conscientiously do what our predecessors did; though indeed we know, from authentic documents, that some of them have suffered banishment in a like cause; however, that we were prepared to yield him every service, even more than our predecessors had done, saving our order; but that new obligations, unknown to the Church, and such as our predecessors were never bound by, ought not to be undertaken by us; first, because it was bad as a precedent; secondly, because your holiness's self, when in the city of Sens, absolved me from the observance of those usages hateful to God and the Church, and from the pledge which force and fear had extorted from me, in a special manner; and after a grave rebuke, which, by God's grace, shall never pass from my mind, prohibited me from ever again obliging myself to anyone in a like cause, except saving God's honour and my order.' You added, too, if you are pleased to remember, that not even to save his life should a bishop bind himself, except saving God's honour and his order. For these reasons we made our promise to the holy men, 'that if the king would fulfil your holiness's mandate,

by restoring us his favour and peace, and our Church, and
what he had taken from ourself and ours, then we would
endeavour with our whole might, saving God's honour
and our order, to serve himself and his children'; but
we stated, 'that, without authority from your holiness,
we might not make changes in a formula which the
whole Western Church acknowledges, and which is
expressed even in those very reprobate usages for which
we are banished. For there it is contained, that before
consecration, bishops elect shall swear fealty to the king
concerning life and limb, and earthly honour, saving
their order. Why is it then that we alone are to be compelled by this captious pledge which is exacted from us,
to drop all mention of God's honour and the indemnity
of our order?' What Christian ever made such a
demand on Christian?

"He has eluded the solicitations of the holy men by
shifting his answers, and, after much saying and un-
saying, has left them, regretting the toils and expense
which have availed nothing. He did indeed pretend
that he would summon the English bishops and consult
them; but in reality what he is waiting for is the return
of his envoys from your holiness. For, as I learn from
those who may be credited, they boast that, as they did
on a former occasion, they will obtain from your holiness what the king desires, either by promises or threats.
I cannot, however, believe that the apostolic see will
compel anyone to suppress God's honour, or prohibit
his mentioning the safety of his honour. And truly, if
your holiness dismisses them, as they deserve, you will
re-establish Church liberty, and the fair fame of the
apostolic see. May it please you to deal manfully; for

most undoubtedly, if it is your pleasure to put the wicked in fear, you will restore peace to the Church and a perishing soul to God. You have already seen what gentleness can effect; now essay the other method. In the severity of justice you will most assuredly triumph. Exact what we have been despoiled of, yea to the last farthing. Let it not get abroad among our contemporaries and posterity, that such rapine has escaped punishment, and thus embolden himself and his successors to repeat it. We have also to request most earnestly, that if the malefactors whom we excommunicated venture into your holiness's presence, or send to you, you will not absolve them to our prejudice. If this had not been done on a former occasion, the Church would have been at this day in the enjoyment of peace.

"If he shall compel us, which, by God's grace, he shall slay us rather than we will consent to do, to submit to this obligation (for we have not forgotten the oath which we made to you and the Roman Church when we received the pall), he will by this precedent compel all the bishops and clergy to do as we have done. And other princes will have no difficulty in following his example. What he demands from us is demanded from knight or peasant in our country."

Wearisome though the correspondence is, one may clearly read in its long-drawn-out protestations and counterchecks that a severe blow was being prepared. So Gilbert Foliot saw, and he, with Jocelin of Salisbury, appealed to the Pope against any censure from Becket. The canonists debated whether this appeal could prevent a deserved censure: Becket was advised that it could not. Accordingly on Palm Sunday, April 13th, 1169, at Clairvaux, he solemnly excommunicated Gilbert Foliot, bishop of London, and the bishop of Salisbury, with several of those who had seized upon Church property. He warned Geoffrey Ridel, archdeacon of Canterbury, Richard of Ilchester, archdeacon of Poitiers, Richard de Lucy, and others, that they too would be excommunicated, on the next Ascension Day, if they did not amend and give satisfaction. The letter to Foliot ran thus—[1]

"Your extravagances we have long enough borne with, and would that the sweetness of our patience which has been above measure detrimental to ourselves, may not be to the ruin of the whole Church. You have abused our patience, and would not listen to the Pope or ourselves in the advice which concerned your salvation, but your obstinacy has become worse and worse, until, from regard to our sacred duty, and to the requirements of the law, we have for just and manifest causes passed sentence of excommunication on you, and cut you off from Christ's body, which is the Church, until you make condign satisfaction. We therefore command you, by virtue of your obedience and in peril of your salvation, your episcopal dignity, and priestly orders, to abstain, as the forms of the Church prescribe, from all communion with the faithful, lest by coming in contact with you the Lord's flock be contaminated to their ruin, whereas they ought to have been instructed by your teaching, and led by your example to everlasting life."

Foliot tried every possible means to avert or resist

[1] *Materials*, vi, 541.

the blow, and Henry wrote strongly on his behalf to the Pope. But the excommunication was delivered in a dramatic manner during high mass at S. Paul's on Ascension Day, 1169. Berengar, a French clerk, the archbishop's messenger, gave a packet into the hands of the celebrant, a priest named Vitalis, as though it were an offering. Holding the priest's hands firmly, Berengar ordered him on behalf of the Pope and the archbishop to give one copy to the bishop and one to the dean and not to celebrate mass till it was read. He ordered William of Northall, the gospeller (afterwards consecrated in 1186 to be bishop of Worcester, on the same day as S. Hugh to Lincoln), and William Hog, the epistoller, to witness, while in a loud voice he cried out "Know ye that Gilbert, bishop of London, is excommunicated by Thomas, archbishop of Canterbury and legate of the apostolic see." Concealed by his companion's cloak, he then escaped through the crowd.

News was brought to the bishop at Stepney, and he summoned his clergy to hear his defence. He brought out among other reasons good or bad his own strange hobby, that London was an archiepiscopal see till the pagans came and destroyed it. The dean, archdeacon, canons, and all the parish priests joined in the appeal, with the abbat of Westminster and others. And letter after letter poured in to the bewildered Pope. The bishop applied to the king: the king offered his strongest support against "that traitor and my enemy, Thomas." Foliot crossed to Normandy and went on to Rome to prosecute his appeal.

The excommunications threatened were delivered on Ascension Day. There was a further threat of interdict for all England on the Purification of the Blessed Virgin Mary, 1170. Alexander saw no way out of the new tangle but through another commission. This was given to Gratian, subdeacon and notary of the Holy See, and Vivian, archdeacon of Orvieto, men erudite and industrious, says Herbert of Bosham, and the former the nephew of Eugenius III of blessed memory; the latter (as it was said) not above being bribed—it is of him that William of Newburgh uses the familiar phrase about Romans and cardinals.

But there were many who thought that as both Gratian and Vivian were lawyers, Henry could not bribe or overawe them. And indeed so it seemed when they saw the king, for when he began to demand the absolution of those who had been excommunicated, and to swear at large by God's eyes, Gratian answered, "Threaten not, sir; we are of a court that has been wont to give the law to emperors." He promised many concessions, but the way in which they were received by the large assembly of bishops, most of them his own subjects, gives some ground for believing that Becket had reason for regarding all his promises as treacherous. On the excommunication question he could not get his way, and he shouted out to Gratian, "Do as you like; I don't care an egg for you or your excommunication." Days were spent in fruitless talk. At last it seemed that there was hope of a reconciliation. They yielded so far as to absolve Geoffrey Ridel, Nigel Sackville and Thomas Fitz-Bernard on an oath of unconditional obedience to their commands. But then Henry demanded the insertion in any agreement of the words "saving the dignity of the kingdom," and they on

Becket's behalf of a "saving the dignity of the Church." Gratian returned to Rome saying Henry was not to be trusted. Vivian made one more attempt.

Meanwhile Becket sent orders to the bishops and the religious orders in England, as primate and papal legate, to publish—if the king should not repent and make amends before then—on the Feast of the Purification, 1170, an interdict on all England. Other names, including that of John of Oxford, were to be added, from Christmas, 1169, to the list of the excommunicates. Henry as a counterblast sent orders into England, that anyone found with letters of the Pope or archbishop should be instantly taken and executed as a traitor; that no one should be allowed to leave England without the king's licence; no appeal be allowed to Pope or archbishop; that anyone from bishop to layman, observing the interdict, should be banished with all their kin and have all their goods confiscated; that all the goods and possessions of those "who favour Pope or archbishop" and those of all their kin of either sex be seized and confiscated; that all clerks return to England under pain of confiscation; that Peter's pence be not sent to Rome but collected for the king.

But this was not Henry's final measure. He still endeavoured to pacify his enemies. He proposed a pilgrimage to S. Denys, to propitiate Louis, and this succeeded. He induced Vivian to meet him at Montmartre, the chapel of the holy martyrdom of the saint, on November 18th, 1169.[1] There Becket had come for one more attempt, it seems, to see his master and old friend. They met, the archbishop of Rouen and the

[1] See M. Halphen, *op. cit.*

bishop of Séez, besides Vivian and Louis, mediating. They seemed to come to an entire agreement: Henry yielded everything: Becket was satisfied with the restoration of the property of the Church as he had held it when he went to the Council of Tours and as Theobald had held before him. "Concerning that word added, *Salvo honore Dei,* about which in the last meeting the whole strife and contention had been, there was not a record nor a mention," says Herbert of Bosham. All seemed satisfactorily arranged, but then—let Herbert tell the tale—[1]

"Thus every storm seemed to be blown over, and we were, as we thought, on the point of entering the harbour, when the archbishop, through the mediators, demanded some guarantee of the conditions; not, as he said, because he suspected the king of treachery, but that he naturally entertained suspicions about some of the courtiers after so long a quarrel, and he wished that some outward sign or token of peace should pass between them. Now the archbishop, being a prudent man, had some days before the meeting consulted the apostolic pontiff what caution he should require, if the king should allow him after so long variance to return to his Church. To this question the Pope replied, that as a Churchman and priest he could not exact a pledge or oath from the king; that the cause between them was one of justice and the peace of the Church, for which, whether in open quarrel or after peace was made, it was precious to yield one's life. None of the ordinary guarantees were therefore to be required in such a case; 'but,' added his holiness, 'If God willing, you could

[1] *Materials*, iii, 449.

prevail upon the king to let a kiss of peace pass between you, with that you might be content, without requiring any other caution, unless it should be spontaneously offered.'

"The archbishop, fortified by this advice, when everything else was arranged, followed the Pope's counsel, and desired that the king should give him a kiss as a token of their reconciliation; but when the king received this communication through the mediators and the king of the Franks, he replied, that he should have been very ready to do as the archbishop required, if he had not formerly sworn publicly that he would never kiss him, even if he should at some future time be persuaded to make peace with him; and that the sole cause of his refusing now to kiss the archbishop was his wish not to break his oath.

"The king of the Franks and most of the mediators hearing this, entertained a suspicion that under the honied words which had hitherto passed between them, they had perhaps been made to drink poison. So they returned in haste to the archbishop, who was waiting in the chapel of the Martyrdom, and reported the king's answer. And being timid men, and now entertaining suspicion, they made no comment on the subject, but delivered duly the king's answer, just as he had spoken it.

"Now the archbishop was one of the most cautious of cautious men, having experienced many things, and as soon as ever he heard the king's answer, he and the others became suspicious and from what he said both secretly and openly he seemed already to see into the future: for he did not wait to consult anyone, but answered absolutely and precisely that at present he would not make peace with the king, unless, according to the advice of the apostolic pontiff, it should be ratified by the kiss of peace. This so absolute answer cut short the conference, just as night was coming on: and the kings had a long journey before them to Mantes, where their quarters had been prepared, which was twelve leagues from Paris.

"The king of the English, tired with the long day, now had a long way to ride by night, often and often on the way cursed the archbishop, reckoning up the various annoyances and causes of vexation which he had given him.

"Whilst the kings thus took their departure, we retired to pass the night in a house of the Templars which is called the Temple, and just outside Paris. As we were leaving the chapel, which is called the Martyrdom, in which the business of the day concerning the pacification had been done, one of our people came up to the archbishop and said thus: 'My lord, this day's conference has been held in the chapel of the Martyrdom, and I believe that nothing but your martyrdom will ever ensure peace to the Church.' Thus answered the archbishop: 'Would that she might be freed, even by my blood!'"

That night after the night office (matins) in the chapel of the Temple, many of the "erudite" came to Becket and told him they could approve his cause no longer. The king had yielded on every point, he had given up his *salvo* and was ready to restore the Church and property. There was no reason now why they should stay in exile: he held out only for that merely personal matter of the kiss of peace. Becket listened carefully and attentively to "the wounding words": then he said that without the kiss the peace could not stand; but that if they so wished, and the Pope would agree, he would gladly go back to England to suffer there what the Lord should decree. Many saw his meaning, says Herbert, and burst into tears.

It is probably to this time that a letter of Becket to Alexander and John, his agents at the Papal Court, may be attributed.[1] Vivian, he says, now sees through the treachery of Henry, and he himself was ready to meet the king in Normandy for a settlement.

"But you must endeavour to persuade the Pope to forbid our incurring any new obligation, not warranted by the customs of the Gallican and Anglican Churches, and not to depart from the form which we sent in writing to the king, to command that a decent portion of our property shall be restored to us, to alarm the king by the threat of an interdict on his continental dominions, to write earnestly to the king charging him to receive us in the kiss of peace, and to issue fresh letters commanding the restoration of the lands which we named as having been taken away from the see of Canterbury, the restoration of which is essential to the peace. He must forbid us to absolve any of the excommunicates unless they submit to take the oath, according to the custom and forms of the Church.[2] For among all the prerogatives of the Constitutions which he claims

[1] *Materials*, vii, 173. No date is given, and the editor regarded it as supplementary to a letter of 1167 (see above, p. 192), but it refers to the meeting at Montmartre.

[2] This is the oath required, on absolution, to obey the decisions of the Church. It was one of the points which, in the Constitutions of Clarendon, the king refused.

to God's prejudice, if we may believe men of experience, this is the most pernicious. If he fails in his presumption on this point, he will not, we trust, insist upon the other, lest he be again confounded. Furthermore, the lord Pope should write and thank the most Christian king for the consolation he has held out to us, pointing out to him what a sin and sacrilege it is to take the property of the Church, and without just cause to defraud ecclesiastics of their goods, and how impossible it is to forgive sin, unless there be repentance and restitution when there is opportunity of making it. If stolen property when it can be restored is not restored, it is but a fantastic repentance, and not the true which leadeth to salvation, but rather accumulates to condemnation.

"We send to you the petition which we offered to the king, and desire that you do not depart from it, unless you can better our cause, also the letter which we sent to Master Vivian, and which, as we have heard, he forwarded to the king of the English. You will thus be better provided for advancing the Church's interests. If any of the chatterers presume to blame us for not entering the king's dominions without the kiss of peace, let them remember the case of Robert de Silly,[1] who was not safe either by the kiss or by the pledge given to the king of the Franks, and unless they are out of their senses, they will not, I think, blame me.

"May God direct both you and me, too, that we may do his will in all things, and whether by joy or sorrow to ourselves, restore liberty to his Church. These things you shall signify from us to his lordship of Ostia, and the other things which I wrote to the archbishop

---

[1] A Poitevin vassal of Henry's.

of Sens, and as he shall advise you, to other of our friends who are waiting for the redemption of Israel.

"The bishop of Lisieux, as you know, persecutes us, though wearing the name of our friend, like the man in Ovid, whose character he has sustained under the guise of a bishop, giving arms at one moment to the Greeks against the Amazons, and the next moment to the Amazons against the Greeks;[1] now assisting the ecclesiastics against the seculars, and now the seculars against the ecclesiastics. See what he has lately written for the bishop of London, whose deserts are well known to you, and then recall to mind the advice which he used to give us. You see how truly he is playing the part of Sinon between the Greeks and the Trojans, and the etymology of that cunning Greek's name well applies to him, for he is always hesitating between Si! and Non! That priest and clerk of his lordship of Pavia has persevered to the end the same as he was in the beginning. What that is, I believe, my lord Gratian knows as well as I. For he sided with him when he was here, and since that he has always stuck to the king."

A letter to the Pope praising Vivian followed this, and another to his agents carried on the tale[2] with exceedingly sharp words about the bishop of Salisbury's archdeacon and son—

"Be zealous in attending to our business, and use continued and unflinching diligence to counteract our adversaries, especially that spurious offspring of fornication, and enemy of the peace of the Church, that son of a priest, Reginald of Salisbury, who is everywhere

[1] Ovid, *de arte amandi*, iii, i, 2.
[2] *Materials*, vii, 181.

defaming our character to the utmost of his power, saying that we have acted treacherously, and that we promised him we would not in any way aggrieve his father. We would no more make such a promise to him than to a dog. He says also that if our lord the Pope was to depart, he would get our name blotted out of the book of life, for he boasts that the Roman Curia is so venal that he could get it to grant him what he likes. He has also suggested to the king of the English to make a petition to the lord Pope, that he shall grant permission to some English bishop to crown the king's son, and consecrate new bishops, and so deceive the Pope. When the king replied to all this, that he did not believe the Pope would consent, Reginald answered, 'Our lord the Pope will act like a thick-head and a fool if he does not grant your requests.' We, therefore, entreat your kindness, for we confide unhesitatingly in your fidelity, to stand firm with our friend Hugotio of Rome, who is just gone back out of France, and with our other friends and your own, in defending our cause, and the justice and liberties of the Church; to the defeat and confusion of that fabrication of falsehood and deceit, that his wickedness may be revealed and recoil on his own head, that he may repent of ever having come to the court, and may be held up to the world as having been defeated in his schemes, as he deserves. For, as you know well, if our lord the Pope were to lend an ear to the king's petitions in such a matter, which God forbid, he may be sure that the authority of the Roman Church in England will for ever fall, and no one shall ever again dare to mention the name of its apostolic authority. But if our lord the Pope, as is best for him to do, sends away the king's ambassadors foiled and baffled, he may be sure that by God's mercy we shall immediately obtain peace. For the king of England insists most on these two points, the coronation of his son and the consecration of the bishops, and he will be compelled to make peace with us, if he sees the Pope firm. Among other things take care not to talk with the above-named Hugotio on our business in presence of the cardinals or any other person, but take an opportunity of speaking to him privately about the settlement of our matters; so that no one may know there is any intimacy between you and him."

A new point appears in this letter: it was that which was at last to bring Becket back to his own land—the question of crowning king Henry's son.

CHAPTER XII

PACIFICATION AT LAST

WHEN Vivian returned from his bootless task Alexander did not give up all hopes of effecting a reconciliation between the English combatants. It was unfortunate, perhaps, that he had no consistent policy; but the papacy in the twelfth and thirteenth centuries never had. The very "customs" for which Henry II was reprobated were allowed a little later to Philip Augustus: what an English king might not do a Sicilian king did without protest; and neither Henry nor Becket knew at what point of principle the Pope could be depended upon to remain fixed. However, the Papacy was great in negotiations, and legations at least paid themselves. On January 19th, 1170, Alexander issued a new commission, to Rotrou, archbishop of Rouen and Bernard, bishop of Nevers, subjects, the one of Henry, the other of Louis, directing them to require from the English king the kiss of peace to the archbishop and the restoration of the property of the deprived clerks.[1] An interdict was to be pronounced on Henry's continental dominions if after forty days the king had not accepted these terms. But, on the other hand, if they had certain hope of peace and reconciliation the legates might absolve those whom the archbishop had excommunicated.

And, three weeks later, the Pope went further, authorising, in a letter of February 12th to the bishop

[1] See the Pope's letter, *Materials*, vii, 198.

himself, the absolution of Foliot; he was formally
absolved by the archbishop of Rouen on Easter Day,[1]
on his way home. When he reached England he published his freedom abroad; he had celebrated mass
publicly before he left Rouen.[2] Thus Becket, writing
to Cardinal Albert, denounced the absolution—[3]

"Would that your ears, my dear brother, were open
to what is published in the streets of Ascalon to the
shame of the Roman Church. Our latest messenger
seemed to have some consolation from the apostolic see
in the letters which he bore from the lord Pope; but
their authority is made void by the letters officially
issued that Satan be unloosened for the destruction of
the Church. For by the apostolic mandate the bishops
of London and Salisbury are absolved, of whom the
former is known to have been from the first the exciter
of schism and the author of all malice, while the latter
did all he could to encourage others in disobedience.
I know not how it is that in the Court of Rome the
Lord's side is always sacrificed, that Barabbas escapes,
and Christ is slain. By the authority of the Curia, our
exile and the calamity of the Church has been prolonged
to the end of the sixth year. With you the wretched,
the exiles, the innocent are condemned, and for no
other reason (on my conscience I say it) than because
they are the poor of Christ and weak, and would not
go back from the righteousness of God, while on the
other hand you absolve the sacrilegious, the murderers,
the robbers, the impenitent, whom I openly declare,

[1] April 5th. See letter to Becket, *Materials*, vii, 275.
[2] This seems to be the true reading of the letter, *Materials*, vii,
278, which Fr. Morris and others misinterpreted.
[3] *Materials*, vii, 279.

on the authority of Christ, that not Peter himself, did he rule the Church, could absolve in the sight of God. ...Let him who dares absolve the robbers, the sacrilegious, the murderers, the perjurers, the men of blood, the schismatics, without repentance. I will never forgive to the impenitent the things which have been taken away from God's Church. Is it not our spoils, or rather the spoils of the Church, which the king's envoys lavish on and pay to the cardinals and courtiers?...For myself I am determined never to trouble the Court more; let those resort thither who prevail in their iniquities, and after triumphing over justice and leading innocence captive, return with boasting for the confusion of the Church. Would to God that the Roman way had not caused for no purpose the deaths of so many wretched innocent folk. Who in the future will dare to resist that king whom the Roman Church animates and arms with such triumphs, leaving a deadly example to posterity?"

It seemed, indeed, that the Roman Church had animated the king towards another triumph. Henry had long desired to establish his throne, which was none too secure, in England by the coronation during his own lifetime of his eldest son, Becket's former pupil. Possibly now, but it is more charitable to suppose earlier, when in 1167 Alexander was at the crisis of his fate during the siege of Rome by Frederick,[1] the Pope had granted the permission—which it was not his to grant.

"Since through our dearest son Henry, the illustrious king of the English, great gains and comforts are known

[1] See *Materials*, vi, 206, where the date is provisionally given as 1167. The day is June 17th. But did Henry or Roger apply for the licence in that year? Böhmer, *Corpus Juris Canon.* See Migne, *PL.* cc. 457.

to have come to the Church in this article of our necessity and as we love him with the more affection for the constancy of his devotion and hold him dearer to our heart, so do we the more freely and promptly desire all such things as lend to the honour, the increase, and the exaltation of himself and his. Hence it is that, at his petition, we by the authority of the blessed Peter and our own, and by the counsel of our brethren, grant that our dearly loved son Henry, the said king's eldest son, may be crowned in England.

"Since therefore this pertaineth to your office we command you by apostolic letters that when you shall be required by the aforesaid our son the king you shall place the crown upon the head of this said son, by the authority of the apostolic see; and what shall be therein done by you we decree to remain valid and firm."

It was on this permission, whenever given, that Roger of York was now ready to obey the king's commands. But on February 20th, 1170, the Pope issued a contrary order[1] to Roger and all the English bishops: "Whereas it has come to our hearing on the report of many that the coronation and unction of the kings of England belongs by ancient custom and dignity of his church to the archbishop of Canterbury, we strictly entreat you by apostolic authority in these our letters, if the illustrious king of the English should wish his son to be crowned and anointed while our venerable brother the archbishop of Canterbury is in exile, from presuming to lay your hands on him or in any way intruding into the matter, which if any of you shall presume to do let him know that it is in peril of his office and order.

[1] *Materials*, vii, 217.

In this matter we refuse all appeal and every occasion of malignancy."

Whatever may be the date of the first letter and whatever the cause of the inconsistency which was the grievous weakness of the papal court through all these years, one cannot wonder at the indignant eloquence of the "co-exiles of Thomas" in the letter which they addressed to Cardinal Albert.[1] During six years they had been persecuted, and neglected by the Pope. To whomsoever had given him the ill advice on which he had acted he might well say, "Get thee behind me, Satan, for thou savourest not the things which be of God." The Curia, shamelessly open to bribes, was the real cause of the long exile, of the neglect of the people destitute of Christ's word, of the corruption of good men by "the Roman way." To such complaints there was no answer. No one has asserted that the papal Curia was honest or uncorrupt.

On June 14th, 1170, Roger crowned the young king in Westminster Abbey. The night before he had received the Pope's inhibition, and a letter from Becket forbidding him to do so, though the ports had been strictly watched by the king's orders. The papal prohibition which Becket sent was probably conveyed by a female hand—that of a nun who either bore the name Idonea or was merely designated by the archbishop as his dear daughter apt and meet for the work of danger. His letter to her is characteristic—[2]

---

[1] *Materials*, vii, 283.

[2] *Ibid.* 307. It has been generally treated as written at the time of Roger of York's suspension, but that letter was sent by a man, and the editors are probably right in attributing this to the present occasion.

"God hath chosen the weak things of the world to confound the mighty.

"The pride of Holofernes which exalted itself against God, when the warriors and the priests failed, was extinguished by the valour of a woman; when Apostles fled and denied their Lord, women attended Him in His sufferings, followed Him after His death, and received the first-fruits of the Lord's Resurrection. We trust that you also are animated with their zeal. God grant that you may pass into their society. The Spirit of love hath cast out fear from your heart, and will bring it to pass that the things which the need of the Church demands of you, arduous though they be, shall appear not only possible but easy.

"Having this hope, therefore, of your zeal in the Lord, I command you, and for the remission of your sins enjoin on you, that you deliver the letters, which I send you from his holiness the Pope to our venerable brother Roger, archbishop of York, in the presence, if possible, of our brethren and fellow bishops; and if not, in the face of all who happen to be present. Moreover, lest by any collusion the original instrument should be suppressed, deliver a transcript of it to be read by the bystanders, and open to them its intentions, as the messenger will instruct you.

"My daughter, a great prize is offered for your toil—remission of sins, a fruit that perisheth not—the crown of glory, which, in spite of all the sins of their past lives, the blessed sinners the Magdalene and the Egyptian have received from Christ their Lord.

"The Mother of Mercy will be with you, and will entreat her Son, Whom she bore for the sins of the world, God and Man, to be the leader, companion, and the patron of your journey. He who burst the bonds of hell, and curbed the violence of devils, can restrain the hands of the impious lest any should hurt you.

"Farewell, Bride of Christ, and ever think on His presence with you."

Roger, bishop of Worcester, the king's first cousin, had been prevented by the Norman justiciar from crossing to England, as he had been ordered to do. Henry II when he returned to Normandy met him three miles out of Falaise—a place which might remind them both that the lineage of the one was not much less spotted than that of the other—and bitterly reproached him, for he knew, very likely, that Thomas had also forbidden him to go; very sharp words passed on both sides, and the courage of the old bishop may well have warned the king that public feeling had become more and more decisively against him. When some of the courtiers tried to truckle to Henry by abusing his cousin he turned angrily upon one of them, a Gascon knight, with the tongue of his race, and said: "Do you think, you base fellow, that if I say what I choose to my kinsman and my bishop that you or any other may dishonour him with your tongue? I can hardly keep my hands from your eyes: neither you nor the others may say a word against the bishop." Henry in fact had begun to see that he might do well to take the advice of his honest kinsman, so he made him ride back with him to his lodging and "after dinner," says Fitz-Stephen, "the king and the bishop talked in private and in amity together, and concerning a reconciliation with the archbishop."

It was high time. Louis, enraged that his daughter should not have been crowned with her young husband, was threatening war. The Pope was besieged with supplications and denunciations on all sides, and it was certain that he could not condone the flat disobedience. Becket quite plainly announced that the threatened interdict would now be issued.

By the end of June, Henry was at Falaise. There the legates came to him and gave him "commonitory" letters from the Pope. He still held out about the kiss. He began his restless hurrying over his domains, so characteristic a resort in a time of stress. Two days later he was probably at Argentan; on the 6th he was at La Ferté Bernard, where he met Thibault of Blois; a little later he was at Vendôme and saw King Louis. Meanwhile the legates had come to Sens, and with William the archbishop had seen Becket. They prevailed on him again to meet the king, when he would be with Louis, in the friendly country of Chartres. On July 20th, two days before S. Mary Magdalen's festival, they met on the open plain between La Ferté, Villeneuil, and Fréteval, on the frontiers, that is, of Louis's land of Chartres and the county of Vendôme.

Fitz-Stephen tells the tale briefly, Herbert more briefly still. Becket's own account is the best. It is to be found in a letter to the Pope announcing, in the happiest vein, the end of his long sorrows and the reconciliation with his friend.[1] He begins with a cry of rejoicing that "God hath looked with an eye of compassion on the Church and at length hath turned her sorrow into joy." If Henry had been successful the

[1] *Materials*, vii, 326.

liberty of the Church would have been entirely destroyed, the Roman pontiff would have been unknown
in England, and the privileges of the Church would
have been blotted out without hope of recovery. It
was the threat of interdict and the knowledge that
"Frederick, the so-called emperor," was not spared
which brought the king to submission. And complete
submission it was.

"For concerning the customs for which he used
with such pertinacity to contend, he did not presume
to speak one word. He exacted no oath from one or
from any of us: he yielded to us the possessions which
he had taken away on account of this dissension, as we
had set them down on a schedule; he promised peace
and security and return from exile to all our companions, and even the kiss if we desired to press him
so far. In every article he appeared vanquished, insomuch that he was called perjured by some who bade him
swear that he would not that day admit us to the kiss."

Then he describes the scene—his own arrival with
the archbishop of Sens, Henry's rushing forward
through the crowd, with uncovered head, and offering
the first salutation, and then his long talk with such
friendly intimacy that it seemed as if there had never
been any division.

"And almost everyone who was present, with the
most joyous amazement glorified God, tears bedewing
the cheeks of many, and blessed the blessed Magdalen,
on whose day it was, that the king was turned from
the former ways, to restore joy to his whole land and
peace to the Church. We corrected him, with such
moderation as was fitting; we plainly showed him the

ways wherein he was going, and the perils which beset him on every side; we besought and warned him to repent and, bringing forth worthy fruits of penance and making open compensation to the Church, which he had not slightly injured, to purge his conscience and redeem his reputation, for from evil counsellors rather than from the motion of his own will both had suffered much hurt. And when he had heard all this not only with patience and also with kindness, and promised amendment, we added that it was necessary for his welfare and for the security and preservation to his children of the power which God had given him that he should give satisfaction to his mother the Church of Canterbury for the matter wherein he had of late grievously wounded her."

And then they embarked on a constitutional discussion as to the right to crown kings. Henry could point to the coronation of William the Conqueror by Ealdred of York, Becket could explain it through the schismatic intrusion of Stigand into the see of Canterbury. Henry I had been crowned by the bishop of Hereford: here Becket's history was at fault; but Anselm was in exile and when he returned Henry came with his diadem and asked him to place it on his head, for only the necessity for immediate coronation had made him allow the breach of the privilege of Canterbury. Then they spoke of the young king, for whom Becket expressed much affection, and Henry with bright face and cheerful voice said that he had a right to give such love, for he himself had given his boy to Becket as a son, and the lad's affection for him was such that he could not endure to look on the face of any of his enemies.

"Then leaping from my horse, I would have humbled myself at his feet, but he seized the stirrup and compelled me to remount, and seemed to shed tears while he said 'What more? My archbishop, let us restore again our old love to each other; let us each show the other what good he can, and be forgetful of the former hatred. But, I beseech you, show me honour in the sight of those who now watch afar off.' And passing over to them he said (because he saw that some of them, whom the bearer of this will indicate to you, were lovers of discord and incentors of hatred), so that he might stop the mouths both of them and of all who should speak evil, 'If I, when I find the archbishop prepared to every good thing, should not be myself good to him, then were I the worst of all men, and I should prove the evil things that are said of me to be true. Nor do I believe that any advice is more honourable or useful than that I study to surpass him in kindness and charity.'"

So they parted for the moment, till Becket was to make his formal request for restitution. It was made, and it was accepted, and they talked together familiarly till nightfall, as of old. Becket added that he did not fear that the king would not keep his word, unless evil counsellors misled him. Arnulf of Lisieux suggested that all who had been excommunicated should be absolved; the archbishop answered that this could not be done without distinction, and that satisfaction must be made. Henry issued a formal act of reconciliation and restoration, promising true peace and firm security, and all the possessions which he held when he was first made archbishop.

The discussions had spread over two days. But then there was delay. Henry fell ill, and when he recovered seemed in no hurry to fulfil his promises. When they met at Tours he avoided giving the kiss—which he had not given—by having a requiem sung instead of the ordinary mass, so that there should be no kiss. And then he got on his horse and rode away so quickly that Thomas could scarce catch him, and when he did they had sharp words. And so again at Chaumont there was an evasion. But orders were sent over to England to the young king to see that the archbishop's property was restored; yet even then this was not done till the king's officers had got the Michaelmas rents. So Becket complained, and Alexander gave him formal authority, as legate, to lay censure, without option of appeal, on any (saving the persons of the king, queen, and their children) who should not restore possession or do justice. The pretensions of York still remained: Becket seems to have claimed that he should admit his primacy. He saw that peace was not really made. "I believe," he wrote to the Pope, "that I shall return to England, but whether for peace or for pain I know not, but what our lot shall be is ordained of God." To Henry he wrote more sharply as to the delay—[1]

"It is known to the Inspector of hearts, the Judge of souls, the Avenger of crimes, Christ, in what purity and sincerity we made peace with you, believing that we should be met with singleness of heart and good faith. For what else, my most serene lord, could we conceive from your words which your kindness addressed to us, either to convince or to pacify us? You sent letters to

[1] *Materials*, vii, 393.

my lord the king, your son, that he should restore to us and to our adherents all the possessions which we had before we left England; what idea could we form from them, but of benevolence, peace, and security? But lo! your honour is at stake, which, God knows, we value beyond your profit, and the sequel shows neither good faith nor singleness of heart. For the restitution, which you commanded to be made to us, is put off to the tenth day under pretence of Ranulf de Broc, whose presence your son's counsellors thought necessary to the performance of your orders. Who those counsellors are, and with what fidelity to you they have acted in this matter, will be a subject for your enquiry, when it shall seem good to you. We, however, are persuaded that these things are done to the injury of the Church and to the loss of your own credit and salvation, if you do not correct them. For the aforesaid Ranulf is, in the meantime, seizing on the property of the Church, and openly storing up in Saltwood Castle the victuals which he has taken from us; and as we have been told by those who can prove it to you whenever you shall demand it, he has boasted in the hearing of many, that we shall not long enjoy the peace which you have granted us, and he threatens to take away our life, before we have eaten one whole loaf in England. You know, my most serene lord, that the man who has the power to correct what is wrong and neglects it becomes a party to the crime. The above-named Ranulf can have nothing to do in the matter, unless backed by your wishes and supported by your authority. Your discretion will be made acquainted with the answer which he returns to the king your son's letter, and you will judge of it according to your good pleasure. And whereas the Church of Canterbury, which is the spiritual mother of the British Isles, is evidently perishing in consequence of the odium which falls on us, we will serve her at the peril of our own life; we will expose our own head, with God's permission, to that persecuting Ranulf and his accomplices; he shall kill us, not once but a thousand times, if God will only, by his grace, give us strength and patience to endure it.

"It was our intention, my lord, to return to you, but woe is me, necessity drives me to my suffering Church. I go thither by your licence and under your protection, to die in its behalf, unless your filial piety vouchsafe speedily to give me consolation. But whether we live or die, we are yours in the Lord, and ever will be: whatever may happen to us and ours, may God bless you and your children!"

It is plain that the strange sense of dread, the premonition which there is no reason at all to suppose was affected or unnatural, weighed down the spirits of the archbishop, who seemed to have won his case. In truth he had received only promises; and men knew what was the value of the promises of the Angevin king.

They had met twice since the reconciliation at Fréteval. The second time Becket had said, "My heart tells me that I shall see you no more in this life," and Henry answered, "Do you take me for a traitor?" "That be far from thee, my lord," were the last words of the archbishop to his old friend.

They were to have met again at Rouen early in November, but Henry wrote that he was detained by disturbances in Auvergne. He sent John of Oxford, schismatic and "jurator," to represent him. It could not have been pleasant to the man who had excommunicated him four years before. When he heard why he had come, he said, "How things change." In this unwelcome guardianship he prepared to return to his own land.

Many urged him not to go, Louis, among them, promising him so long as he lived "the riches of Gaul." But it would have been cowardly to delay. He said to the bishop of Paris, "I go to England to die." No one seems to have been ignorant of his forebodings.

On November 24th he went to Wissant. On the 30th he sent letters suspending the archbishop of York and excommunicating the bishops of London and Salisbury, or rather replacing them, by papal authority, under the sentences from which they had been irregularly released. The letters were delivered to the three prelates as they were waiting next day at Dover to cross to the king. On the same day Becket landed at Sandwich. Even the pilot had warned him. But from the moment of reconciliation at Fréteval he was determined to return to his see, whatever might befall.

CHAPTER XIII

THE MARTYRDOM

OUT of the voluminous records of these years of strife and out of the sheaves of letters which when all was over seemed to become almost sacred relics, there emerge a few personalities which time has been unable to efface. Henry, the great king, duke and count, whose vast territories were not wide enough for his unresting activities, a strong man with the wisdom of a statesman and a lawyer, impetuous, savage, relentless, treacherous, of unbridled passions and indomitable will: he is the commanding figure in the English history of his age. There can be no wonder that he was not a popular king: he was too restless, too heartless, too exacting in his demands on his servants, too fickle in his affections, too determined in his statecraft.

Round him clustered the ablest body of ministerial officials that medieval England had seen, judges, soldiers, ambassadors, financiers, priests, men who could turn their hands to any work and could do it well, who were devoted to him, who served him without sparing themselves, and learnt from him so well that they could carry on for years after his death the fabric of government which he had built up, when his own guiding brain was replaced by a recklessness which exaggerated one part of his nature and then by a treacherous baseness which parodied another.

In the Church there were still leaders, men who had filled a great place and some who would have filled it

if they had not been under the heel of one greater than
themselves; Henry of Winchester, trained as a Cistercian but practised as a statesman, now in his old age
unflinchingly on the side of the Church's claims as
represented by the Primate, but yet too eminent and
too grave in his silence to be oppressed by the Angevin
lord; Roger of York, growing lethargic in his vast
province but full of ambition and enmity to the last,
not overburdened by ecclesiastical scruple, a tool whom
men more astute might use; Gilbert of London, learned,
pedantic, scrupulous over mint and cumin, of restless
temper and untamed fire, denying ambition yet obviously critical, bitter, jealous, implacable; Jocelin of
Salisbury, timid and self-indulgent; Hilary of Chichester, vain and garrulous; Roger of Worcester, simple,
manly, obstinate, unlearned: these are the chief among
the ecclesiastical officers of the land. Below them there
are a herd of bishops, deans, canons, monks, who are
swayed to and fro by the news, or the danger, that
comes their way; but who veer steadily towards the
king's side, from that conservatism, that dread of thinking evil of dignities, which has ever been an ingrained
character—and often so beneficially—of the English
Church, but which led them, as in some other ways,
into time-serving, greediness of promotion, unwilling-
ness to pay the cost of uprightness. Yet, then as always,
men who served both Church and State could still
preserve their honour and their faith: Ralf of Dissay
was an example of the success, as John of Oxford of
the failure, to serve both the king and the cause of
right.

On the other side was the small band of Becket's

friends, small in England because persecuted almost out of existence, but stronger overseas because welcomed at foreign courts as men who suffered for principle, and men, too, of wisdom and wit, leaders of thought or examples of piety. From these came many of the biographers of the archbishop, as from them came a great mass of the correspondence which agitated the palaces and monasteries of Europe during the years of strife. No more gracious figure is there among them than the gentle, kindly, wise, John of Poitiers, and none more expressive of the best thought of the time than John of Salisbury, political philosopher and ecclesiastic, brilliant writer and man of sound judgment and true heart. All these, and many more, scores of writers and thinkers and men of action who filled a great place in the history of their day, revolved, for some part of their lives, round the central personage whose changeful and dramatic career filled men's minds and hearts for generations after he had been on men's lips as "second after the king in four realms."

Of Becket himself, in spite of all the records, and after centuries of discussion, it is still more difficult to judge than of any of his contemporaries. But as his life unfolds itself in his own letters and in the memorials of his friends it is not difficult to see a personality of striking force, which it is easy to misjudge, and which lends itself almost obstinately to harsh criticism. Thomas Becket was a strong man and a genuine man, not so strong perhaps as his master and enemy, but vastly more sincere. What his mind saw to do he did with all his might; and wherever what seemed to be the voice of duty called him there unflinchingly he went. When he was the king's servant he obeyed his master implicitly and trusted his judgment more absolutely than he trusted his own; but criticisms and objections of others, good clerks and saintly men though they might be, he passed by as the idle wind. So when he became arch-bishop. He had already an ideal of what a primate should be, how absolutely he should be devoted to the interests of the Church, how meekly and resolutely he should be set to deny himself and to walk humbly, as monks walked, in the way of the Lord. But humility he always found hard to learn: he was too eager to know what was right, too vehement to do it, to consider into what paths of personal assertion the call might seem to lead him. Of conscious striving to assume a character which he did not really possess, a minute and unpre-judiced study finds it quite impossible to accuse him. He never dreamed of playing a part as an actor plays one: a character seemed to be set upon him by his con-secration, and he yielded—not without hesitations and restlessness—to its impress. He deliberately and pain-fully set himself, not to assume a part, not to qualify for a position, but to accept what the ecclesiastical theories of his age, exclusive, ascetic, separatist, set up before him.

Out of the lives of the saints which he read, and out of the stress of conflict in which he found himself involved, there seemed to rise the vision of a character, determined, ascetic yet humane, gentle towards the weak, but unyielding to the proud, which took Christ for Ruler and Captain, perhaps even more than for Example and Pattern. There was the ideal, and to-wards the making of it went the histories of holy men and the memories of his own predecessors—Old Testament heroes, the Apostles Paul and Peter, popes like Hildebrand, primates like Lanfranc as well as like Anselm. It was hard for Becket's own stubborn nature to fit itself into the mould; but he tried with all his might and main to make himself worthy.

Though he had a personal charm of manner, of brightness and affectionateness, which attracted men to him and fixed their friendship as years went on into a real devotion, he never conquered an abruptness, an impetuosity, a passionate assertiveness which made him bitter enemies. He had a warm and true heart: pity that he wore it on his sleeve. An utter contrast to Henry of Anjou, Thomas Becket could never suppress or even conceal his emotions: it seemed to him a sort of disloyalty to truth to attempt it. Acutely sensitive in mind as in his power of hearing, Becket was one of those men who suffer inevitably in the judgment of those who disagree with their opinions. Sometimes, as he did, they arouse bitter animosities; always they lead hard lives.

Becket's hard life was now drawing towards its end. On the first day of December, 1170, it seemed as if his troubles were over and he had come to his own land in peace. For ensign his ship bore the primatial cross, set up as it drew nigh to land. The fisher-folk and the poor of Sandwich saw the holy sign and gathered to the beach; they ran into the water to draw the boat to land; they knelt on the shingle among the waves to beg their archbishop's blessing—one lad among them, George by name, remembered it in after years, says William of Canterbury: some wept, and many cried, "Blessed is the father of orphans, the judge of widows, blessed is he that cometh in the name of the Lord!"

But hardly had he landed when there was a rude contrast to the affection of the poor. The sheriff of Kent, Reginald of Warenne, and Ranulf de Broc, who had come from Dover, where they had seen the excommunicated bishops, beset the primate, demanded that the bishops should be absolved, and, but for the sympathetic crowd and the judicious moderation of John of Oxford, might have attempted violence. The archbishop made a quick and dignified protest, and they went away.

The next morning the primate went the twelve miles to Canterbury. It was a triumphal procession.

"When it was known at Canterbury that the archbishop had landed," says William Fitz-Stephen,[1] "they all in the city rejoiced from the least to the greatest. They decorated the Cathedral. They put on silks and costly raiment. They prepared a great feast for many people. The archbishop was received in solemn procession. The church resounded with hymns and music, the hall with rejoicing, the city everywhere with fulness of joy."

Herbert of Bosham tells that as he drew nigh to the city he was received as a lamb for a burnt offering, or as an angel sent from heaven, with ovation or with prayer. Herbert loves these quaintnesses of speech. "But why do I say with ovation? Rather Christ's poor received him as the Lord's anointed. So wherever the archbishop passed crowds of poor, small and great, old and young, ran together, some throwing themselves in

[1] *Materials*, iii, 119.

his way, others taking their garments and strewing them in the way, crying and exclaiming, 'Blessed is he that cometh in the name of the Lord.' Likewise the parish priests with their flocks met him in procession with their crosses, saluting their father, and, begging his blessing, called out again that oft-repeated cry, 'Blessed is he that cometh in the name of the Lord.'...You would have said, had you seen, that the Lord a second time approached His Passion, and that among the children and the poor and the rejoicing people again He Who died once at Jerusalem for the salvation of the whole world was now again ready to die at Canterbury for the English Church. And though the way was short yet among the thronging and pressing crowds scarce in that day could he reach Canterbury, where he was received with the sound of trumpets, with psalms and hymns and spiritual songs by the poor of Christ, his children, and by his holy monastery with the reverence and veneration due to their father."

He passed barefoot through the streets[1] and went

---

[1] Canterbury to-day retains many a noble memorial of that distant time, many a building that Becket's eyes must have looked on in the last weeks of his life. From the first it had been the ecclesiastical capital, and the dignity, splendour and beauty of the English Church had been concentrated there. In Becket's day it was not the capital of the kingdom. That honour then belonged to Winchester and soon would belong to London, but in neither of these famous cities has there ever been so rich a store of the ecclesiastical glory of the early Middle Age. Still the Norman keep survives, though in ruin: still the church of S. Martin on the hill marks the spot where the earliest English Christians worshipped. The church of S. Dunstan has a memory of king Henry's penetential pilgrimage to the shrine of Becket, and through the earlier Westgate he passed that day. Ancient walls and churches and gardens recall the day when the archbishop passed by them in his hour of short-lived triumph.

straight to the cathedral church. "Then," continues Herbert, "might you see at his first coming into the cathedral the face of this man, which many seeing marked and wondered at, for it seemed as though his heart aflame showed also in his face."

In the choir he received the monks, one by one, giving them the kiss of peace; he had prepared the way by sending John of Salisbury to absolve and reconcile those who had communicated with excommunicates during his absence. Herbert said to him, "Now, my lord, it is no matter when you depart hence, for in you to-day the Bride of Christ has won the victory. Christ conquers, Christ reigns, Christ rules." The archbishop looked on him, but answered nothing.

Then in the chapter-house he preached a sermon, says Fitz-Stephen. "He preached a most instructive sermon, taking for text, 'Here we have no continuing city, but we seek one to come.'"[1]

The next day came the sheriff of Kent with Ranulf de Broc and others, clerk and lay, and they demanded the absolution of the bishops against whom, they said, he had plotted. He answered, in a phrase he had often used, that they wished to drink his blood, "and they will"; but absolve them he could not without the customary oath. This their emissaries, taking stand on the Constitutions, refused. So they departed unsatisfied; and the archbishop of York said he would spend money lavishly at the papal court to overwhelm his rival.

After a week at Canterbury Becket determined to see the young Henry, his old pupil. He sent to him three destriers, whose beauty Fitz-Stephen eulogises, and

[1] Heb. xiii, 14.

prepared to follow the propitiatory gift. During the latter part of 1170 the young king was at Winchester. Becket sent Richard, prior of Dover (afterwards archbishop) to see him there, but he refused to see the archbishop. The lad had his father's orders, and he was weak enough himself. As "Benedict of Peterborough" says later, he was like wax. It was a bitter blow. Becket was ordered to return to Canterbury. Already he had passed through Rochester, where Walter, the brother of his old patron, Theobald, and once archdeacon of Canterbury, received him with stately welcome, and came to Southwark, to the palace of Henry of Winchester, where crowds of visitors, clerk and lay, made him a kind of court. In the midst of this triumph it was startling to meet with a rebuff from the young king whose father had represented him as so warmly his friend. It was a sign that the old king had still a strong political party at his back and that the archbishop was never to be forgiven by the partisans of the Constitutions. Already a woman in Southwark had cried out, "Archbishop, beware of the knife."

He returned to Canterbury. On the way he stayed at his manor of Harrow, where first he had come to Theobald. Friends came freely to him, among them the rich and generous abbat of S. Albans, who paid on his behalf another ineffectual visit to the young Henry. Gladly, said the primate, would he have spent Christmas in the abbey of the first English martyr: the record of his last sayings to their ruler was kept in the great abbey. But foes were equally active. Ranulf de Broc had seized a ship-load of French wines sent to him and beaten and imprisoned the sailors; but an order from the young

Henry caused amends to be made. When he was again at Canterbury the nobles kept away from him, and the Brocs attacked and beat his men, stole his deer, robbed his convoys of provisions, and insulted him by cutting off the tail of one of his poor tenant's horses.

In the midst of his petty vexations he wrote a letter to the Pope:[1] it was his last, or at least his last on any matter of personal concern. He told the whole tale of his return, and of the trouble that he found awaiting him; and he ended by repeating the justification of his action with regard to the excommunicated prelates: "That the same bishops had before been excommunicated by me, and had not obtained absolution, though they had besought with much solicitation, until they had taken this oath. And if my sentence could not be dissolved without an oath from the bishops, much less could yours which was far stronger and incomparably more potent than mine or any other mortal power. At which answer (so those who were present told me) the bishops were so much moved that they decided to come to me and to receive absolution after the manner of the Church, not considering it safe that they should for the sake of preserving the customs of the realm impugn the apostolic decrees. But that enemy of peace and disturber of the Church, the archbishop of York, dissuaded them, counselling that they should go to the king, who was their protector, and send messengers to the young king that I intended to depose him, when, God is my witness, if he were well-disposed to the Church, I would rather that he had not one realm only but the largest and the most of any king on earth. My archdeacon was

[1] *Materials*, vii, 401.

the ensign bearer of this legation, since the archbishop of York and the two bishops hasted to cross the sea that they might win over the king and excite his anger against the Church. And they caused to be summoned six clergy of the vacant sees that in the king's presence by their counsel, contrary to the canons, and in a foreign land, in the absence of their brethren, the election to the vacant bishoprics in my province should be made. But if I refuse to consecrate those so elected, they will have an occasion of sowing discord between me and the king. For there is nothing which they fear more than the peace of the Church, lest perchance their works should be seen and their excesses corrected. My messenger will supply many things which for the sake of brevity I have not inserted in this letter. May it please you favourably to hear my petition. My dearest father, may your holiness ever fare well."

So the Christmas festival came on.[1] Warnings came to him from every quarter, but he would never again leave his diocese. He resumed the habits of his first days as archbishop, sitting in his court as judge, and going to the choir offices in the cathedral church. On Christmas Eve he celebrated mass at midnight. Again he celebrated high mass on the festival itself and preached on the Vulgate text, "On earth peace to men of good will." It was a contrast to the absence of peace where men's wills were evil; and he spoke of the martyr whom Canterbury had already produced, S. Alphege, and

---

[1] For the last days of Becket and the martyrdom there is no more vivid picture, nor (on the whole) any so careful and complete as that of Dean Stanley's *Memorials of Canterbury*, which I have had constantly at hand while writing these pages.

declared that it might not be long before there was another. Then he indignantly denounced the men of evil will, and ended by excommunicating the brothers Broc for their outrages, and two clerks for their seizure of his churches of Harrow and Throwley. Says Herbert—

"Truly had you seen these things you would have said that you saw face to face that animal of the prophet's vision, with the face of a lion and the face of a man." The day ended with peaceful festivity. "He who had shown himself so devout at the Lord's Table showed himself happy, as was his wont, at the table of this world; and it being the Feast of the Nativity, though a Friday, he partook of meat as on another day, thus showing that at such a festival it was more religious to eat than to abstain."

It was the last time the faithful Herbert was to be at his side. On S. Stephen's Day the master called "the disciple who wrote these things" and told him to go to the Frankish king and the archbishop of Sens and tell them what fate had befallen their friend—how there was no peace but rather war. Herbert could not keep back his tears, and said, "If I go I know that I shall see thee in the flesh no more. I was determined to abide faithfully with thee, and now thou seekest to deprive me of my share in thine end, who have been with thee in thy temptations: now I shall not be a sharer of thy glory who have been a sharer of thy woe."

Becket answered, also with tears: "Not so, my son, not so; thou shalt not be deprived of the fruit, who fulfillest the command of thy father, and dost follow his counsel. Nevertheless what thou sayest and mournest

is true indeed, that thou shalt see me in the flesh no
more; and nevertheless I will that thou depart, especially because the king hath thee in the cause of the
Church more suspect than the rest."

On S. John Evangelist's Day they parted for the
last time. With Herbert went Llewelyn, the candid
cross-bearer.

Meanwhile the bishops had gone to the king, and
Roger of Pont l'Evêque (says Fitz-Stephen) had told
him that he would never have peace so long as Thomas
lived. Henry burst forth in rage. "Fools and dastards
have I nominated in my realm who are faithless to their
lord and none of them will avenge him on this low
clerk." It was not the first time he had said such words,
but now there were men at hand who would act on
them. Four knights of the household, Reginald Fitz-
Urse, William de Tracy, Hugh de Morville, Richard
Breton, set off instantly, urged, says Guernes, by Roger
of York. They arrived, by different ways, at the archbishop's castle of Saltwood, now occupied by the Brocs,
on the Holy Innocent's Day. The king sent after them
to stop them, and with his message despatched an order
for the arrest of the archbishop. But on the next day
they were at Canterbury with a band of followers,
collected in the king's name. Clarembald, abbat of
S. Augustine's, received them into his house.[1] All

---

[1] As an illustration of the little care with which popular writers
have studied the life of Becket it is perhaps worth noting that when
this book first appeared a reviewer wrote that in the case of the
archbishop there was "the rivalry which almost every medieval
bishop has with his chapter carried to its furthest point. The
dean, or, as Mr Hutton more correctly calls him, the abbat, put
up the four fighting men who had come to Canterbury to kill

night they had sat planning their work. They were ready to execute it. A citizen came to the archbishop to warn him. He answered, "They will find me ready to die. Let them do as they will. I know that I shall die a death of violence; but they shall not kill me outside my church."

About four o'clock in the afternoon the knights—"non jam milites, sed miseri ac miserabiles"—came to the palace. Dinner was over, the archbishop had withdrawn into an inner room and was at business, but a crowd still lingered in the hall. The knights were politely welcomed and the servants offered them food. It was scornfully rejected, and they demanded to see the archbishop.

They were admitted, and found him sitting on a couch. He had prepared himself, men thought afterwards, for his end. He had said matins at midnight in his own room, and then looking out of the window had asked if he could reach Sandwich by daybreak. Easily, he was told; but then they heard him say, "God's will

S. Thomas." And he added that "these conditions are strange.... They require explanation, and this neither Mr Hutton nor most English writers provide." Neither I nor any other writer could possibly explain the conditions which the reviewer thus stated, for they did not exist. There was no rivalry between Becket and his chapter. They were firm friends. There was no dean of the chapter nor do I call him an abbat. He was a prior. The abbat who "put up" the "fighting men" had no more to do with the cathedral chapter than the dean of Westminster has with S. Paul's. He was abbat of S. Augustine's, which was, and is, a very different place from the cathedral. And he was a lifelong enemy of Becket. I am glad to possess the letter an eminent historian wrote to me at the time in which he said "the review was the most pompous and incompetent piece of impertinence I have read for a long time."

be done: Thomas will wait on God's ordering in his own church." He had been present at mass and visited all the altars, made his confession to the Benedictine Thomas of Maidstone, and had thrice undergone the discipline. Besides this, there was that terrible scourge which the strange asceticism of the age advised, the hair shirt, which he wore with its moving life.[1] At dinner he had eaten pheasant, and a monk had remarked on his cheerfulness. He answered, "One who must go to his Maker should needs be cheerful." It was a saying which a few hours later bore a new interpretation. One writer adds that he had drunk more wine than usual, and when it was quietly whispered to him, said, "He who must lose much blood, must needs drink much wine." The knights were admitted. Then let Edward Grim, who had but recently come to him from Cambridge and was now with him till the last, tell the story, with comments and additions which we may glean from others—

"They sat for a long time in silence and did not salute the archbishop or speak to him. Nor did the man of wise counsel salute them immediately they came in, that according to the Scripture, 'By thy words thou shalt be justified,' he might discover their intentions from their questions. After awhile, however, he turned to them, and carefully scanning the face of each one he greeted them in a friendly manner, but the wretches, who had made a treaty with death, answered his greeting with curses, and ironically prayed that God might

[1] A fragment of this is preserved in a monstrance in the sacristy of Santa Maria Nera at Lucca. Mr T. Brocklebank kindly sent me a photograph in 1910.

help him. At this speech of bitterness and malice the man of God coloured deeply, now seeing that they had come for his hurt."

Fitz-Urse said they had a message from the king. Becket had sent away his clerks, but now he called them back, that all might hear. In the moment when the knights were alone with him the thought came to one of them to kill him with the shaft of his primatial cross, but the others returned quickly. Then Fitz-Urse reproached the archbishop for the excommunications, and said that they proved that he would take away the crown from the young king. Becket said that rather would he wish him all the crowns of the earth and help him to win them by right and justice. Nor was there cause of offence in that his people had welcomed him so warmly and followed him in crowds. Even now he was ready to satisfy the king in all things, but he had been forbidden his presence. But the excommunications he could not take off: he could not loose those whom the Pope had bound. Then they said it was the king's command that he should depart from the kingdom with all his men. He answered: "Let your threats cease and your wranglings be stilled. I trust in the King of Heaven, Who for His own suffered on the Cross: for from this day no one shall see the sea between me and my church. I came not to fly; here he who wants me shall find me. And it befits not the king so to command; sufficient are the insults which I and mine have had from the king's men, without more threats."

"You have basely followed your own passion and turned out of the Church his servants. We will stand by our lord's orders," was their answer.

He said, "No one shall have mercy at my hands who disobeys the orders of the Roman see or the laws of the Church of Christ, and," he added, "I wonder at you, who are bound to me"; for Fitz-Urse, Tracy, and Morville had been his men.

Then they rose angrily to their feet and said, "You have spoken in peril of your head."

"Come you to kill me?" he answered. "I have committed my cause to the Judge of all; I am not moved by threats, and as your swords are ready so is my soul for martyrdom. Seek him who flies: I stand firm in the Lord's battle."

They went out, Fitz-Urse calling on all to hold the archbishop that he might not escape. He said, "Here, here shall you find me," laying his hand on his neck.

The monks urged him to fly, while the knights, binding his porter and one of his armed men, had gone into the city to collect soldiers and weapons. John of Salisbury said, "You will never take anyone's counsel. Why must you make them more angry by following them to the door?"

"What would you have me do? I have already taken counsel, and I know what I ought to do. We must all die, and the fear of death must not turn us from righteousness. I am more ready to die for God and righteousness and the Church's liberty than they are to kill me."

The doors had been barred when the knights went out, but they found their way back through the orchard by another way. Thomas went calmly, waiting even for his cross to be carried before him by a clerk of Auxerre, to vespers in the cathedral church. The

private door, not often used, that led from the palace
to the cloisters, was found closed: the court was filled
with armed men, so they did not go in the usual way.
But two cellarmen of the monastery opened the door
from within, and the crowd of clerks hurried the archbishop on. He went along the north side of the cloisters,
then eastward, as the cloister turned—and for a moment
detached himself from the pressure by going into the
chapter house—and so by the door of the north transept
below the steps which led up into the choir.

The service was being sung, but it was interrupted
by boys who cried out that soldiers were breaking into
the monastery and the palace. Many of the monks fled;
but the archbishop, still standing outside, commanded
them to go on with the service. They fell back from
the doorway, and, asking what they feared, he turned
back to see the armed men who, the terrified crowd
cried out, were in the cloisters. "I will go out to them,"
he said. As he spoke the knights rushed along the south
side of the cloisters. In spite of his protests the monks
clapped to the door, and barred it, leaving outside some
of the clerks who had followed him, and tried to drag
the primate up into the choir. He broke from them
and called out loudly, "Away, ye cowards! On your
obedience I charge you not to shut the door: the Church
must not be made into a castle." He opened the door
himself, and called in the monks—"Come in, quicker,
quicker!"—and then turned to meet his murderers.
Fitz-Stephen tells how of all his clerks only three stood
by him: Robert of Merton, the oldest of his friends,
Edward Grim, and Fitz-Stephen himself. It was five
o'clock on a winter night, and the others easily hid

THE DEATH OF BECKET

themselves in the darkness: so, they thought, might he do in the hiding-places they had shown him. But he stood quite unmoved. The door was open, and the knights, with Hugh of Horsea, a degraded clerk, rushed in.

As they came the three friends were urging the archbishop up the steps from the transept on the western stairway which leads into the choir. At the south-west of the transept where he stood, and which still, though altered, remains in much of its old features and now bears the name of "the martyrdom," was the altar of the Blessed Virgin, at the east end of the north aisle of the nave; at the east end of the chapel the altar of S. Benedict; and in the middle was a pillar, which supported the gallery above leading to the chapel of S. Blasius. There, as they stood in the gathering darkness, let Edward Grim, one of the faithful three who stood by their lord, again take up the tale—[1]

"Inspired by fury the knights called out, 'Where is Thomas Becket, traitor to the king and realm?' As he answered not, they cried out the more furiously, 'Where is the archbishop?' At this, intrepid and fearless, as it is written, 'The just, like a bold lion, shall be without fear,' he descended from the stair where he had been dragged by the monks in fear of the knights, and in a clear voice answered, 'I am here, no traitor to the king, but a priest. Why do ye seek me?' And whereas he had already said that he feared them not, he added, 'So I am ready to suffer in His name Who redeemed me by His Blood: be it far from me to flee from your

---

[1] *Materials*, ii, 431 *sqq.* I follow the translation which I gave in my Bampton Lectures, *The English Saints*, pp. 258 *sqq.* (second edition), with a few words altered.

swords, or to depart from justice.' Having thus said, he turned to the right, under a pillar, having on one side the altar of the blessed Mother of God and ever Virgin Mary, on the other that of S. Benedict the Confessor: by whose example and prayers, having crucified the world with its lusts, he bore all that the murderers could do with such constancy of soul as if he had been no longer in the flesh. The murderers followed him: 'Absolve,' they cried, 'and restore to communion those whom you have excommunicated, and restore their powers to those whom you have suspended.' He answered: 'There has been no satisfaction, and I will not absolve them.' 'Then you shall die,' they cried, 'and receive what you deserve.' 'I am ready,' he replied, 'to die for my Lord, that in my blood the Church may obtain liberty and peace. But in the name of Almighty God, I forbid you to hurt my people whether clerk or lay.'"...

They wished to avoid the guilt of sacrilege, but they could not drag him from the pillar to which he clung; they had thought to kill him outside the church, or— as they afterwards said—to make a prisoner of him. They tried to put him on Tracy's shoulders, and so drag him out, but he resisted and Grim held him in his arms. The strong archbishop, strong still as when he unhorsed the knight at Toulouse, threw Tracy on the pavement. In vain cried Fitz-Urse, "Come with us, you are our prisoner." "I will not come, abominable wretch," was the answer; and with the word of shame, "pandar," the archbishop adjured him not to touch his lord to whom he owed fealty. In fierce rage Reginald waved his sword and cried "Strike!"

Grim thus continues: "Then the unconquered martyr, seeing the hour at hand which should put an end to this miserable life and give him straightway the crown of immortality promised by the Lord, inclined his neck as one who prays, and joining his hands he lifted them up, and commended his cause and that of the Church to God, to S. Mary, and to the blessed martyr Denys. Scarce had he said the words than the wicked knight, fearing lest he should be rescued by the people and escape alive, leapt upon him suddenly and wounded this lamb who was sacrificed to God on the head, cutting off the top of the crown which the sacred unction of the chrism had dedicated to God; and by the same blow he wounded the arm of him who tells this. For he, when the others, both monks and clerks, fled, stuck close to the sainted archbishop and held him in his arms till the one he interposed was almost severed.... Then he received a second blow on the head, but still stood firm. At the third blow he fell on his knees and elbows, offering himself a living victim, and saying in a low voice, 'For the name of Jesus and the protection of the Church I am ready to embrace death.' Then the third knight inflicted a terrible wound as he lay, by which the sword was broken against the pavement, and the crown, which was large, was separated from the head; so that the blood, white with the brain and the brain red with blood, dyed the surface of the virgin mother Church with the life and death of the confessor and martyr in the colours of the lily and the rose. The fourth knight prevented any from interfering so that the others might freely perpetrate the murder. As to the fifth, no knight but that clerk who had entered with the knights, that a fifth blow might not be wanting to the martyr who was in other things like unto Christ, put his foot on the neck of the holy priest and precious martyr, and, horrible to tell, scattered his brains and blood over the pavement, calling out to the rest, 'Let us away, knights; he will rise no more.'"

So the vigorous life was ended, and the strong soul, struggling almost to the last, was taken to the judgment of God. Over the city burst a great storm of thunder and lightning, and men's hearts failed them for fear.

The hours of horror and dismay that followed need not here be told. The knights fled, at first in triumph, afterwards, men said, in shame and remorse. Strange tales were told of their after life, due most of them to the imagination of the people, or the monks, who would not let such murderers live the ordinary life or die the common death of men.

When terror had at length subsided the monks took the body of their archbishop, marvelling at the sign of his asceticism which they discovered, and at the calm beauty of the face, as it were asleep with a calm smile on the lips. They collected some of the blood in little vessels: already a citizen had dipped a cloth in it, as the holy relic of a saint. A red glow from heaven, the Northern Light, hung over the great church and lighted up the choir where the body had been laid, and men thought they saw the right hand of the martyr raised in blessing of those whom he had left to be witnesses of his fate.

The next day, December 30th, 1170, the body was buried in the crypt, in a new marble tomb, behind the

THE SCENE OF THE MARTYRDOM

altar of the Blessed Virgin, and not far, it seems, from the tomb of S. Dunstan.[1] No mass was said: the altars were stripped, and for a year no voice of public prayer was heard in the great cathedral church where the blood of its archbishop had been shed.

[1] See Dart's *History and Antiq. of the Cathedral Church of Canterbury*, 1726, and appendix in Vol. ii, of Fr. Morris's *Life of S. Thomas*.

No one can follow the life of Becket without feeling that it is open to criticism at every point. The attempt to make of such a character a "plaster saint" fails utterly. He was violent, impetuous, resentful of injuries, impatient of opposition, bitter in tongue, stubborn in heart. But the conception of saintliness which involves impeccability is utterly foreign to the Christian idea; still less is it consistent with Christian history that one who is considered to have been a martyr should have lived a whole life of holiness. Becket was canonised within three years of his death, and no canonisation in English history was ever so popular, while none was more strictly justified according to the rules of the Western Church before the Reformation.

The archbishop who laid down his life on December 29th, 1170, was a brave strong man, who had lived a strenuous life. He was as sensitive as he was courageous. He had great personal influence, great power of fascination. But it was not these things, or the high place he filled during his years of power, that made him so famous for four centuries after his death. Rather did he become a popular English hero, and a maker of national history, because he was believed to have fought a good fight for the right, and to have died rather than yield.

To-day in England we have no sympathy with clerical separatism. Henry's ideal, of the equality of all men before the law, is ours. But the achievement of personal liberty, the establishment of constitutional rule as we know it, is very largely the result of the struggles of the Middle Ages for class privilege. There is no reason to suppose that the generality of mankind had a greater affection for the ministers of religion in the twelfth century than they have to-day. If the power of the clergy seemed greater then, it was open to abrupt exceptions and conclusions which have as certainly passed away. But clerical privilege, the right to be tried in separate courts, to make special rules in separate assemblies and to make them binding on the highest in the land, seemed to men then to be a not unreasonable claim, and it even became, as in Becket's days, a popular cry, because it was merged in the claim of liberty for each different class. Merchants, lawyers, villeins, barons, felt themselves in danger of being stifled by an overmastering central power, the power of an unrestrained and arbitrary king. Such a danger could only be averted by the struggle of each class in turn. And the Church alone could fight with any prospect of success, for it alone had a solidarity in different lands, and could invoke forces in its support which would prevent its isolation in one small quarter of the globe. If the barons tried to conquer, to rule men as they willed, they discovered that that was a game which the king also could play, and generally could play better. They could not resist him when they were alone. Still less could other classes, save only the estate of the Church. Thus it was that the poor looked to the Church for protection: her ideals were utterly different from those of the other classes, and when she rose to them men found shelter against oppression under the covering of her wings. Slowly by her action in defence of her own claims she made national liberty possible. So Stephen Langton, one of the heroes of English Liberty, who gave to Magna Carta what it had of national beneficence, found in Becket a predecessor whom he delighted to honour. So the citizens of London when they stood up against the kings called upon his name, as their fellow-citizen and the champion of liberty. And so Thomas of Canterbury ranked in the minds of men, for generations, as one of the makers of national history, because he had striven, as they thought, for freedom, the freedom which was won so gradually and as the result of so many struggles. Political liberty seemed to owe its origin not a little to ecclesiastical claims; but when it was won it could not tolerate any exceptional treatment of a class which might seem to substitute exclusiveness for freedom.

Becket had claimed rights for the Church as against the State. The claim, whether right or wrong, was simple enough in regard to Church courts and Church property. It was a claim as to which good men and wise men might at that day think differently. But it was not for this claim simply that Becket died. He died because he refused to take off a sentence of excommunication at the command of men who threatened his life. Whether the sentence was originally right or wrong does not enter into the question: no one can doubt that Becket, however wilfully, thought it right. But unquestionably it was within the spiritual not the secular sphere. Bossuet seized the real point when he declared in his sermon on S. Thomas that the discipline as well as the faith of the Church needed martyrs. The contention of the archbishop was that terms of communion can only be settled by the Church with which communion is held: they cannot be laid down by the State, whose province does not touch men's souls: still less can they be dictated by individuals. Here modern sentiment and modern judgment must be entirely on the archbishop's side. The Church must have as much right to fix its own limits as the State has to enforce its own obligations. If Anselm was right in the contest concerning ecclesiastical investitures, Becket was right in the contest concerning ecclesiastical censures. Thus, he took his place, by the insistent approbation of his contemporaries, among the saints of the English Church.

The claim to saintliness in the Middle Age was inevitably involved in an atmosphere of miracle. The age of Becket was an age of wonders. Men saw portents in the sky, in strange conjunction of events, in tales of hearsay that took on wonders as they passed from mouth to mouth—like the green children whom William of Newburgh, a man of most sound judgment, records to have appeared in his day. It has been well said that the men of those days looked for the supernatural to explain all events, however simple, and would have thought it impious to do otherwise. The step from this to belief that the goodness of a good cause must be attested by miracles is not a long one. Thus, within a very short time of the murder of Becket, a number of cures took place at Canterbury, and they were attributed to his merits. Drops of his blood, diluted with much water, were stored in bottles to give to the sick; and results which modern knowledge of psychology does not suffer us to consider impossible were declared to have followed.

Now at first there was no glory but rather danger to be apprehended from a declaration that the saintliness of the murdered man was proved by miracles. "In the spring of 1171 no one dared to mention the miracles abroad."[1] Soldiers of the Brocs guarded the gates and bridges to watch those who came as pilgrims to the cathedral. It was the poor folk of Canterbury who gradually made them known: they "persisted, so to speak, in being cured, at a time when such cure was unfashionable or even dangerous."[2]

The first portents were visions. Thrice the saint appeared to Benedict of Canterbury. It was while still, even in the monastery of his own cathedral, some doubted, as Grim tells us, whether he ought to be regarded as a martyr, "having been slain as the reward of his own obstinacy." On the third day after the murder a Sussex knight's wife, appealing to Becket as Saint Thomas, found her sight, which had been affected by weakness, restored to her, and in six days she was able to rise from her bed.

By Easter time miraculous cures had become common, and within a few months they grew from what might easily be explained to what it is impossible to believe. Imagination gave place to invention. But still there remained the mysterious influence of a great personality, acting on the faith of men, and working

---

[1] Dr Edwin A. Abbott, *S. Thomas of Canterbury, his Death and Miracles*, i, 223, a work of the greatest interest which in some respects I closely follow in the pages dealing with the miracles.
[2] *Ibid*

effectively in a way which it is mere question-begging either to describe as supernatural or to explain by credulity or superstition.

Within three or four years, a biographer was able to write that "The glory of the noble martyr to-day far surpasses the insults he formerly endured. So much are the towns and villages, the castles and cottages, throughout England all affected by it, that nearly everyone from the least to the greatest desires to visit and honour his sepulchre. The same spirit of devotion has attracted thither clerics and laymen, poor and rich, the common people and nobles, fathers and mothers with their children, masters with their servants. On the roads leading to Canterbury, in the hostelries and inns, one constantly sees as eager crowds as on the public market days in the largest cities. By night no less than day, in winter as well as summer, travellers continue to come, and it even seems that the more severe the season is, the greater the pleasure they find in accomplishing their pilgrimage."[1] Already the famous Canterbury pilgrimage was begun.

The occurrences at Canterbury, the healing of the sick by the merits of S. Thomas, and the cures effected by Canterbury water, are beyond the scope of biography.[2] With no scepticism of explanation, which

[1] "Anonymus Lambethensis" in *Materials*, ii, 140, 141 (paraphrased). The date of this is unfixed, but as Henry's reconciliation at Avranches, 1172, is mentioned but not his pilgrimage to Canterbury, July, 1174, and the author is stated to have been an eyewitness of the murder, the work may reasonably be considered to be of about the date suggested above.

[2] For the subject of medieval miracles in general I may venture to refer the reader to *The English Saints* (*Bampton Lectures*, 1903), appendix to lecture vi, pp. 277–98, second edition.

modern science would condemn as foolish, we may simply assert that in most discussions of the matter we have the old confusion on the subject of the supernatural. Bishop Butler has long ago told the world that man's ideas of what is natural or supernatural are relative to his knowledge of the works of God. We are as yet only on the fringe of the vast subject of mysterious cures. If we cannot idly brush them away as "faith-healing," it is because we do not in the least know what "faith-healing" is. The history of the miracles of S. Thomas has its modern parallels—yet not exact parallels—in the nineteenth century. The declaration that those who do not believe a special "miracle" to have been wrought in these cases are un-Christian sceptics is untrue: they are often earnest believers who recognise their ignorance of much in God's world both of nature and grace. We are not atheists because we see no reason to believe that God has specially distinguished the water of Lourdes and the last fifty years of our era. Nor do we cease to be historical students because we deal with the miracles of S. Thomas as illustrations of the deep influence of his life and death, his character and his principles.

It had been asked, "Did the miracles result from the man or from the circumstances?"[1] Was it the nature of his death that brought the miracles? If he had died in his bed, he as mere archbishop Thomas Becket, it is said, "would have rested, an unhelpful corpse, with other commonplace corpses of ordinary archbishops in an unvisited grave."

"This is so far true," says Dr Abbott, "that we must

[1] Dr Abbott, *op. cit.* ii, 300.

admit at once that Becket, dying an ordinary death, would probably not have cured a single spasm of rheumatism. But it by no means follows, either that other saints would have made up for his deficiency, or that he is so far to be separated from his death that it is to be called an accident instead of an act. If Becket had died in his bed, pilgrims might still have gone to S. Edmund, S. James, the two Apostles in Rome, or the Tomb in Jerusalem; but it would have been in the old slack and (comparatively) lifeless and formal way. There is no more reason to doubt that Becket caused a religious revival, than that Wesley and Whitefield did. The two chroniclers of miracles agree in asserting that the miracles brought with them an uprising of moral and religious fervour, and indirectly prove it by multitudinous details recorded without controversial purpose. It was brief indeed, but it was powerful while it lasted. The churches built by the archbishop's former enemies as well as by his countless worshippers, are outward monuments of a strong inward protest against the violent and oppressive character often assumed by the secular forces of the time—or at all events of concessions from the strong to the strength of such a protest from the weak. It was not the Saxon against the Norman, it was the poor and weak oppressed against the rich and strong oppressor, that everywhere—alike in England and France and through the Latin-speaking world—rose up in the might of S. Thomas the Martyr, and decreed that he must be a saint, even before the papal edict had made him one. Most of those healed in the days of the earliest miracles have English names. But their passionate reverence and their wonder-working faith did not arise in their hearts from patriotic motives, because they were 'English born.' It was because they were wronged or liable to be wronged, that they took up the cause for which the New Martyr of the English had shed his blood. The Church, though sometimes defective and corrupt, was nevertheless felt by the poor to be often their only protection against outrage, and the martyr typified her championing spirit."[1]

The miracles, then, may take their place among the signs that, by his death, Becket conquered in the great strife with the king, and that he conquered as the representative of the people of England.

Henry's horror when the news reached him was genuine. The description of his frenzied outcry, followed by stupor, which comes to us in a letter from Arnulf of Lisieux, reads like a true description of the grief of a man so passionate. The interdict which followed was not unexpected, nor was the penance undeserved. It was not till May, 1172, that Henry was admitted to make oath that he had never commanded or wished the primate's death, though his rash words had occasioned it; he accepted severe terms of reconciliation, and he abandoned the Constitutions.

On February 21st, 1173, the decree of canonisation was issued by Alexander III, and the festival was fixed for the day of martyrdom. On July 12th, 1174, Henry II did notable penance at the martyr's tomb.

Further honour was delayed by a great fire (September 5th, 1174) which destroyed the choir built by Conrad, prior in the time of S. Anselm. Then William of

[1] Dr Abbott, *op. cit.* ii, 301.

Sens set to work at the rebuilding, 1175 to 1178, which was completed by William the Englishman in 1179. The body of the saint had rested in the crypt, which remains to-day much as it was—in medieval phrase—on "the day when he was alive and dead." The choir was finished in 1184, the new cloisters were begun in 1190; in 1220 the corona was consecrated and the body was removed to its new shrine. From this date the dedication to the Holy Trinity became commonly recognised as affixed to the whole cathedral church. Alan of Tewkesbury, as early as 1185, had urged the Translation to the new unfinished chapel of the Blessed Trinity: behind this there was the new apse, built in imitation of the church of the Holy Sepulchre at Jerusalem. It was this which now received the name of "Becket's Crown," and here the body was taken on July 7th, 1220.

The Icelandic Saga, preserving the impression of an eye-witness, says that:[1] "Concerning this the master relateth that he may not tell the number of the multitude of folk that assembled on the said day at Canterbury, for the city of Canterbury and the villages around were so filled with folk that many had to abide in tents or under the open sky"; and the assembled monks with the king, Henry III, and Stephen Langton, the patriot primate, were "surrounded by each baron and every kind of mighty folk, therewithal bishops, abbats, priors, and other states of learned men from different parts. Now, in God's name, cometh the third hour of the nones of July, at which hour the bishop standeth robed together with the other bishops and orders of learned

[1] *Thomas Saga*, ii, 202.

men afore-named, who then proceed amidst solemn singing down into the crypt where the chest was kept. The solemnity with which it was brought thence up into the church and was placed over the altar, where pre-parations had been made for it, may be best told in these few words, that the Church of Canterbury showed forth freely every honour which she could do to her father, in bells rung, in song, and vestments, not only inside the church, but also in the joyance in which the city showed its solemn delight, the King and all other folk deeming themselves as partakers of a divine gift if they might in any way minister to the new festival. It is a matter not soon told, what sort of thanksgiving was performed that same day for the honour of the blessed Thomas, for that very ceremony grew so long for the sake of the offerings and the devotion of the people that it seemed as if it were never coming to an end at all."

The shrine itself,[1] which was for three centuries to gather to itself the gift of countless pilgrims, the riches of kings, the offerings of distant nations, was prepared soon after. Of it the Saga[2] tells: "The next thing done by lord Stephen, archbishop of Canterbury, was that in his devotion he resolved to turn the offerings made to the holy Thomas into a shrine for him. And when this had been settled by the urging of the king and other mighty folk in the land, the archbishop procureth for the work the greatest master of the craft that could be found within those lands. But when the commonalty

---

[1] For the history of the shrine see Wall, *The Shrines of British Saints*, pp. 152 *sqq.*

[2] *Thomas Saga*, ii, 210.

of England got full certainty of this, the love which the people owe to S. Thomas was soon revealed, since they would hear of his shrine being made of no other metal than gold alone, which indeed had to be done. Hence the pilgrims to S. Thomas's shrine repeat the saw of the English, that after that time England never grew so wealthy in gold as before, and for that they give thanks to God. Now, by their mighty cost and choice workmanship, the shrine was the most excellent work of art that had ever been seen, being set all round with stones, wherever beauty and show might thereby be best set off. When the shrine was finished the archbishop layeth therein the holy relics of the worthy martyr, archbishop Thomas, and placed it above the middle of the high altar, only so high that it rested on the upper table thereof, one face of it pointing eastwards, the other westwards."

So Stephen Langton, the champion of English liberty against John, king Henry's son, commemorated the patriot whom king Henry's father's words had sent to death.

A plain wooden altar marked the place of martyrdom in the chapel of S. Benedict.

There in honour and glory the body rested till the days of Henry VIII, and year by year came pilgrims to the shrine. Descriptions, at different dates, show its extraordinary richness, the most famous that of Erasmus, only fourteen years before it was destroyed. In September, 1538, came the destruction by order of Thomas Cromwell, Vicar-General for the king, possibly after a sort of mock trial of the long-buried saint. Two months later a proclamation, speaking of Becket as a "rebel and traitor to his prince," and a "bearer of the iniquity of the clergy," ordered all pictures and images of him to be put down and all mention of him in church books to be obliterated.

Of the destruction of the body there seems to be little doubt. The Consistorial Acts at Rome announce the destruction of the shrine and the order that the body should be burnt and the ashes scattered to the winds. Stow, in his *Annals* (1565), records that this was done.[1]

There remained more abiding memorials. Hubert Walter, archbishop of Canterbury, had in 1192 recognised the new military order, of men who were both knights and canons, bearing the name of S. Thomas Acrensis (of Acre). It had been founded, within a few years of the martyrdom, in the Holy Land, and may possibly have had its origin in the penance accepted by Henry II of maintaining five hundred knights at his own cost for a year in the Crusade; and it is not unlikely that the curious legend of the Saracen mother which is found in a MS. (1264–70),[2] and in the Lives and Legends possibly by Robert of Gloucester, which cannot be many years later, may have found its origin

---

[1] In 1888 it was believed, however, that the bones had been discovered. On examination they did not tally with the original statements as to the injury to the skull, and there seems no reason to doubt that the burning really took place. The matter can be followed out in Morris, *Life*, ii, 597 *sqq.*, and *The Relics of S. Thomas*, 1888, and in A. J. Mason, *The Bones of S. Thomas*. A paper by Mr G. W. Warner in *The English Historical Review*, vi, 756, gives an account of a forged (late seventeenth century) account of the rifling of the tomb of Becket; "a plausible admixture of truth and falsehood." See further in Appendix I.

[2] See Kingsford, *Song of Lewes*, pp. xi, xvi–xvii.

in this connection. The order lasted till 1538, when it met its fate in the dissolution of the monasteries. But it had helped to perpetuate the martyr's memory in an enduring way.[1]

The most important influence in the history of hospitals in England was undoubtedly that of Becket. To his shrine came the greatest pilgrimages of sick and whole. At Canterbury and Southwark, hospitals were soon founded in his name, and before long similar buildings were erected at most of the southern ports and all along the Pilgrims' Way. Sick and whole, even lunatics, came to seek benefit from S. Thomas. Every pilgrim who stayed a night in the house at Canterbury received fourpence. He was regarded as the best of all saintly healers: a sign, which could be bought at Canterbury, bears that legend. Thus the name of S. Thomas became the most common dedication, after the twelfth century, of English hospitals. The order of S. Thomas of Acre, though some of its houses were called hospitals, was of course military, not medical, but it had taken charge of the very earliest hospital that was named after the saint. His sister had established a house for the sick in Cheapside, on the site of the house where her brother was born. This she gave to the knights and by them it was retained till 1538, when the site was bought by the Mercers' Company: on it now stands their chapel and hall. More famous because of its continuous history is S. Thomas's Hospital in Southwark, newly founded by the citizens of London in 1552 on the site where an Augustinian

[1] The posthumous influence of S. Thomas is admirably summarised by Dr Tout in the essay mentioned above, p. 37, note.

hospital had been set up, with the same dedication, in 1228. This again may trace its origin to the "Xenodochium" erected "in honour of God and the blessed martyr Thomas in London, at Southwark"—as described in a letter of Gilbert Foliot to the people of his diocese in 1179.[1] S. Thomas's Hospital preserves the name of Becket eight centuries after his life in the way in which it may most fitly be remembered.

But there are other memorials no less enduring. Far away in Sicily, the Norman kingdom with which he ever kept up a close relation of kinship, exists a mosaic in the cathedral church of Monreale, which is dated not more than twenty years after his death, and of the same time is a sculpture over a porch at Bayeux. On the south porch of the cathedral church of Chartres is a representation of the martyrdom not later than the thirteenth century. At Sens, in the south choir aisle, is a seated figure in stone, which is said to have come from a house in the city where he once resided, before, it may be supposed, he was lodged in the abbey of S. Colombe.[2] His own seal has a portrait which has strong claims to be regarded as authentic,[3] and there is another (dated no later than 1220) in the Black Book of the Exchequer in the Public Record Office. Among later representations are a fourteenth-century panel formerly in the court of Henry IV, the Becket window

---

[1] *Materials*, vii, 579. See also Miss Norgate's article on Thomas of London in the *Dictionary of National Biography*.

[2] See above, p. 124. It is reproduced as the frontispiece to this book.

[3] The late Canon Edward Moore informed me that there is no impression at Canterbury, but there is a copy in the Lambeth Library.

at Canterbury of the thirteenth century, some stained glass at Lincoln of the same date, other glass at Trinity College, Oxford, the miniatures of the thirteenth century illustrating an anonymous French poem, some frescoes (now destroyed) at S. John's, Winchester, and at Pickering, and a single figure at Stoke Charity Church, Hampshire. Nor does this exhaust the list.

Still more famous, and more enduring, are the memorials which remain in the literature of Europe. But for the pilgrimages to the shrine of the "holy blissful martyr" there would not have been the immortal *Canterbury Tales*. They stand apart in a glory of their own which owes little to the saint himself and does little for his memory. But of literature which is directly concerned with him there is abundance indeed. Hardly a country in Europe but tells of the life and death of Becket in its annals: among the very earliest of them is the work of the historian of the Latin kingdom of Jerusalem, William of Tyre, archbishop and crusader, and a little later there was in existence in Iceland the romantic Saga, which embodies the records of an English priest whose own work appears to be irretrievably lost.

The "Becket cycle" is one of the treasures of medieval literature. In the first place are the letters which cover almost the whole life of the saint. They occupy three stout volumes of the *Materials*, collected and edited from earlier editions and from manuscripts by the late Canon J. C. Robertson, of Canterbury, who devoted so much of his life to preserving the authentic memorials of the archbishop. Like the letters of Gregory VII or of S. Bernard, these authentic records bring the Middle Ages close to us in the veriest intimacy of their life. We see the impetuous spirit of the chancellor and archbishop overflowing on to the parchment on which the scribe—or very often, it may be, the archbishop's own hand—records the passions of the moment, the affections, the anger, the bitter irony, the despair and sorrow unto death, and, through all, the unflinching determination which marked his character from the first days of his advancement to the last hours of his martyrdom. Some letters bear the signs of careful composition, are stately, affected, legalistic. Even in Becket's own there is often a pose of pedantry, an assumption of learned literary pomp, which belonged, like the rich habit of the chancellor, to the habits, the *étiquette*, of his day. There are signs, too, of his following a literary model, whose matter as well as manner he was not unwilling to adopt—Hildebrand, the great asserter of the Church's extremest claims. But again and again there breaks out, even in the most laboured passages, a note of personal feeling, of genuine indignation, of pathos, of friendship, which reveals the true man, whom his enemies hated so bitterly, his disciples admired yet criticised, and the poor almost worshipped. Round the central letters cluster those of friends and foes. John of Salisbury, full of insight; John of Poitiers, full of sympathy; Gilbert Foliot, full of bitterness; Pope Alexander, full of hesitation and change. Henry's abrupt angry periods read as if they were dictated by himself. Cardinals write things soothing, bishops cry peevishly when they are scolded, clerks strive to show a knowledge of law, and monks a knowledge of the world. All through there is a sense of actuality, of the feelings of men who deal with difficult crises and great principles, which no later collection of historical letters has surpassed. We are brought face to face with the men of a great age, in their habits as they lived.

When chroniclers sit down to write their impressions of what they had heard or even seen we are still in an atmosphere charged with the electricity of partisanship. In so great a mass of material the general annalists of the time may be cursorily dismissed, even when they have each an extraordinary personal vivacity of his own —Gerald de Barri, most diverting of romantic, self-admiring Celts; Roger of Hoveden, solemn recorder of fact; Ralph of Dissay, thoughtful priest, learned in statecraft; Gervase of Canterbury, monastic antiquary; William of Newburgh, wise impartial student of affairs, "the most independent chronicler in the whole list of our medieval historians."

There are many more in whose pages the fame of the martyr found place, but the professed biographers stand apart by themselves. A few words may roughly describe the most important of these. William of Canterbury, who became a monk at Christ Church during the primate's exile, was ordained deacon by him, and received from him the habit on his return. His book was originally a collection of the miracles at the tomb, and he began to write it within eighteen months of the murder. It gradually grew into a Life, depicting the archbishop, from the monastic point of view, as the hero of Christ Church, ascetic and "filling up the spiritual man with merits." The collection of miracles, of which it seems that William had some official cognizance and perhaps kept the official record, was presented to Henry II by the monks; but they probably did not show the king the work in which his repudiation of concern in the archbishop's death is referred to in a tone of scarcely concealed irony. The king's conscience disturbed him not, and he took oath on the Gospels that he had neither ordered the murder nor wished it: no one would voluntarily take such an oath when he could have by money or penance won absolution without risking damnation. William had himself been with Becket in S. Benedict's chapel: he had heard Fitz-Urse call out "Strike, strike"; but he was one of those who forsook him and fled.

Next to William may be placed another Canterbury monk, Benedict, who rose to be prior of Christ Church, and died as abbat of Peterborough in 1193. His biography only exists in fragments, but his collection of the miracles is perhaps the earliest and certainly in some ways the most important of all. It is the candid work of a candid man, full of touches of minute observation. He is described as among Becket's familiar attendants, and he may have been with him in the cathedral church before the martyrdom.

"Benedict, who was the first appointed to report the miracles, seems to have been well adapted for the task; a man of (comparatively) simple and unaffected style, peculiarly accurate (for those times) in matters of chronology, free from exaggeration, and disposed to suspect exaggeration and imposture in others. Hence great weight must be attached to his accounts of the early miracles. The diseases healed by them were for the most part (as might have been anticipated) nervous disorders, such as might be cured by a strong emotional shock. In some cases Benedict frankly tells us that the cure was not at first perfect; in others that it was followed by relapse. In one case he informs us that the reputed water of S. Thomas was not S. Thomas's at all. It was a fraudulent imitation; yet it performed the desired cure."[1]

As regards the miracles then, in their earliest aspect, as they appeared to the men of Becket's own day, the work of Benedict is of great value; and it is probable that it was the first that was set down.

Guernes, or Garnier, of Pont Ste Maxence, began to collect materials within a few months of the martyrdom, and formally to write in 1172, the second year after the martyrdom. He finished his work in 1174, and later he added a few lines of epilogue. He wrote not the clumsy Latin of the earlier martyrologists but his native French, and in verse; and he was rewarded with a fine horse with proper harness by Mary, abbess of Barking, the archbishop's sister; and the nuns, too, were generous.

> "—e les dames m'unt fet tut gras
> chescune d'eeles de sun dun."

His own memory of his hero went back to the time when he led the English troops[2] and was chancellor of the English king. He took infinite pains to amass materials. He questioned everybody, went to Canterbury, submitted his book to the correction of the monks, and read it aloud for the edification of the pilgrims. He has a remarkable eye for detail and is one of the most vivid of all those who recall critical scenes in the life. His knowledge of the exile and of the French king's

---

[1] Abbott, *op. cit.* i, 224.
[2] E jeol vi sur Franceis plusurs feiz chevalchier (v. 359).

feeling towards his dangerous guest is especially valuable. Guernes, who went about among the poor folk of Canterbury, embodies better than anyone else what the common people felt: he himself had true sympathy for them, for he alone raised his voice against the Constitution which forbade the ordination of villeins, and knew that of old God called to His service not "dukes and persons high" but "men born of low estate."

Edward Grim claims a place by himself, for he alone risked his life for his hero. A secular clerk from Cambridge, he had come to Canterbury for the express purpose of seeing the primate who had suffered exile for the Church, and the terrible scene which he witnessed stamped its mark on his own life. Serious, restrained, methodical, his biography is the tribute of a commonplace trusty nature to a high spiritual ideal. He felt intensely and the feeling struggles through the shackles of a tongue imperfectly learnt, and shines in many a passage of power and convincing truth. Among all those who loved or admired the hero, Grim stands first, for his sturdy sincerity and the courage of his candid words. He wrote in 1171-2.

If Grim stands apart there are three other biographers who, each unlike the other, yet possess claims very similar to the attention of all who would learn what Thomas really was as well as what he did. John of Salisbury was unquestionably the ablest of the three. Of about the same age as Becket, he had a training more exclusively literary and more exact. For nearly twelve years, from 1136, he studied in France, and he was the pupil of the great Abailard, and of all the most famous teachers of the time. He was probably attached to the service of Pope Eugenius III from 1147, and was with him when Henry Bishop of Winchester paid his visit to Rome in 1148–9. It was then that the bishop bought the "veteres statuas" about which to the present day antiquaries are so much excited, and very likely it was the witty John who as a grammarian with a long beard mocked at him for so doing.[1] Commended by S. Bernard, and the familiar correspondent of popes and kings, there was no European scholar of his day to surpass him in learning. From 1154, when he entered the service of archbishop Theobald at Canterbury, when he returned to England, he had a close knowledge of Becket and was his constant correspondent and his vigorous defender, and he was his critic to the last. But at the supreme moment his courage failed him, and he turned away from his friend's side. He wrote, it seems probable, almost immediately after the murder. He was as convinced a believer as anyone in the miracles: perhaps remorse predisposed him to believe. He died in 1180 as bishop of Chartres, the faithful city which had welcomed his master, where the memory of the saint was to be preserved among the matchless sculptures of the cathedral church.[2]

Herbert of Bosham had none of the restraint and none of the critical faculty which made John of Salisbury the most candid of all Becket's intimates: he hardly aspired to be a friend: he was "the disciple who wrote these things," yet he records many expressions,

---

[1] This is thought probable by Dr R. L. Poole who, in a most valuable paper in the *English Historical Review*, July 1923, elucidates much that was suggested by Pauli, *Zeitschrift für Kirchenrecht* xvi, 265–87. Dr Poole's paper is a triumph of elucidation of difficulties.　　　　　[2] See above, p. 286.

many momentary thoughts or hasty words, which give an extraordinary expression of reality to his long and often prosy tale. His Life of the saint and his *Liber Melorum* are works which human patience will scarce endure to read through; and yet there is, ever and again, a touch in them so pathetic and so simple as to bring to the reader's eyes the tear that one feels sure were never far from his own when he wrote of his dear lord, whom he loved with such reverence and yet with such intensely human affection. In Herbert of Bosham, if sometimes the real Thomas eludes us, we come very near to him in the impression which he made on those who knew him well.

Herbert's chief work was finished probably before 1187; ten years earlier William Fitz-Stephen began his life, which is perhaps the best of all. He describes himself—and the fact needs no proof outside his book—as the archbishop's fellow-citizen. He was, he tells us, his remembrancer in the chancery, his subdeacon when he said mass, and in his archiepiscopal court he was his clerk and sometimes his deputy. He was present at Northampton: he was an eyewitness of many things that he tells of the life: and he saw the martyrdom and stood by the martyr to the last. He was one of the king's justices later on, and seems always—or at least in later years—to have been an official of the king. He stands out clearly before us, and he writes boldly, as a man of affairs, for men who can understand the great work that falls on statesmen and bishops. But a mystery hangs over his book. No contemporary mentions it: he is not named among the saint's companions. Save for his record his connection with Becket would have been utterly forgotten. But the book itself is his passport to fame. It shows him a man of the world, who can tell the points of a horse and note the humours of travel and the strange tricks of self-assertive men. Every descriptive touch of the archbishop shows a knowledge as intimate as the power of observation is exact. No biographer tells more certainly what really happened and how it happened, or sees with more sure insight the thoughts which moved men to their words and deeds.

In spite of the silence of contemporaries, no one doubts that Fitz-Stephen's is a genuine record; and indeed several manuscripts are of a date little later than that in which the book must have been first composed; and one comes from the abbey which Richard de Lucy founded in memory of the saint who had excommunicated him.

Besides these there are a number of anonymous but contemporary lives, that which Mr Freeman (and others before him), as well as M. Walberg, consider to be the work of Roger, a monk of Pontigny, perhaps the most important among them. The identification with Roger is not certain: it has been suggested that Robert of Merton, the archbishop's oldest friend, may have been the author; but the evidence is really strong enough for us to accept the authorship of the Pontigny monk, and its date as 1176–7. The two salient points in the book are the intimate knowledge of Becket's early life, which of course might have come from his own stories of his youth, and the very close resemblance in many points to Guernes. The writer certainly knew the archbishop also in exile. Another anonymous life (*Lambethensis*: the MS. is at Lambeth) is candid in declaring

that once the writer thought his hero's "life madness"
—a reminiscence of the Book of Wisdom, of course—
and contains matter which shows some personal knowledge. Others give new details.

And beside these anonymous sources there are still
two more primary authorities. There is the life by Alan,
once a monk and prior of Christ Church, and afterwards abbat of Tewkesbury, where his tomb still stands
behind the high altar of the abbey church. He was a
contemporary but not an eye-witness, a collector and a
skilful investigator. For the years of exile, and the
month before, his assistance is most valuable. There
is—or was—Robert of Cricklade, prior of S. Frides-
wide's, Oxford, some of whose memories, very quaint
and vivid, are preserved in the inimitable Saga of Iceland, a book which is as happy in its accounts of the
saint's life as its rich enjoyment of his miracles.

But the tale is an endless one. French metrical lives,
English poems, jostle one another in the bibliography,
and sermons innumerable were preached in honour of
the saint, by English archbishops, like the great Stephen
Langton, and foreign clergy of every grade.[1] For a
hundred years one almost feels that no man of letters
could keep his pen from the life of the martyred primate
of all England.

Individual biographies were soon gathered into collections of gems. In 1198 a *Quadrilogus* was begun,
which had a new edition in 1212. Elias of Evesham,
who first composed it, took the Gospels for his model,

---

[1] *E.g. Zwei Mittelalterliche Declamationen über Thomas Becket* by
Dr Otto Günther in *Nachrichten der Kgl. Gesellschaft der Wissen-
schaften zu Göttingen*, 1892.

and made his collection from John of Salisbury, Herbert of Bosham, William of Canterbury and Alan of Tewkesbury. Roger of Crowland, his reviser, introduced several of the Letters, and prepared his work for the Translation in 1220, when it was presented to Stephen Langton. Another but inferior cento was that of Thomas of Froidmont.

Thus the Middle Age was satisfied with ample knowledge of the saint. The sixteenth century was supplied by the Romanist Thomas Stapleton (1535–98) with a new version of his *Tres Thomae*: the seventeenth saw the publication of the first *Quadrilogus* by Lupus (Christian Wolf) at Brussels in 1682; the eighteenth the rival volumes of Berington and Lord Lyttelton; the nineteenth the rediscovery of the real Becket by the brilliant Richard Hurrell Froude, leading to the enthusiastic but inadequate labours of Dr J. A. Giles; and, forty years later his brother, James Anthony Froude, by his hasty onslaught evoked the retorts of Edward Augustus Freeman. Among many other, and often excellent books, the work that endures is not polemical. It is the *Materials for the Life of Archbishop Becket* which were published in seven volumes in the series issued under the direction of the Master of the Rolls, the crowning work—though he did not live to complete it—of James Craigie Robertson, canon of Canterbury, who had first written the archbishop's Life in 1859. And beside it we may now put the edition of the metrical life by Guernes (Garnier) de Pont-Sainte-Maxence by E. Walberg, in the *Skrifter Utgivna av Kungl. Humanistiska Vetenskapssamfundet i Lund* (1922).

But perhaps the memory of Becket to-day owes more to the genius of the great Victorian poet than to any scholar's toil. Tennyson in his play has revived the true spirit of the medieval hero, to which a great actor gave inspired embodiment.

Principles waver, party cries grow old, burning questions die down into ashes, but the loving memory of a great nation cannot wholly fade away, and personal courage and human faith—even though chequered and distorted—in things unseen, abide beyond the breath of change.

Truly did the great poet see the inspiration of the martyr in that thought of him among men which made him the most popular of all English saints.[1]

"The voice of the Lord is in the voice of the people,
The voice of the Lord is on the warring flood,
And He will lead His people into peace!
The voice of the Lord will shake the wilderness,
The barren wilderness of unbelief!
The voice of the Lord will break the cedar-trees,
The Kings and Rulers that have closed their ears
Against the Voice, and at their hour of doom
The voice of the Lord will hush the hounds of Hell
In everlasting silence."

And so the poet preserves the thought of the man who says—

"But I must die for that which never dies."

---

[1] *Life of Tennyson*, ii, 197. Lord Tennyson says of these fine words that "some of the last lines which my father ever wrote are at the end of the Northampton scene, an anthem speech written for Irving."

BECKET'S BONES

IN 1888 some bones were discovered in Canterbury Cathedral which were taken by some to be those of Becket concealed at the time of Henry VIII's order to prevent their being burnt. A good deal was written at the time on the subject, *pro* and *con*. I think I have read all that has been written, and to me the most important studies seem to be those of Father J. Morris, S.J., *The relics of S. Thomas* (1888), Mr M. Beazley, *The Canterbury Bones* (undated, ?1913), Mr. W. Pugin Thompson, *Becket's Bones* (3rd ed. 1922), Dr Edward Moore, *Studies in Dante* (4th series, 1917), and Dr A. J. Mason, *What became of the Bones of St Thomas?* (1920). Of these Dr Mason's study is by far the most important and complete, and (I think) Dr Moore's the most nearly approaches to convincing the reader that the bones were really those of Becket. Now the amount of evidence as to details of the murder is very great indeed, and there is a great deal of evidence too as to the destruction of the shrine by Henry VIII and the disposal of the bones. All the original evidence is most carefully discussed by Dr Mason, and I think I can best sum up the whole matter, so far as I am able to do so, by basing my opinion entirely on his book. Dr Mason tells his readers that in making this study he obeyed a wish of the Archbishop of Canterbury that he should "put together the documents bearing on the question whether the bones discovered in 1888 were

those of his great predecessor or not." He has done so
with patient assiduity. There is nothing, so far as I
know, in any book that has any claim at all to be an
ancient authority which he has neglected—though this
is rather a hazardous thing to say when the subject has
so enormous a literature belonging to it. To modern
writers, and rightly, he has paid little attention: he
mentions Robertson and Stanley (who were occupants
of the stall he now holds), and Dr Edward Moore (once
a colleague of his own) and hardly anyone else. There
would be, of course, an interest in having set down
here what other modern authors thought about the way
in which Becket's bones were disposed of. Dr Mason
is a little impatient with the late Father John Morris,
whose pamphlet on the subject held the field till now,
and does not think it worth while to mention other in-
vestigators. I think he is fully justified, for it is simply
a matter of evidence, and only the oldest evidence is of
value. Nevertheless it is worth noticing that the letters,
most vivid and interesting, written in 1888 by Miss
Agnes Holland (afterwards Mrs Bolton),show that most,
if not all, of those who saw the bones when they were
unearthed, and compared them with the accounts of
the martyrdom, were convinced that these were not
Becket's bones and also, from the other evidence, that
Becket's bones were burnt. The most interesting argument the other way is undoubtedly that of Dr Moore,
because it quotes the parallel cases of the bones of
Dante and those of S. Cuthbert, where we may certainly conclude that the real bones were concealed and
rediscovered. The utmost that Dr Moore would say
of the evidence in favour of the view that the bones

discovered in 1888 were really those of Becket was that "the conclusion remains, and ever must remain, doubtful," but that "the balance inclines very strongly to the side of its probability." Dr Mason is much more decisive. He thinks the facts "seem to point to the conclusion that the bones are those of the great Archbishop." If I am less certain, it is not from any disparagement of the labours of the learned Canon. On the contrary, I feel sure that he did the best that could be done to set forth the facts clearly. But do they warrant the conclusion he advocates?

Several points need to be remembered. First, and most important, What was the actual wound which proved fatal? That, no doubt, which severed the crown of the head from the head. Herbert of Bosham, who was not an eye-witness but (as Dr Mason very truly says) "was usually well informed," says of the murderers, after the first blow, which glanced aside and wounded Edward Grim, "hinc inde feriunt et referiunt, feriunt inquam et referiunt donec coronam capitis separarunt a capite." Here I may interject that Dr E. A. Abbott takes *corona* to mean the crown of the head, and this is most certainly the natural translation. Dr Mason, with Dean Stanley and the modern Roman Catholic writers, would translate it as that part "which had received the tonsure and the unction." But the real question is, was any large portion of the head cut off? The balance of contemporary testimony undoubtedly is that it was. Let us quote Dr Mason's excellent and candid summary:

"William Fitz-Stephen says that 'the whole crown of the head was cut off,' and that Hugh drew out the brain 'from the cavity of the severed crown': he speaks of 'what was left' of the head after this mutilation. Edward Grim says that the stroke by which he was himself wounded 'shore off the top of his crown'; but he supposes that the final stroke, when the Archbishop was prostrate, 'so severed the crown from the head' as to mingle the brain with the blood. Benedict affirms that when the martyr was on the ground one man 'cut off the greater part of his head'—this being an enlargement of the former wound. John of Salisbury implies that it was after the Archbishop's death that 'they cut off the crown of his head.' Garnier only mentions that the 'cupel' was taken off from the crown. Herbert, as we have seen, considers that the result of blow after blow was to 'sever the crown of the head from the head.'"

Now it must be remembered that every one of these is a contemporary authority, and probably all but one are eye-witnesses. Is it conceivable that they should have said that the crown of the head was actually cut off if they had not seen it separate? Certainly all the later Middle Age believed that this severance had actually occurred. The only rebutting assertion is that of the difficulty of replacing the severed part and binding up the whole head, as it certainly was bound before burial. This seems to me a far smaller difficulty than would follow from rejecting all this weight of evidence. Dr Mason finds it difficult to believe that the corona was "very neatly fitted" on to the head again. But why should it have been "very neatly" fitted? It was covered the eye-witnesses say, with a cloth, which was bound round it, and (perhaps before it was bandaged thus) a "kind of circlet of blood" was visible. The Icelandic Saga, which certainly represents a very early authority, states that the piece struck off was put on and buried with the rest of the head. I see no difficulty in this. Now, if the crown was actually severed, the head found in 1888 was not the head of Becket. "If at the time of the martyrdom a large part of S. Thomas's skull was severed from the rest, then this is not the head of S. Thomas," says Dr Mason. This is certainly true.

The second point, the decision of which may be equally conclusive, is—What became of the bones when the shrine was rifled by the orders of Henry VIII? For this there is the evidence of the king's general letter for taking away shrines and images, which says that he has ordered all such to be taken away, but (says Dr Mason truly) "does not specify the means adopted for the purpose"—nor (I may add) what was to be done with them. Commissions are quoted for the taking away of the shrines, but that for Canterbury is not forthcoming. No order is given in any of the commissions extant for the burning of the bones. But Becket stood in a special position. He was supposed to be a special offender against the Royal Supremacy, and he was especially reverenced by Englishmen as the first of their race born in England who was Primate of all England after the Norman Conquest. What special treatment Henry VIII meted out to him we do not know from any written evidence of the king's orders. But we do know that Pope Paul III excommunicated the king on the ground (among others) that he had had the bones burnt. Cardinal Pole, who certainly had independent sources of information, states the same thing.

In the same year "Hoby, the English Ambassador in Spain, reports the offence given by 'the burning of the saint's bones.'" Nicholas Harpsfield, who was before long Archdeacon of Canterbury, and would surely have corrected his statement later if it were wrong, also asserts the burning. Dr Mason, on what grounds I do not know, states that he does this "without any independent investigation." The MS. of his history has not yet been published, but when it is we may know more. A MS. note to Wriothesley's Chronicle also states that the bones were burnt. Stow in 1580 says the same, and in 1615 repeats it. "His bones scull and all, which was there found, with a peece broken out by the wound of his death, were all brent in the same church by the Lord Cromwell" (1580): "then and there burnt" (1615). Holinshed (1586) agrees. The exculpatory statement, a draft of which exists in the Record Office, is considered by Dr Mason "positively and somewhat indignantly" to deny the burning of the bones. I do not find any such statement in it. It asserts the burning of some relics, and, while stating that the actual head was found with the bones and that another head which had been reverenced (presumably that seen by Erasmus) was "but a feigned fiction," adds merely: "if this head was brent, was therefore S. Thomas brent? Assuredly it concludeth not." It is to be observed that there is no denial that the bones of S. Thomas were burnt, but only a denial that the burning of other bones is evidence that they were. The only evidence that they were not burnt is that of "Il Pellegrino Inglese" (1552), and of the author Dr Mason admits that "it may be doubted whether" he "had first-hand and independent knowledge of the facts"; nor does even he explicitly deny the burning. The fact is that all the contemporary evidence states that the bones were burnt; and that this was never, so far as I know, explicitly or authoritatively denied.

If the bones were not burnt, why were they not discovered and honoured in the reaction under Mary? The case of S. Cuthbert is hardly parallel. There Dr Raine conclusively proved the identity of the bones still remaining in Durham Cathedral. In the case of Canterbury, when Mary came to the throne there was every reason to declare what had really happened. Nicholas Harpsfield was archdeacon of Canterbury under Mary, and he states quite plainly that the bones were burnt. (MSS. are at Lambeth and in the British Museum.) Dr Mason thinks that "as he wrote 'burned' it becomes plain that he took his 'facts' straight from the Pope and the cardinal [Pole] without any independent investigation." Why? Living at Canterbury he must have known persons who remembered the fate of the martyr's bones. I can scarce believe that he would not have discovered them if they existed.

But if I cannot accept Dr Mason's conclusion as proved, and must regard all the rest of his book, besides the points I have mentioned, as in the strict sense irrelevant to the issue, I should be dull indeed if I did not recognise its learning and candour and the interesting sidelights it sheds upon medieval and sixteenth-century history, and did not feel myself guilty of some audacity in disagreeing with its contention.

SOME MEMORIALS OF S. THOMAS

For this list I am greatly indebted to the kindness of the Rev. George Herbert, who has given prolonged and careful study to the subject. He does not regard it as complete. (See also Keyser, *A list of the buildings in Great Britain and Ireland having mural and other painted decorations of dates prior to the latter part of the Sixteenth Century*.) The wall paintings etc. often give valuable evidence for the traditional view of the nature and details of the murder. Those no longer existing (or concealed) are enclosed in square brackets and several of the others survive only in a mutilated condition.

In addition to these there are a large number of MSS. in the British Museum and the Bodleian containing representations of the murder, and the miniatures of an anonymous poem, thirteenth century, were published for the Société des Anciens Textes Français (ed. Paul Meyer) in 1883. There are also many painted representations on screens and other woodwork (including those inside the chapel of the Holy Trinity in Canterbury Cathedral), sculptures, and much glass (mostly of late medieval date).

It is to be observed the earliest representations almost always show the saint wearing a beard.

LIST OF WALL-PAINTINGS

Bramley
[Brentwood]
[Burford]
[Burgh St Peter: sketch exists]

Burlingham St Edmund
Canterbury (Eastbridge Hospital)
Eaton
Faversham
Hadleigh
Halstow, Lower
Hauxton
Hereford Cathedral
Hingham
Maidstone
[Mentmore]
[Merstham]
North Stoke
Pickering
Preston
St Albans Cathedral
Shorthampton
[South Newington]
Stoke Charity
Stoke d'Abernon
[Stoneleigh]
Stow
[Stratford-upon-Avon]
[Sulhampstead-Abbots]
Upchurch
Wellow
[Whaddon]
[Winchester, St John's]
[,,   Magdalen Hospital]
[,,   St Cross]
Wootton Bassett
Yarmouth, Great

INDEX

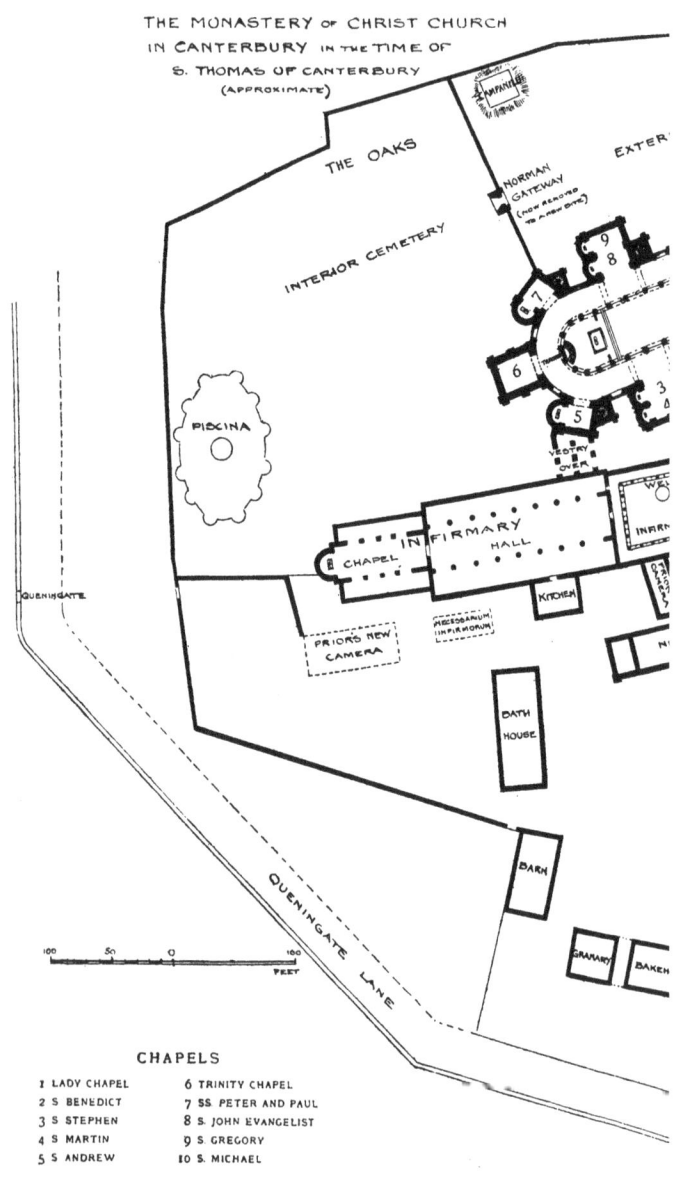

THE MONASTERY OF CHRIST CHURCH
IN CANTERBURY IN THE TIME OF
S. THOMAS OF CANTERBURY
(APPROXIMATE)

THE OAKS

EXTER

NORMAN
GATEWAY
(NOT REMOVED
TO A NEW SITE)

INTERIOR CEMETERY

PISCINA

QUENINGATE

VESTRY
OVER

WE

CHAPEL   INFIRMARY   HALL   INFIRM

PRIOR'S NEW
CAMERA

MESSUANIUM
INFIRMORUM

KITCHEN

BATH
HOUSE

BARN

QUENINGATE LANE

100   50   0   100
FEET

GRANARY   BAKEH

CHAPELS

1 LADY CHAPEL	6 TRINITY CHAPEL
2 S BENEDICT	7 SS. PETER AND PAUL
3 S STEPHEN	8 S. JOHN EVANGELIST
4 S MARTIN	9 S. GREGORY
5 S ANDREW	10 S. MICHAEL

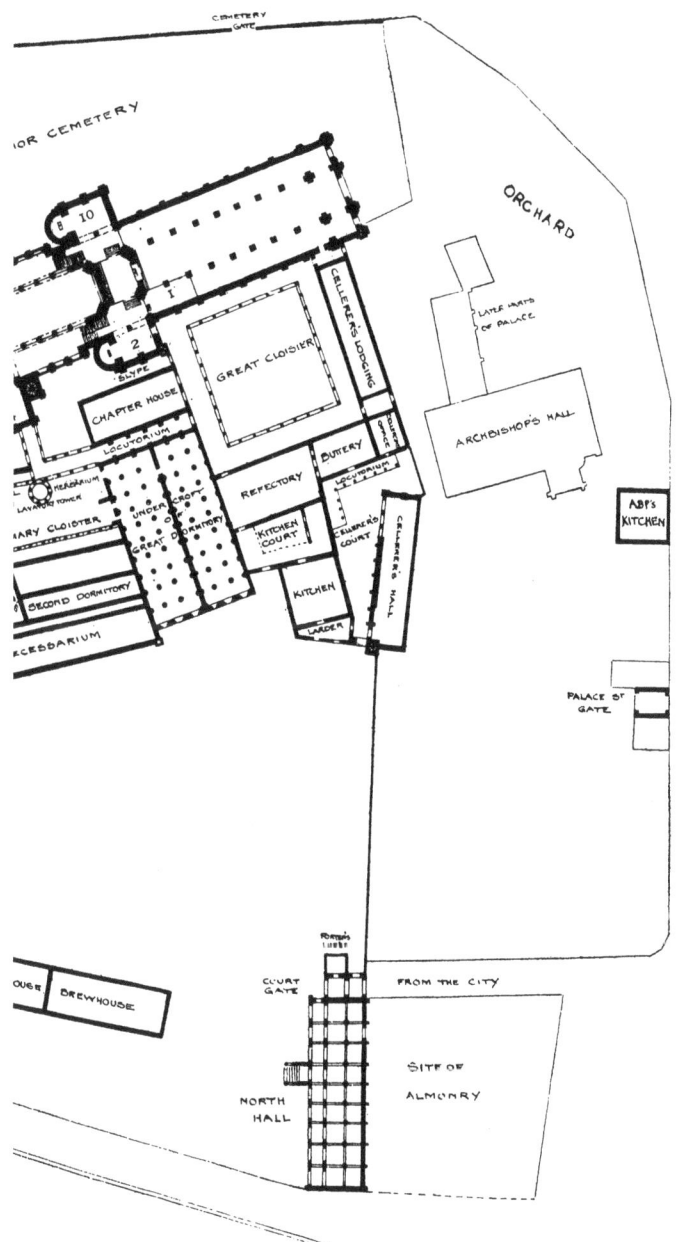

CEMETERY GATE

OR CEMETERY

ORCHARD

10

LATER PARTS OF PALACE

ARCHBISHOP'S HALL

ABP's KITCHEN

CELLERER'S LODGING

GREAT CLOISTER

1

SLYPE

2

CHAPTER HOUSE

LOCUTORIUM

REFECTORY

BUTTERY

LOCUTORIUM

LAVATORY TOWER

HERBARIUM

UNDER CROFT

GREAT DORMITORY

KITCHEN COURT

CELLERER'S COURT

CELLERER'S HALL

MARY CLOISTER

SECOND DORMITORY

KITCHEN

LARDER

ECESDARIUM

PALACE S.T GATE

HOUSE

BREWHOUSE

PORTER'S LODGE

COURT GATE

FROM THE CITY

SITE OF ALMONRY

NORTH HALL

For EU product safety concerns, contact us at Calle de José Abascal, 56–1°, 28003 Madrid, Spain or eugpsr@cambridge.org.

www.ingramcontent.com/pod-product-compliance
Ingram Content Group UK Ltd.
Pitfield, Milton Keynes, MK11 3LW, UK
UKHW040249270426
470322UK00028B/146